# Development in Africa's Informal Settlements

## Below the Proletariat

**A. R. Pashayan, Ph.D.**
Professor, American University – Washington, DC

**Series in Economic Development**

VERNON PRESS

www.vernonpress.com

| | |
|---|---|
| *In the Americas:* | *In the rest of the world:* |
| Vernon Press | Vernon Press |
| 1000 N West Street, Suite 1200 | C/Sancti Espiritu 17, |
| Wilmington, Delaware, 19801 | Malaga, 29006 |
| United States | Spain |

Series in Economic Development

Library of Congress Control Number: 2023947204

ISBN: 978-1-64889-836-5

Also available: 978-1-64889-774-0 [Hardback]; 978-1-64889-828-0 [PDF, E-Book]

Cover design by Vernon Press. Cover image by A. R. Pashayan (Polluted Viwandani, shot in 2023).

*To George "Mongololoh" Mungai Njuguna, a Kenyan whose struggles in life represent the struggles of all who live in the slum of Mukuru, and to the development professionals who serve the extreme poor.*

# Table of Contents

# List of Figures

# List of Tables

# About the Author

## A. R. Pashayan, PhD

Dr. Pashayan is a full-time lecturing professor at American University, School of International Service in Washington, DC. She teaches Global Inequality, Power & Practice in Development, Gender and Development, and Introduction to International Research at the university. Pashayan serves as Faculty Advisor to graduate students and works at the American University campus in Nairobi, Kenya, during summer leading experiential learning for the AU Abroad students. She has also held adjunct teaching positions at LSE, CSUN, and Howard University. Dr. Pashayan founded a Community-led Nonprofit Organization specifically to help residents of Informal Settlements. She regularly attends the World Bank Spring Meetings, interned two years at USAID, and worked for the former US Ambassador to the African Union on Impact Investing. The combination of experience in academia, as a practitioner, and as a development professional gives Pashayan a unique advantage in identifying gaps in service to the people experiencing poverty. With the current youth bulge across Africa, Pashayan seeks to address development gaps that could lead to what Pashayan calls "a potential youth bomb," leaving the continent into deeper poverty. This book represents her dedication to problem-solving for the best approaches to reducing extreme poverty in slums.

## More work by Dr. A. R. Pashayan

### American University Faculty, Dept. of Environment, Development, and Health
https://www.american.edu/sis/faculty/apashayan.cfm
Contact: apashayan@american.edu

### Commentary Interview with African Growth Initiative at Brookings Institution Washington, DC
https://www.brookings.edu/articles/learning-from-the-people-of-nairobis-mukuru-slum/

### Website for development program in Mukuru Slum
www.yodinternational.org

### Angela Pashayan's website
www.angelapashayan.com

### Dissertation
https://www.proquest.com/dissertations-theses/different-approach-poverty-reduction-kenyas/docview/2716515245/se-2?accountid=8285

# Abstract

This book discusses the effectiveness of international development programs to reduce extreme poverty in African informal settlements (slums). It is equally about the people affected by development programs. The intention is to foster dialogue among professionals about the effectiveness of development programs to better serve their clients (the poor). This book expressly examines the communication and critical thinking disconnect between development professionals and slum dwellers regarding the types of programs offered versus the types of programs needed to reduce extreme poverty in slum communities. With a sample of 500 residents from Mukuru Slum in Nairobi, Kenya, and 100 development professionals with expertise in poverty reduction in slum communities, this book sheds light on the similarities and differences of programs identified as key to effectively reducing extreme poverty. Most importantly, this book provides a theoretical way forward (The Theory of Extreme Poverty Reduction) based on Freirean pedagogy to stimulate authentic dialogue among slum dwellers that leads to the critical consciousness necessary for successful poverty reduction.

# Acknowledgements

The journey of authoring this book began during the first course of my Ph.D. program at Howard University. Learning from Dr. Cotman, now retired, set the pace for more profound academic scholarship and writing. A method of analysis was instilled in me that resulted in deeper arguments and critiques of the literature on international development. I revel in his expertise and acknowledge his emphasis on being a voice for people without a voice. I cannot thank you enough, Dr. John Cotman.

Similarly, I acknowledge the time given to me by Dr. Richard Seltzer to discuss research methodology for human research conducted as part of this book. He recognized my drive and confidence in successfully conducting research in the middle of an African Slum. To his surprise, I always succeeded in what he thought vc would be impossible. I remain in your gratitude, Dr. Seltzer.

Acknowledging Dr. Eleanor King is like acknowledging my own alter ego. Being understood is paramount to fostering the best in the human condition. Without much dialogue, Dr. King understands what I am thinking and where I am heading in my writing process. Unlike others, Dr. King also understands the time, funds, and energy I have outlaid in fieldwork before writing this book. She inspires me because she believes in me. The best in me salutes the best in her. Namaste, Dr. King.

During the day, I split my time between Howard University, the Library of Congress, the Wilson Center for African Research, and the Center for Strategic and International Studies (CSIS). I listened to research presentations and industry professionals who shed light on various issues of poverty reduction in Africa and international development. At CSIS, I met John Simon, former Ambassador to the African Union. John provided me with insight into international development from the perspective of a seasoned diplomat who has held top positions at the Overseas Private Investment Corporation (OPIC), the National Security Council (NSC), and the Millennium Challenge Corporation (MCC). He also served as an advisor to the President on AIDS and Malaria relief, as Deputy Assistant Administrator at the United States Agency for International Development (USAID), and is the current CEO of Total Impact Capital, Impact Investments. That someone of this stature meets with me to discuss international development means that my work is relevant. Thank you kindly, John Simon.

At CSIS, I also met Susan Fine, former Senior Deputy Assistant Administrator at USAID, who helped me frame my dissertation abstract. Subsequently, she recommended that her retired husband help me edit the body of the work. I assumed her husband worked in a different sector and had much time on his hands. Her husband, Patrick Fine, had recently stepped down as CEO of Washington, DC' preeminent development company, FHI360. Patrick graciously provided the "industry" edit of the writing. His support and opinions are heavily weighted in the development sector.

Patrick served as a former Senior Fellow of Global Economy and Development at Brookings, Vice President of Operations at the MCC, Sr. Deputy Assistant Administrator at USAID's Africa Bureau, Mission Director in Afghanistan for USAID, and remains a frequent writer on international and human development issues. Moreover, Patrick Fine studied under Paulo Freire, the expert whose theory led me to my Theory of Extreme Poverty Reduction in this book. Thank you, Susan and Patrick.

None of this work would have been possible without my family. My parents were community leaders and problem-solvers in marginalized Compton, California. On the opposite spectrum, my brother-in-law sailed around the world with Chapman University Afloat. It was he who introduced me to a world beyond Compton. Moreover, my deepest thanks go to my husband, Don, and three sons, Johnathan, Kevin, and Maxwell. They put up with my constant travel around the world, including ten years of hanging out in what seemed to be the most dangerous place ever, the slums of Nairobi. Specific thanks go to my Johnathan, who once said, "Mom, you have already done the work of International Relations; why not get the degree?"

Finally, I thank the Kenyans in Nairobi who have supported my work. Many have escorted me through various informal settlements and provided me with knowledge of their lived experiences. They welcomed, trusted, and helped me build the social capital necessary to be accepted in the slums. To John Ombasa, George Obell, Moha Mahamood, Peris, Janet, Mongo, Ras, Bobby, Kevin, Ibrah, Chu-Chu, Mickey, Papa Choxx, Brother Frank, Krees, Nani, Tobias, Steve, Shakur, and countless others, "Mungu akubariki na nashukuru sana."

*May God Bless everyone who has nudged my life*
*toward the culmination of this work.*

# Acknowledgements

The journey of authoring this book began during the first course of my Ph.D. program at Howard University. Learning from Dr. Cotman, now retired, set the pace for more profound academic scholarship and writing. A method of analysis was instilled in me that resulted in deeper arguments and critiques of the literature on international development. I revel in his expertise and acknowledge his emphasis on being a voice for people without a voice. I cannot thank you enough, Dr. John Cotman.

Similarly, I acknowledge the time given to me by Dr. Richard Seltzer to discuss research methodology for human research conducted as part of this book. He recognized my drive and confidence in successfully conducting research in the middle of an African Slum. To his surprise, I always succeeded in what he thought vc would be impossible. I remain in your gratitude, Dr. Seltzer.

Acknowledging Dr. Eleanor King is like acknowledging my own alter ego. Being understood is paramount to fostering the best in the human condition. Without much dialogue, Dr. King understands what I am thinking and where I am heading in my writing process. Unlike others, Dr. King also understands the time, funds, and energy I have outlaid in fieldwork before writing this book. She inspires me because she believes in me. The best in me salutes the best in her. Namaste, Dr. King.

During the day, I split my time between Howard University, the Library of Congress, the Wilson Center for African Research, and the Center for Strategic and International Studies (CSIS). I listened to research presentations and industry professionals who shed light on various issues of poverty reduction in Africa and international development. At CSIS, I met John Simon, former Ambassador to the African Union. John provided me with insight into international development from the perspective of a seasoned diplomat who has held top positions at the Overseas Private Investment Corporation (OPIC), the National Security Council (NSC), and the Millennium Challenge Corporation (MCC). He also served as an advisor to the President on AIDS and Malaria relief, as Deputy Assistant Administrator at the United States Agency for International Development (USAID), and is the current CEO of Total Impact Capital, Impact Investments. That someone of this stature meets with me to discuss international development means that my work is relevant. Thank you kindly, John Simon.

At CSIS, I also met Susan Fine, former Senior Deputy Assistant Administrator at USAID, who helped me frame my dissertation abstract. Subsequently, she recommended that her retired husband help me edit the body of the work. I assumed her husband worked in a different sector and had much time on his hands. Her husband, Patrick Fine, had recently stepped down as CEO of Washington, DC' preeminent development company, FHI360. Patrick graciously provided the "industry" edit of the writing. His support and opinions are heavily weighted in the development sector.

Patrick served as a former Senior Fellow of Global Economy and Development at Brookings, Vice President of Operations at the MCC, Sr. Deputy Assistant Administrator at USAID's Africa Bureau, Mission Director in Afghanistan for USAID, and remains a frequent writer on international and human development issues. Moreover, Patrick Fine studied under Paulo Freire, the expert whose theory led me to my Theory of Extreme Poverty Reduction in this book. Thank you, Susan and Patrick.

None of this work would have been possible without my family. My parents were community leaders and problem-solvers in marginalized Compton, California. On the opposite spectrum, my brother-in-law sailed around the world with Chapman University Afloat. It was he who introduced me to a world beyond Compton. Moreover, my deepest thanks go to my husband, Don, and three sons, Johnathan, Kevin, and Maxwell. They put up with my constant travel around the world, including ten years of hanging out in what seemed to be the most dangerous place ever, the slums of Nairobi. Specific thanks go to my Johnathan, who once said, "Mom, you have already done the work of International Relations; why not get the degree?"

Finally, I thank the Kenyans in Nairobi who have supported my work. Many have escorted me through various informal settlements and provided me with knowledge of their lived experiences. They welcomed, trusted, and helped me build the social capital necessary to be accepted in the slums. To John Ombasa, George Obell, Moha Mahamood, Peris, Janet, Mongo, Ras, Bobby, Kevin, Ibrah, Chu-Chu, Mickey, Papa Choxx, Brother Frank, Krees, Nani, Tobias, Steve, Shakur, and countless others, "Mungu akubariki na nashukuru sana."

*May God Bless everyone who has nudged my life*
*toward the culmination of this work.*

# List of Abbreviations

| | |
|---|---|
| ADB | African Development Bank |
| AGOA | African Growth and Opportunity Act (2000) |
| AU | African Union |
| AUDA | African Union Development Association |
| BUILD | Better Utilization of Investments Leading to Development (2018) |
| CDC | Center for Disease Control |
| CBO | Community-Based Organization |
| CSO | Civil Society Organization |
| DAC | Development Assistance Committee |
| FDI | Foreign Direct Investment |
| GBV | Gender-based Violence |
| IBRD | International Bank for Reconstruction and Development |
| IDRC | International Development Research Center |
| IMF | International Monetary Fund |
| KENSUP | Kenya Slum Upgrading Program |
| KES | Kenyan shillings |
| KISIP | Kenya Informal Settlements Improvement Project |
| MENA | Middle East and North Africa |
| NEPAD | New Partnership for Africa's Development |
| NGO | Non-governmental Organization, |
| OECD | Organization for Economic Cooperation and Development |
| ODA | Official Development Assistance |
| OPIC | Overseas Private Investment Corporation |
| PAC-DBIA | Political Action Committee-Doing Business in Africa (2015) |
| PPP | Public-private Partnership |

| Q7 | A reference to the question number in the survey |
| RFP | Request for Proposal |
| SDG | Sustainable Development Goal |
| SDI | Slum Dwellers International |
| SPA | Special Planning Area |
| UN | United Nations |
| UNDP | United Nations Development Program |
| UNEP | United Nations Environment Program |
| UNESCO | United Nations Education, Scientific, and Cultural Organization |
| UN-Habitat | United Nations Human Settlements Program |
| UNHCR | United Nations High Commissioner for Refugees |
| USAID | United States Agency for International Development |
| USG | United States Government |
| VSLG | Village Savings Loan Groups |

# Introduction

In 2010, a retiring board member of the Sivananda Nonprofit organization hired me to develop and set up a feeding program to feed the "poorest of the poor." Sivananda is a global organization with several centers throughout India, Canada, Europe, Asia, Israel, Latin America, the Bahamas, and the US. I met the retiring board member in San Francisco, where I sought yoga volunteers to travel and help me with international poverty reduction programs. Considering the retiree's age, health, mobility issues, and race, I chose to avoid the continent of Africa. The thought of setting up a white liberator with a permanent limp in the middle of a poor African community was unsettling. The development program to liberate hungry souls could turn into his call for liberation from the dangers of being a conspicuous outsider with access to cash.

I researched extreme poverty in Latin America, Southeast Asia, Indonesia, and India to provide my client with information on viable locations where I could set up his program. I urged him to choose locations such as Vietnam or the Himalayas, where Sivananda had a branch that could assist him if necessary or if his health issues worsened. He refused Vietnam and the other locations I found.

I probed deeper with questions about his life to better understand his intentions and discovered that he was a white South African who lived through apartheid in a household that upheld the system. His desire to feed the "poorest of the poor" was to make amends for the past.

He swiftly declined the proposal to return to South Africa but remained open to other African countries. My research on extreme poverty in Africa led me to informal settlements, more commonly known as slums. Surprisingly, I learned that nearly 50% of African citizens live in slums. Knowing that my client would only be satisfied working to feed the poorest of the poor, I conducted a comparative analysis of country politics, economics, safety, transportation, access to healthcare, tourist attractions, and expatriate population.

Extreme poverty was in every region. However, East Africa prevailed with the most benefits for my client to thrive, particularly in Arusha, Tanzania. I could develop a well-planned feeding program in a location where my client could also enjoy breaks in the Serengeti or the white sandy beaches of Zanzibar. The politics of Tanzania were moderate, election violence was uncommon, and the population often worked in the service industry hosting western tourists. My thoughts were to attract volunteers to serve in the feeding program, then send them off to enjoy the world's finest safari and beaches. I arranged a trip for myself and my client that included a week in Tanzania to meet community leaders, primary school administrators, area chiefs, youth leaders, and local civil society organizations. Unsure he would be satisfied working with people living at this level of poverty, I had a similar tour organized in Nairobi as a backup.

The slums of Nairobi were considerably poorer, and my client realized how few desperately poor people he encountered in Arusha. The flight to Nairobi was short, and we met community leaders from five slums in a matter of hours. The next day, our tour through the slums led my client to decide that Nairobi would be the perfect location to set up his feeding program. I had consumed so much information about Nairobi and formed so many community contacts that I inadvertently became connected to the slums.

Although my experience spans ten years in Nairobi's slums, my ethnographic notes for this book are from 18 months of visits, from two to four weeks at a time. Having spent so much time in the slums of Nairobi with families, single mothers, fathers, youth, and children, I decided to start my own nonprofit. Knowing I could not be present full-time like my client, mine would be a community-led nonprofit that could run itself. The structure of my nonprofit was more organic than that of my client, yet I developed both for different purposes. The community-led approach to development was not "a thing" at the time. I designed such a system because it made sense to engage the community in self-help and because my life and family were in the US. To this day, this organic community-led nonprofit remains located in Mukuru, Nairobi's largest slum by ground space.

The consulting experience led to my return to academia. Having earned a BA in Psychology at UCLA, I was ready to take what I learned experientially into a master's degree course. I had so much to write about, discuss, analyze and compare. I applied for and was accepted at Norwich University in Vermont, School of International Relations and Diplomacy. The oldest of six military colleges recognized by the US Department of Defense, Norwich, founded in 1819, became open to non-military students in 1972. I chose this university because soldiers have a wide breadth of on-the-ground experience with members of the communities where they serve. More than just toting guns, soldiers often get to know the locals, and some even start projects to help the community. Earning an MA degree from Norwich was a strategic choice. I shared similar ethnographic experiences, seeing extreme poverty, illness, death, and hardship of everyday people. To bring those realities to class for analysis, international relations, international development, diplomacy, and foreign policy come to life.

After Norwich University, I returned to the field for another four years of ethnography, spending two to six weeks at a time in Nairobi. During this period,

I watched community members lose their lives to illness, uncontainable slum fires, childbirth complications, and some went missing due to sex trafficking. My time in Mukuru is likened to the Peace Corps in an area where there will never be a peace corps, an unplanned urban location filled with great poverty that governments have not legitimized, duplicated across all 54 countries of Africa. Half of the population of the continent of Africa lives in slums. It is through my experiences, together with academia, that I write with a vantage point from different approaches to reducing extreme poverty.

It was 2018 when my time in Mukuru was interrupted once more. I moved to Washington, DC, the seat of power where development initiatives are born. Accepted into the Ph.D. program in Political Science and International Relations at Howard University, I began preparing to conduct the research you are about to read. This book is based on my dissertation research. However, it includes ethnographic notes taken over five and a half years during visits to Mukuru. It is these notes that add human relevance to the research and, most importantly, to validate the voices and lives of slum dwellers I have come to know.

# Tools for Instructors and Practitioners

I currently teach International Development as a professor in Washington, DC. My courses emphasize development in informal settlements of Africa and follow an interdisciplinary approach. It is the interdisciplinary approach that blends subject matters used for programming by practitioners with those of academia. Bridging this gap brings international development closer to reducing extreme poverty and finding effective solutions to reach the SDGs.

To fellow academic colleagues in Washington, DC and beyond, I have included a section at the end of each chapter that outlines key points for classroom teaching. The points serve well in lectures, slide presentations, and quizzes. Discussion questions are also found at the end of each chapter which can be used for essay questions. Some chapters include experiential exercises that are most effective when followed by a post-exercise written reflection. Teaching with an interdisciplinary approach will welcome students interested in a variety of fields, all of whom will gain valuable knowledge. The material in this book will carry them farther along in their career paths to spearhead innovation in development for the largest category of people living in extreme poverty. We know from the world poverty clock and World Bank Data that Africa has the largest amount of poverty as compared to other continents, and those living in informal settlements make up over 50% of the continent. Students interested in gender studies, food security, climate change, policy, WASH, climate change, and health, including maternal and child health, will gain knowledge from the primary research in this book conducted in Nairobi's second most populous slum.

To fellow practitioners in Government Agencies, Multilateral Organizations, NGOs, and Civil Society, the discussion questions at the end of each chapter will benefit your teams by providing prompts for dialogue that help improve our understanding of the dynamics of poverty. The prompts were developed from direct quotes made by your client – people living in extreme poverty – and are, therefore, central to effective program planning. These prompts hold within them the voices of Mukuru residents. For many agencies and large organizations, the prompts may be the most direct communication that office-based teams have had with their client aside from that of local missions and contractors. Furthermore, the experiential exercises in this book will help your teams relate to the lived experiences of their clients.

This book is filled with primary data gathered for you. It comes directly from Mukuru residents and from Nairobi-based development professionals who are likely to have some connection with the agency organization you work for.

For that reason alone, the contents hold significant relevance to the future of effective development programs that *"build back better," "leave no one behind,"* and promote Community-led Development.

To the general public, you will undoubtedly enjoy reading this book to learn about life in extreme poverty. You may encounter some reading points that sound a bit academic, but overall, you will gain an insider's view of the development sector, including the progress and setbacks that aid organizations have made along the way.

Typically, when I am discussing living conditions in Mukuru with professionals or anyone who has not walked through a slum, a disconnect remains between the words I speak and the understanding of the listener. I'll say, 'the homes have no toilets,' and immediately thereafter I hear statements about how locals must have strong bladders and need good shoes since they walk a long distance to reach a port-a-potty. The reality that excretions occur in open air near the house never crosses their minds.

It is in full transparency that this book is written with the goal of helping poverty reduction organizations "get it right." Communication is difficult enough with our neighbors, let alone understanding the needs of those from different continents, cultures, and socioeconomic backgrounds. Add to that, having been oppressed and having the most visible differences in appearance to the rest of the world, together seen as objectionable, efforts to reduce extreme poverty in Africa are fraught with misunderstandings that this book seeks to make clear.

*Each chapter ends with the opportunity to engage in deeper thought about its contents. Key points are noted as well as discussion questions, case studies, and/or experiential exercises. Definitions of industry terminology can be found in Appendix A.3 for reference or for testing students.*

# Chapter Overview

**Chapter one** is intended to help you understand the material life of residents who live informally. The chapter points out indicators of lack that correspond with how life in the slums is far from reaching any of the Sustainable Development Goals. I also discuss perceptions of poverty reduction program effectiveness and Freirean theory that explains the commonality of a disconnect between those with learned versus lived experience who devise the programs. The goal of this chapter is to provide the reader with an experiential encounter through the predicaments and daily habits of a long-time slum resident named George.

**Chapter two** is an introduction on how and why the informal settlements were formed with reference to Rostow' stages of growth and failed approaches in the modernization of African states. The discussion provides context for the history of Nairobi's slums and narrows the further discussion to the slum of Mukuru. Indigenous customs regarding family heritage and bonds with land are discussed to explain the affinity that residents of informal settlements have with the slum. My research questions and hypothesis are stated along with the significance of the research to the cannon. Assumptions and limitations are noted as well as delimitation, followed by definitions of key terminology used throughout the book.

The background statement in this chapter provides a full breadth of information regarding failed development models and statistics from the 2019 Kenyan Census that correlate with information about the informal settlement of Mukuru. The chapter continues with a brief discussion of *inclusive development*, which follows "the concept that every person, regardless of identity, is instrumental in the transformation of their own societies." (USAID, Operating Policies, ADS Chapter 205). This chapter concludes with the relevance of this research and the urgency for innovative ideas toward long-term solutions in a post-COVID-19 world.

**Chapter three** covers the existing theory and pertinent literature, including primary and secondary work that supports the theoretical implications of my work. It begins with an explanation of Paulo Freire's Theory of Critical Consciousness and how it relates to my work, blending lived experiences with learned experiences on extreme poverty reduction. The remaining parts of the chapter are organized into four categories of existing work on: (1) development and ethnography, (2) social theory and hermeneutics, (3) primary work in critical consciousness, and (4) works from the development sector.

The first category is a continuation of Rostow's failed approaches in the modernization of African states, where I discuss the work of Scott (1985), Bates (1981), Moyo (2009), Gendzier (1985), Rodney (1982), Carothers (2004) and Lancaster (2006). Scott, an ethnographer, and Bates, an economist, explain how modernization affects communities, both rural and urban, leading to social discord and corruption. Moyo, also an economist, offered a way forward toward modernization and development by refusing foreign aid (Moyo, 2009). Gendzier, Rodney, Carothers, and Lancaster explain the overall fundamentals (and ills) of aid in terms of state-building and Euro-centric approaches to development.

The second category expands with human-centered theorists, including Cernea (1991), Bourdieu (1977, 1993), Marimba (1994), and Garvey (1937). Pierre Bourdieu's theory about *habitus* and the embodiment of cultural capital is offered as a way of understanding social dynamics in informal settlements. Bourdieu describes habitus as the most influential type of social capital. Habitus is the physical embodiment of cultural capital based on the ingrained habits, skills, and dispositions that one possesses due to one's life experiences (Bourdieu, 1977). His model includes valuable information about culture, embodied, objectified, and institutionalized capital in social settings. Cernea's triumph is his work amending the Millennial Development Goals to include putting people first in development programming. The work of Marimba and Garvey bolstered the Afrocentric perspective that was missing from most development initiatives.

The section continues with perceptions and approaches to poverty reduction with a discussion on the hermeneutics of Taylor (1985), Kuhn (1962), Koltai (2016), and Sen (1970) shed light on perspectives and paradigms. As part of the literature review, perspectives are related to how development professionals versus residents of informal settlements view solutions to extreme poverty. Koltai makes it clear that his approach to poverty reduction is job creation (Koltai, 2016), while Sen's notion that development is about enhancing human freedom adds to interpretations that can be justified by collective choices, unanimity, and social welfare functions (Sen, 1970). Kuhn's paradigms equate to the shift needed for better development programs to reduce extreme poverty.

Chapter three concludes with the fourth theme on research findings anchored in Paulo Freire's theory of critical consciousness. Studies by Zimmerman (1992), Boone et al (2019), Godfrey and Wolf (2016), and Deimer and Li (2011) are founded on principles of consciousness, empowerment, and human agency. Deimer and Li conducted research on agency and political participation based on psychological empowerment theory. Zimmerman's work on self-analysis of agency relates to the work of Godfrey and Wolf in their search for what impedes vs promotes consciousness and agency. Both pieces of research lead to North, who identifies that *extended consciousness* is necessary for one to achieve mastery over his or her life. Boone et al. conduct research on how to raise critical consciousness by instituting a new praxis structure that removes the "us" vs. "them" power positions during participatory development planning. At the end of chapter three, there is a chart of existing program successes and failures for easy review of "what has already been done," in development to reduce extreme poverty.

**Chapter four** represents the approach to inquiry using mixed methods for specific reasons. Focus groups with slum-dwellers were purposely selected because group dialogue is a communication method that keeps with cultural and social norms. Questions that foster critical consciousness are sprinkled amongst other questions into the dialogue about effective development. While focus groups are appropriate for slum-dwellers, I conduct interviews with development professionals to learn about program development and the effectiveness of those programs. Responses from slum dwellers and development professionals are coded and quantified for statistical analysis. Research design, setting, and sample are explained as well as data collection and the method of data analysis. The research question and hypothesis are re-stated with variables and coding described.

**Chapter five** shares the data, findings, and analysis of my inquiry. Cross-tabulations appear in this chapter and in the appendices. Qualitative quotes are discussed in terms of relevance to the research questions and hypothesis. Statistical significance is discussed, as well as unexpected findings.

**Chapter six** concludes the book with a summary of key takeaways, prominent themes, top causes of poverty, and inter-sectoral approaches to reducing poverty. Comparisons are made between approaches with further analysis and implications. The application of Freirean principles used to create The Theory of Extreme Poverty Reduction is examined and explained in terms of utility to produce effective development programs. Communities of Inclusion and Self Reliance (CISRs) are explored for social and economic potential and as further support of the new theory. Recommendations are offered that blend theory with research implications and practitioner knowledge. Recommendations include viable solutions that could be used in development programs.

Chapter 1

# The Proletariat

**Proletariat** 1: **the laboring class,** especially the class of industrial workers who lack their own means of production and hence sell their labor to live. 2: the lowest social or economic class of a community. *Merriam Webster*

The proletariat is a term used by Leon Trotsky to describe poor working people who were shunned and disregarded by the middle and upper classes. They were farmers and factory workers, bakers, butchers, and everyday people who spent long hours working to barely make ends meet. They represent the backbone of most countries, reaping few benefits from the cosmopolitan world that thrives around them. Every country has a proletariat class. However, I argue that the poor living in informal settlements live below the proletariat.

### 1.1. George

George is approximately 37 years old. His parents moved to the Mukuru Slum of Nairobi, Kenya, in the 1960s, shortly after Kenya gained independence from colonial oppression. George is the second eldest in a family of five children. His sister, a few years older, does not bear the responsibilities of George as the eldest male. When the remaining siblings were born, George assured the family's safety when the parents were away from the house. When George was six or seven years old, his mother died mysteriously. She died in a tragic way that left the children in trauma, particularly the second to last child, Bobby. The youngest son, Dan, was too young to comprehend what occurred. A few years later, the father died of AIDS, leaving all five children on their own. George was nine years old. Displaced children in the slums live a life of severe hardship. If there are family members nearby, they are not inclined to take in extended family. To do so is to willfully add to the detriment of their own children. Survival is literally at stake. For a family that eats one meal a day to take in displaced relatives means eating every other day. George and his siblings had to find their own way. This is living below the proletariat.

George's house consisted of four concrete walls enclosing a 15x10 foot area. Everyone slept in the same space. Lack of privacy prevailed during marital sexual activity, menstruation, and other normal developmental activities. There was no kitchen or toilet, no sink or shower, and no place to hang or fold clothing. This was the case not just for George's family but for the whole community. Daily defecation occurred in the open near the river or in plastic bags thrown outside to keep the smell away from the house. These "flying toilets" often landed on heavily trafficked walkways and stomped into crevices of existing dirt paths. Such paths make up the dizzying array of narrow, informal and unnamed streets in the slum.

The youngest was taken by the state to an orphanage. The others fled to the streets. The second youngest, Bobby, was cared for by nine-year-old George. Like a father, George did his best to keep his brother warm and fed. Dependent on hand-outs and donations of milk, the two lasted in the streets for about three months until George relinquished his brother to an unknown older white woman who vowed she would take good care of Bobby. George refers to her as "Grandmother Veronica." George continued to live on the streets, committing small crimes in order to eat until he was rounded up by the state and sent to a vocational school outside Nairobi. When asked which vocation was of interest, his answer was "none." As a result, he was placed to study art (painting).

After two years, he left the program and returned to Nairobi to forge his life as a young adult. With no relevant industry skills or a job, George returned to the only home he had ever known, Mukuru. Like others in the slum, he worked odd jobs: masonry, carrying scrap metal for recycling, selling items, clearing stones from construction sites, etc. When there was no work, George would paint, having slept near art-store dumpsters to obtain discarded materials. In his search to find members of his scattered family, he learned that Grandmother Veronica had died and his brother, whom he had cared for in the streets, was living with a different mzungu (white) and finishing grade school (grade 8). George found Bobby, and with a fatherly bond, the two decided to share a life together in Mukuru. George taught Bobby how to paint, and he taught others as well. He created an informal family of slum dweller artists who tried to sell their work in addition to earning income from the normal daily hustle.

Eventually, George located his elder sister and other brothers. The baby of the family, Dan, surpassed the others in education. He earned a bachelor's degree in Social Work yet remains unemployed. Dan returned to Mukuru and joined his brothers in their struggles in a continual effort to make ends meet. The persistence of poverty remains to date as their now weary bodies push through hunger, illness, and post-traumatic stress.

## 1.2. UN SDGs

The United Nations (UN) created 17 Sustainable Development Goals (SDGs) on behalf of the poor around the world. The goals were initially to be reached by the year 2000. The year was pushed back to 2020, 2030, and now 2050 due to various factors that the international development sector cannot seem to rectify. The first goal is the eradication of extreme poverty, the kind that George and his brothers endure. Statistics from the World Bank inform us that the development community has not been on track to meet the SDGs since 2019 pre-pandemic. Instead, poverty is *increasing* in most countries across Africa. As foreign aid and development organizations look for different approaches to reduce extreme poverty, people like George continue to suffer, and multi-dimensional issues of poverty begin to compile.

Multidimensional poverty is easily understood intellectually, but here's what it looks like in reality. I asked George a question about his morning habits living in the slum. When he did not answer me, I told him what I did...wake up, turn the lights on, go to the toilet, brush my teeth, change out of my pajamas, and make coffee and toast. I knew the answer from my ethnography in the slum, but I wanted to hear and experience what his answer would entail. For three days, he ignored my question. His silence spoke volumes. George had no lights or toilet, no piped water or basin for brushing his teeth, and no pajamas. Making toast in the morning would require keeping bread in his shelter, something that attracts rodents. Making coffee would require many extravagances; ground beans, spoons, cups, water, a fire or stove to boil water, a pot, and sugar or cream becomes indulgent.

After three days, George responded to my question about his morning habits. It was as if he had been embarrassed to talk about it. But my gut feeling was that George had never thought critically about his daily habits in comparison to other people's habits. In doing so, I contend there was a lag in time of communication while George processed the realities that he and his neighbors live with as compared to others. This is what critical consciousness is all about; thinking deeply about what you do and do not have, what you need and do not need, and what you do and do not wish to improve. George's ultimate response to my question came with no embarrassment. It was conveyed with a matter-of-fact candor;

*"I wake up and go "shoo-shoo" (urinate) in the corridor near my home. The way I go to sleep is how I wake up (no changing into pajamas). I don't brush my teeth, I go down to the riverside 200 meters and make toilet (bowel movement). I return to my house, grab my sac and go hustling (to earn money). I come back at 10 am and cook tea with the family. To cook, we use charcoal or kuni (firewood). After, I go hustling again. Sometimes I come back at lunchtime, or I keep hustling until evening when I return for dinner and then I sleep."*

George's morning is an example of multidimensional poverty where one issue of poverty is compounded by another, leading to hunger, lack of water for hygiene and good health, environmental pollution on land and in rivers, no access to affordable energy, all of which increase inequality and more poverty. These represent eight of the SDGs experienced in lack by one person at the start of his day.

**Figure 1.1.** United Nations Sustainable Development Goals

Furthering our conversation on habits at home, I asked George about marital intimacy. The SDGs include health and well-being but nothing in terms of fostering child development through reducing first-hand exposure to sexual activities in the home. As USAID launches a $50 million global child-care campaign (USAID, 2022*) in accordance with Joe Biden's infrastructure initiative, a learning curve is likely to be experienced by development professionals in terms of at-home impediments that counter external childcare programs. While the prevalence of teen pregnancy, early marriages, or rape cannot be blamed on early exposure to sexual intimacy, being awakened regularly by your parents having sex may reduce fear and increase curiosity about sex. George explains.

> "About 'pam-pam-pam' (sex), when the kids sleep is the time we do 'pam-pam-pam.' The house is one single room, so everything is there – the kitchen, the bedroom, everything is there. There is no two bedrooms just one mattress for all."

As the day progresses, George will experience a lack of eight more SDGs, including a lack of industry, decent work, peace and justice, education, responsible consumption, a sustainable community, and partnerships to help him improve his life. The last SDG, which George will undoubtedly experience from October homes with the lowest rent, are perched along the riverbanks.

Each year to December, is a lack of climate action. The Ngong River flows directly through the slum and floods the area during this time. Many of these homes collapse and float down the river, adding to the fecal debris already in the water. The overflow makes its way into the rest of the slum, creating muddy pathways that made me wonder if I was walking on dirt or human feces from the river. The debris brings illness and disease to residents, many of whom suffer from symptoms they ignore. When the flood recedes, one can find all kinds of things along the riverbanks: clothing, couches, corrugated tin from housing, jerrycans, cooking utensils, and dead animals like chickens.

**Figure 1.2.** Ngong River, Nairobi – Flooding in the slums

Mukuru is Nairobi's largest physical slum, spread across three sub-counties and home to 825,000 residents. The winding unnamed pathways through the slum overflow with small businesses offering chapati (flatbread), tomatoes, plastic tubs, jerry cans (for water), raw meat for cooking, hair salons, and sellers of clothing obtained from shipments originating from western donors like the salvation army. Though there are port-a-potty toilets in some locations, bathrooms, or lack thereof, are along the Ngong River. The predicament is the same for taking showers, which are mostly non-existent. Residents fill their jerry cans with non-potable water for free, obtained at a pump typically half a mile away. Potable drinking water is available for a fee and often further away. A half-mile walk means another half-mile all the way back carrying a filled jerry can.

Cooking is done in one pot over charcoal. Like George, most households go without electricity unless it is obtained through cartels at three times the cost of standard electricity rates. Families live together in a one-room mabati (temporary structure) made of corrugated tin, of which rent is paid to someone who may or may not really own the property. It is normal for someone to show up and claim ownership of the property, at which time all occupants must leave immediately. The slums are unplanned urban areas not recognized or serviced by the government. That means no postal service or address, no police or fire service, no plumbing, electricity, water or sewage. Mukuru is a self-managed city and one of 19 slums surrounding Nairobi. George's story is common. To work and live in the slum is to live below the proletariat.

### 1.3. The Proletariat and the Development Professional

A disconnect exists regarding what works best to reduce extreme poverty in informal settlements. To bridge the disconnect is to make a significant breakthrough in the field of development and the goal of the theory in this book. The ineffectiveness of development programs lies not in a lack of capacity but in the non-recognition that certain conditions are necessary to provide a foundation for successful poverty reduction efforts. The Proletariat lives with the psychological impacts of colonialism passed through generations. They recognize the patterns of apathetic local contractors who conduct whatever service development professionals pay them to do. While the development professional may seek to back innovations that give autonomy to the proletariat, the development sector does not have the lived experience to understand its client.

Comparing perceptions of program effectiveness is the beginning of identifying the disconnect. Development professionals may perceive an intervention as effective, while the residents of the Mukuru slum in Nairobi, Kenya, may perceive the same as ineffective. Both may seek relief from the same problem but in different ways. The disconnect between lived and learned experience is part of the issue.

Paulo Freire wrote about the disconnect in *Pedagogy of the Oppressed* (1968). Freire emphasized the importance of critical consciousness to come to an understanding of different worlds. In this case, it is an understanding between development professionals and the poor. Freire used critical consciousness in the favelas of Brazil to help slum dwellers understand broader subjects in a way that helped them communicate better with their historical oppressors. This book follows the theories of Freirean critical consciousness to help bridge the communication gap between slum dwellers who live below the proletariat and development professionals who serve them. With emphasis on the importance of lived experiences as a person oppressed, this book is written to foster a path toward a clearer understanding of poverty issues at the experiential level and the conditions necessary for successful development in informal settlements.

## Chapter 1 - Key points

**Families living in extreme poverty may:**

- Have a family history of poverty
- Be affected by family trauma
- Experience social dysfunction
- Endure dietary health issues
- Suffer from Poverty PTSD
- Experience daily lack in terms of SDGs

**Development professionals may:**

- Be disconnected from the effectiveness of programs
- Have not considered how many SDGs are not reached daily by people living in extreme poverty

**Paulo Freire's theory of critical consciousness:**

- Illuminates different ways to gain an understanding
- Provides a path to blend lived and learned experiences

## Chapter 1 - Discussion questions

1) What SDGs should be focused on first to make effective changes to reduce extreme poverty? Should the SDGs be re-introduced in stages, i.e., two to three at a time?

2) What serves as the best measurement of achieving the stages of SDGs you identified in the previous question? Should measurements be made in informal settlements? Are there key countries where measurements should be made? Who should make the measurements?

3) Program effectiveness can be perceived differently. Have development professionals considered that programs that reach certain indicators still may not be perceived as effective by their clients? If asked directly, could the client be unsure how to answer due to the power dynamics of being historically oppressed?

4) Paulo Freire posits that critical consciousness needs to be cultivated to improve intra-understandings of lived and learned experiences.

Do you think the critical consciousness of the poor should be focused on, or the critical consciousness of the development professional, or both? Why?

5) Considering political history, gender norms, social and cultural dynamics, economic conditions, and place-based conditions such as weather and types of foods that are available, what are some of the ways development professionals can get it wrong in terms of programming?

6) Knowing the daily habits of George, share one thing that the development sector could offer to improve his life.

## Notes

* On April 28, 2022, USAID announced plans to invest $50 million over five years focused on global childcare. The funds would come from the World Bank's Childcare Incentive Fund intended to expand access to quality childcare and early learning programs in low and middle-income countries around the world. Partners in this initiative are the Bill & Melinda Gates Foundation, the Ford Foundation, the Hewlett Foundation, the Governments of Canada and Australia, Conrad Hilton Foundation, Echidna Giving, and the LEGO Foundation. https://www.usaid.gov/news-information/press-releases/apr-28-2022-usaid-announces-plans-invest-50-million-global-child-care

Chapter 2

# Context and Significance

In low-income countries[1], human capabilities, collectively and individually, are epistemologically connected to Eurocentric values. The bar for human and social development is set by outsiders, while the insiders who are economically marginalized are persuaded to follow along. The belief that the outsider knows best acts as informal governance of the psyche, which can alter a native identity. Thus, the economically marginalized become psychologically marginalized. Community self-help is needed to break the cycle, but a path must be opened for the thoughts and voices of the marginalized to be heard, firstly amongst themselves. Community-led development alternatives are the first steps in enabling marginalized peoples to restore authentic values, self-confidence, and self-determination to develop themselves. This book examines a pathway to accomplish community-led development through effective communication and analysis of the best approaches to extreme poverty reduction.

## 2.1. Scope and Setting - Mukuru

The Mukuru informal settlement (slum)[2] in Nairobi, Kenya, is home to over 825,000 residents (Kenya census, 2019). The name Mukuru means "dumping site" in the Kikuyu language[3]. Historically, Mukuru began as grazing land and during colonization, it served as a quarry. Kenyans who worked the quarry lived in nearby settlements or informal housing. At Kenya's independence, most of the land in the area was sold to private owners, including former Kenyan President Moi (Muungano Alliance, 2017). It was purposed for light industry to create jobs during the post-independence, initial modernization era. The state guidelines for development made it difficult to succeed: (1) development had to occur within two years, (2) owners could not borrow against their land until it was developed, and (3) owners could not sell their land until it was developed (Muungano Alliance, 2017). Information regarding the owners of the land is difficult to track. Muungano Alliance spent considerable time trying to find documentation of land titles starting in 2010 (Muungano Alliance, 2017). They succeeded to some extent, and their findings are used as the basis of the data presented here.

Some factories were successfully built, and the railway was added in the early 1970s for the transport of goods[4]. The largest factory was an air, sea clearing, and freight forwarding service named Express Kenya Ltd. It was owned by a white man named Mr. Ruben. The Nairobi River runs throughout the area, making it easy for factories to dump waste from production. Hence the common name of the area is "Mukuru," which translates to "dumping site" in Kiswahili. Mr. Ruben employed many laborers, thereby increasing the number of settlers in Mukuru. Within a few years, Mukuru became one of Nairobi's landfills adjacent to petroleum pipelines and power companies.

In the 1980s, Mr. Ruben abruptly closed his business. Other landowners of parcels near Mr. Ruben's factory reclaim their plots, threatening eviction and demolition of the informal housing settlements by locals. The evictions occurred with no formal, legally recognized process of appeal (Lines & Makau, 2018). As segregation during post-colonization shifted from race to class, informal settlers continued to migrate from rural areas to Mukuru and other informal settlements, mainly because there was no affordable land for the poor in the city of Nairobi (Lines & Makau, 2018).

Geographically, Mukuru spreads across three sub-counties of Nairobi, yet the informal settlement does not exist officially per the Kenyan government. Since Mukuru does not officially exist, government services are not mandated to be offered. Thus, Mukuru remains a residential area with little to no basic services for health, sanitation, electricity, and education. Mukuru is one of several informal settlements in Nairobi, chosen as the focus of this research among the other informal settlements because of its size, accessibility, and my years of experience working with the community. The following paragraph is written to frame my work in Kenya and add relevance to the question of why Mukuru was selected among Nairobi's many informal settlements.

In 2010, I was hired as a consultant to scout a location and set up a non-profit business for a retiring board member of a San Francisco company. His goal was to feed the hungry who live in extreme poverty. My previous travels for poverty reduction work did not include the continent of Africa, his ideal location. I chose East Africa due to its relative stability. I selected Arusha, Tanzania and performed due diligence there before arranging his site visit, at which time he concluded the poverty was not extreme enough. My second choice was Nairobi, Kenya, where I had been corresponding via email with a local community organization.

I coordinated with three community organizations and arranged the visit for my client and me. We toured several informal settlements, and my client elected me to move forward to set up his food sustainability development program in Kibera, Nairobi's largest informal settlement. I, however, was struck by the community in Nairobi's second largest informal settlement, Mukuru. Informal settlements in Nairobi are so large they contain villages within them. While Kibera's villages were cohesive and well-functioning, the villages of Mukuru were less coordinated and in need of more help. Mukuru is centrally located, with easy access from several key entry locations. While finishing my consulting work, I decided to launch my own non-profit programs in Mukuru. Since 2010, I have visited and worked in Mukuru for 4 to 5 weeks on average, four times a year. Across ten years, it equates to approximately 150 weeks or three years of on-the-ground experience in Mukuru. I have witnessed death, open defecation, illness, drugs, corruption, deformities, disease, and gender abuse in Mukuru. I have also witnessed birth, happiness, pride, late homework nights, women's camaraderie, entrepreneurship, art, and resilience amidst abject poverty. This is critical to my research in that others do not have such access to an informal community.

The concept of development in and of itself is problematic; cultural norms, government corruption, and the massive needs of fellow human beings are daunting to navigate, not to mention the implicit bias toward Western modernization. Although billions of dollars have been spent since the late 1960s on foreign aid across Africa, poverty persists (World Poverty Clock[5]). Nairobi's informal settlements alone are home to approximately 2.5 million people in a city with a total population of 4.4 million (Kenya census, 2019). Some sources report that 60% of Nairobi's population lives in informal settlements (Van Noppen, Aden, 2013), thereby highlighting the urgency of creating aid programs that work here. This research addresses the problem of identifying the disconnect between residents of informal settlements like Mukuru and development professionals regarding what works best to reduce extreme poverty.

## 2.2. Theoretical Premise

A Brazilian educator, Paolo Freire, wrote Pedagogy of the Oppressed,1970, to underscore a method of educating the oppressed. Freire believed in educating people based on academic and lived experiences to help bring clarity to teaching material. He did this through dialogue.

Freirean dialogue is a conversation that brings out a deeper understanding of the situations and predicaments that surround a particular issue. This type of dialogue is needed when working in informal settlements because those whom we seek to help are sometimes unsure about what kinds of programs will help them become sustainable. For example, when people in need are given food, shelter, education, and job training through development programs, they assume these are the kinds of programs they need most, which may or may not be true.

It is also essential to take into consideration how dependency theory affects human agency (Rodney, 1972). Colonialism across the African continent bred docile bodies (Foucault, 1977) and stripped Africans of their sense of autonomy and dignity. The colonizers oppressed Africans to the extent of the latter being entrapped, immobilized, and overwhelmed. Karl Albrecht writes about Multiple Intelligence Theory and social intelligence in human interactions (Albrecht, 2006), proposing that intelligence cannot be defined as a single general ability but as multiple intelligences.

Howard Gardner agrees and adds that people are born with different intelligences, and new ones can be learned (Gardner, 2011). Examples of different kinds of intelligence are spatial, linguistic, intra-personal, interpersonal, logical-mathematical, musical, and kinesthetic. The theory is applicable to colonizers in that they lacked the intra-personal intelligence (introspection) to treat people humanely and imposed onto Africans the feeling of being paralyzed, imprisoned, smothered, or otherwise controlled by circumstances beyond their control. The African body was mutilated for the slightest use of human agency, as was the African Consciousnesses (Fanon, 1963). Albrecht states that a fear of annihilation or extinction arouses anxiety (Albrecht, 2006). This is the anxiety that development professionals may believe is gone from the African psyche or emotional DNA, that all fear has been consciously forgotten, and conversation with former colonizers is void of any apprehension. I argue that the ego-death or fear of humiliation, incapability, and unworthiness remains hidden in the African psyche (Albrecht, 2006; Fanon,1963).

In the case of Mukuru residents, the development sector is asking the residents to identify and shape programs using human agency and intelligence that their ancestors were beaten into submission to avoid. Colonizers have wiped their consciousness (Fanon, 1963), and trust must be regained with particular attention to fostering dialogue in appropriate cultural settings. The purpose of this research is to evaluate what residents of the informal settlements identify as effective program elements necessary to live a sustainable life and to analyze their input based on the critical consciousness theory of Paolo Freire. Freirean dialogue is key to addressing the disconnect between what informal settlement residents versus development professionals believe to be most effective at reducing extreme poverty.

Neither this research nor Freirean theory seeks to "raise the consciousness" of Mukuru residents by imposing Western ideology. Freire calls this the "dumping" or "banking" model of obtaining information and is highly against it (Freire, 1970). Critical consciousness is about Mukuru residents coming to their own awareness about how they entered poverty and what they believe are effective programs to reduce extreme poverty, allowing them to better participate with development providers in program planning for long-term sustainable living[6].

Additional theoretical relevance from Ivan Illich (Tools for Conviviality, 1973) points out the detrimental effects of modernization on humanity at large. Illich defines conviviality as the opposite of industrial productivity (Illich, 1973:11). Conviviality embraces a "triadic relationship between persons, tools, and a new collectivity to enlarge the range of each person's competence, control, and initiative" (Illich, 1973:xii). What Illich promotes is the use of modern tools controlled by public interest, lest a person is deprived of "using his own physical power" (Illich, 1973:27). An example of progress for Illich is to have organic mechanisms work side by side with mechanical ones. He advocates against timekeeping and accounting to quantify productivity, instead promoting a "personal balance between the workman and his tools" (Illich, 1973:30).

Illich is concerned that mankind cannot live a convivial life of fulfillment and happiness under a grinding mode of production imposed by Western standards. And as conviviality is reduced, no amount of productivity can satisfy the needs it continually creates. For example, knowledge is viewed by most as a commodity, but it continually needs improvement. Furthermore, and directly related to poverty reduction, Illich argues:

> "People first cease to trust their own judgement and then want to be told the truth about what they know. Overconfidence in 'better decision-making' first hampers people's ability to decide for themselves, and then undermines their belief that they can decide. The growing impotence of people to decide for themselves affects the structure of their expectations." (Illich, 1973:86-87).

Education as a tool of conviviality seems reasonable. However, the twelve stages of enlightenment (grades 1-12) have become something sought by the poor as if it had the magic to produce a new type of man or woman. And, for those who earn low to mediocre grades in school, society discards them as "unprepared for the good life in a man-made world" (Illich, 1973:19). The "poverty of the unschooled" is compounded with "discrimination of the uneducated" (Illich, 1973:19). While Illich is not against education as a commodity, he is against it as an institution that makes those who cannot attain it feel purposeless. Illich says, "The poor learn to fend in dignity where no education could teach the rich to survive" (Illich, 1973:58).

Like Scott, Illich is not proposing to abandon modernization but to provide developing countries with "the choice of its own unique social arrangements" (Illich, 1973:14). Both scholars are intimating that what is "good" is not always aligned with what is "right" in terms of paths to modernization and finding a place on the global stage. Unlike Freire, neither Illich nor Scott differentiate between the lived and learned experiences of people living in poverty but rather advocate for alternative modes of programs to increase productivity in a post-industrial age.

As someone who has spent ethnographic time in the slums of Nairobi, conviviality counts. Before modern medicine, there were alternative natural remedies and practices for good health. Many still occur in the present day, such as childbirth at home in Mukuru. A midwife is present, the pregnant mother squats, and ironically, she does not yell much from labor pain. In India, there is a natural tree from which children and adults break off a small twig (datun), and chew as a form of teeth cleaning. Neem bark has antibacterial properties and active ingredients, some of which are found in toothpaste. The ingredients in neem bark help reduce gingivitis, serve as a breath freshener, and relieve dental pain. This is not to say that I concur with Scott or Illich in full but to emphasize that Freire's clarity on the importance of lived experiences combines elements of both scholars. That schools and hospitals are needed, yes; however, there may be versions of schools and versions of hospitals that serve countries better on their developmental path. Could there not be programs developed that embrace both?

> "...open our eyes to the possibility of a society where work and leisure and politics would favor learning that could function with less formal education" and "permit us to set up educational arrangements that favor self-initiated, self-chosen learning..." (Illich, 1973:61).

In the spirit of blending lived and learned experience for more effective development for informal settlements, some ascribe to leveling the slums and "modernizing" slum-dwellers by introducing apartments to replace their informal homes. Another quote from Illich portrays the result of this approach best:

> "To accommodate more people on less land, Venezuela and Brazil experimented with high-rise tenements. First the police had to dislodge people from their 'slums' and resettle them in apartments. Then the social workers had to socialize the tenants who lacked sufficient schooling to understand that pigs may not be raised on eleventh-floor balconies, nor [that] beans [could not be] cultivated in their bathtubs." (Illich, 1973:63).

Illich can be criticized for selling low-income countries short of reaching their greatest potential. Much like the thoughts of Booker T. Washington, Illichs 'convivial tools can be viewed as limiting and thwarting the development of one's full potential. Nevertheless, there remains something to be said for the respect and worthiness of doing housework, farming, bartering, masonry, and providing grassroots health services.

There are differences between technocrats applying solutions to problems and those who research culturally preferred solutions to problems side-by-side with communities. And there is no reason why the three should not join forces to solve one of the world's most persistent issues – poverty. The poor, nor anyone else, should not have their way of being produced for them. They should be facilitated to think critically about what kind of support is needed for a productive livelihood and allow practitioners to plan accordingly. This is where Freirean theory can level the playing field. In the case of extreme poverty reduction, practitioners and clients share lived and learned experiences to create effective poverty reduction programs.

A further point of contention to be clarified is the use of the word "slum." The term itself is abrasive and dehumanizes those who, by no fault of their own, live there. This is more of a discourse for Westerners, as the locals who live in the informal settlements (from my experience) do not have a problem with the term. They remain proud citizens of Nairobi, some touting remarkable success in education (MA degrees) and other entrepreneurial endeavors. The name of the informal settlement in this research (Mukuru) means "dumping site," a term that locals do not object to, nor take offense at or seek to change. I align with the residents of Mukuru in using the terms "Mukuru" and "slum" to defy the softer term "informal settlement." Mukuru residents are strong, proud, and stand tall against any dehumanization. One can be born in a "dumping ground" and still command respect by their character without changing or softening the truth about the living conditions of where they are raised for others to feel more comfortable. In addition, the development sector uses the term "slum" to differentiate between other types of informal settlements that are not overcrowded and located in rural areas.

The research question and hypothesis are exploratory. There are many questions about the who, what, and why of poverty reduction; each nuanced by our own curiosities. Using Freirean pedagogy in this research is also exploratory. The development sector has approached extreme poverty reduction in external ways but not in ways that raise consciousness, as Freire did with his students in the Brazilian favelas. Since the issues and methods are vast for effective programs to reduce extreme poverty, a good research question and hypothesis stand to unveil additional answers to questions one might ask about extreme poverty reduction. Additional answers will be discussed in the findings and analysis.

## 2.3. Research Questions and Significance

In order to test the authenticity of expression, a theory on critical thinking and communication serves well to improve or identify potential communication gaps between community residents and development professionals. Using such a theory, independent and dependent variables may include self-beliefs, group-beliefs, beliefs about others, and feelings of self-blame.

The significance of this research is to help the development sector in Kenya reach the UN Sustainable Development Goals (SGDs) for the long-deserved alleviation of extreme poverty in the informal settlement of Mukuru and potentially other urban informal settlements. The SDGs placed "poverty eradication" as the first goal to reach by the year 2030 (UN Foundation). The goals were built on several iterations of humanitarian ideals. In 1993, the Development Assistance Committee (DAC) of the Organization for Economic Cooperation and Development (OECD) created a policy for ordinary people in countries receiving aid to participate in the shaping of their lives (Goldsmith, 2001). In 1998, the UN Economic Commission for Africa called for the same (Goldsmith, 2001). Because poverty eradication is a top goal, along with people participating in shaping their own lives, this book will make the following contributions to the existing literature on development, the work of development experts, and the lives of informal settlers; it will serve to:

1.   *Maintain the DAC and OECD's goal of having ordinary people shape their lives*

2.   *Help large development organizations create more effective programs*

3.   *Help the development community achieve the top priority of the UN SDGs*

### Research question:

"Are residents of informal settlements using their knowledge to help development professionals understand what kinds of programs will effectively reduce extreme poverty?"

### Hypothesis:

Residents of Mukuru are not expressing how they feel about the effectiveness of poverty reduction programs offered by development professionals.

I contend that most expatriate development professionals lack an understanding of the everyday components of life in poverty. They have no lived experience. They do not consider that poor people will accept whatever program is offered to them, even if it is a waste of time. From my own lived experience[7], the poor will very rarely turn down a program because they may never get another program in its place. In other words, program feedback may not be authentic. Development professionals in-country with lived experience are frequently paid by large foreign countries who provide a checklist of poverty reduction efforts that must be completed, useful or not. My hypothesis is that a disconnect exists between development professionals and residents of the informal settlement of Mukuru regarding what works to reduce poverty[8].

The research contributes to the work of development professionals in foreign aid. The Mukuru informal settlement of Nairobi, Kenya, serves as the case study in this book, though it is my hope that this work may be applicable to poverty reduction efforts around the world. This book will address extreme poverty by looking at the role critical consciousness may play as a tool for residents of informal settlements to successfully co-create development programs for long-term resilience.

This work assumes that the US Department of State supports the UN SGDs and that agencies such as USAID, the Millennium Challenge Corporation, the US Development Finance Corporation, and other US government agencies engaged in human development share the same goal. The World Bank, an independent agency, is also among those vested in human development. The research in this book has limitations in funding and time to ascertain the root cause underlying the research question and deeper exploring theory behind the hypothesis. Additional limitations of human error in terms of the truth not being reported, particularly in focus groups. Human error is present in all research on human beings and bears no additional relevance to this research. Humans are unpredictable, and there is no preventative measure that can be applied to deter this reality. Delimitations for types of participants, locations, and sectors used for this book are residents of informal settlements in Nairobi, Kenya and the development sector that intends to serve them. The definitions of key terms and acronyms used in this book are listed in Appendix A.3.

### 2.3.1. Significance to Pre-colonial History

Pre-colonial Africa has a rich history, inclusive of urban growth before the fifteenth century, particularly regarding trade to Europe and Asia along the coasts of West and East Africa (Reid, 2011). The falsification of history regarding the role of Africans as "pioneers to mankind on the road to civilization" begins as early as 2300 B.C.E. in Mesopotamia (Diop, 1974:43). Egyptian civilization dominated culturally in Africa throughout the Old, Middle, and New Kingdom (2675-1075 B.C.E.), up to the Roman and Byzantine

Empire (C.E. 642), the time of Augustus Ceasar (University of Memphis Institute of Egyptian Art & Archaeology)[9].

The end of Egyptian domination intersects with the emergence of the Sudanese Kingdom of Kush, which contributed to the culture and political landscape of north-eastern Africa for nearly a thousand years up to 1500 B.C.E. (Hafsaas-Tsakos, 2009). As part of Nubia, the Kush-Nubian culture was sophisticated in commerce, serving Africa's interior with trade in the Mediterranean basin. The Nubian culture helped Sub-Saharan Africa trade ebony, gold, ivory, and animal pelts. Nubians imported incense, olive oil, timber, and bronze from the Mediterranean through ports along the Nile and the Red Sea (Hafsaas-Tsakos, 2009). Ethiopia's city of Axum also represents prosperity in African development. Axum's growth from the year 100 C.E. to 715.

C.E. demonstrates growth in economic and political development and international trade (Butzer, 2017). Success with crop growth continued until the C.E. 800s when ecological degradation shifted farming to other, still fertile lands. We also know that Ethiopia was never colonized (Geda, 2006).

The African continent was not devoid of skills and intelligence pre-colonialism. There are marked differences across the regions, such as highly skilled hunting groups in the Congo and the Kalahari Desert, Galla pastoralists, educated Mandinga, Bozo fishermen, nomadic Fulani herdsmen, and international tradesmen (Rodney, 1972). When there is a discussion about pre-colonial Africa, a Eurocentric perspective accompanies, whereby an automatic comparison of civilizations ensues (Rodney, 1972). "Culture is a total way of life" (Rodney, 1972:34). In this light, the discussion of development must include the originating background and success of African civilization.

Beginning in the 1600s, foreign countries ravished the natural and human resources of the African continent (Matunhu, 2011). Kenya was no exception. When Kenya gained its independence in 1963 under the leadership of President Jomo Kenyatta, modernizing efforts started by colonizers were unsuccessful. The Western development model of industrialization that began with rural agriculture to increase trade did not work (Bates, 1985). Societal norms in Africa were not conducive to this approach. An example of differing norms is demonstrated in the Western approach of growing the same type of agricultural crop twice a year and in large quantities (Bjornlund et al., 2020). Norms of the continent were to grow different types of crops, which would produce one harvest per item (Bjornlund et al., 2020). The Western norms were extraction-heavy, different from the continental norms of producing food for the community while protecting the soil quality for the long-term health of future crops. Likewise, Rostow's stages of economic growth (Rostow, 1960), widely accepted as the standard for modernization, failed because there was insufficient social and physical infrastructure to support broad-based westernized commercial expansion. Slow economic growth, limited wealth creation, and inequitable distribution of wealth during the colonial and post-independence eras created the need for external investment and technology transfer from the US and Europe. However, what was distributed most was foreign aid in the form of loans and poverty reduction programs for human development according to Western standards. During the 1960s, at the height of the Cold War, foreign aid also included security programs (Gendzier, 1985) that addressed the needs of US state interests. Carol Lancaster reminds us that the business of state-building in terms of U.S. interests is paramount, i.e., promoting good governance, leadership, conflict prevention, peacebuilding, national security, trade, foreign investment, and the evolving role of Africa globally (Lancaster, 2006). It was the United Nations that intervened much later to clarify and forge consensus on the goals of foreign aid with the Millennium Development Goals (MDGs), later reformed as the Sustainable Development Goals (SDGs)[10].

The SDGs intend to magnify development with dignity that is people-centered, planet-safe, aiding state prosperity, justice, and partnerships and improving the wellbeing for the people being served. With uneven reforms of the colonial system left behind, African states were at an economic disadvantage at the onset of independence. The continent struggled to modernize using Euro-centric methods and lacked knowledge about how to change the colonial blueprint that was set up to foster profit for government elites and not for the broader citizenry.

Some of Africa's rural workforce (Bates,1981) relocated from rural farms to urban cities, hoping to gain jobs during the modernization era. In Kenya specifically, people from the countryside moved to Nairobi and erected temporary, informal dwellings on government land near landfills and dumpsites. The purpose was to occupy space where they would least likely be ordered to leave. With urban lots in high demand, there were few affordable alternatives.

Moreover, the dumpsites offered discarded items that were useful for everyday living. Temporary dwellings became permanent. Nairobi did not attract adequate foreign direct investment or manage its economy sufficiently to place its citizens in steady jobs (World Bank Country Report, Structural Adjustments, 1980). As a result, people remained living in informal settlements because they could not afford to move out. Most informal settlements across the continent of Africa formed this way (Fox, 2014; Muungano Alliance, 2017)[11].

Kenyans have an affinity for ancestral land. It does not matter whether it is rural or in informal settlements; the affinity lies wherever generations of your family have lived. Ancestral land is more than a birthplace; it signifies identity (Naidu-Hoffmeester, 2018), family traditions, culture, and a deep connection with nature and life. For many Indigenous cultures, the land holds significance beyond commodification (Tafira, 2015). It is where traditions are born and knowledge is passed down (Lemmen et al., 2015).

Land in informal settlements is different than the rural land of ancestors. Yet for residents of slums, the land has become an additional place of family heritage, including the normative, customary rights to continue living on the land due to multi-year, uninterrupted occupation of it (Kibera Facts, 2020; (Bourdieu,1993). Some families have lived informally for up to four generations. Life in informal settlements has become a formal way of living. For some, informal settlements like Mukuru are considered home in the same way as ancestral rural land.

The US provides the largest amount of development aid to foreign countries. Despite US foreign aid being targeted at low-middle income countries across Africa beginning in the 1960s, as of sixty years later (2022), informal settlements remain in Kenya and other African states[12].

Though the US is not directly responsible for alleviating poverty in Kenya or other African countries, there is no exit strategy to allow the Kenyan government and the Kenyan people to address the issues directly in a more productive way. Poverty is defined by the World Bank as those earning $1.90 or less per day. This is henceforth referred to as the poverty line, different from the poverty rate or ratio which is the number of people whose income is below the poverty line. The poverty ratio measurement is different than the actual number of poor. For instance, the poverty rate in Africa had fallen from 54% in 1990 to 41% in 2015 (World Bank, 2015).

However, the number of poor in Africa increased from 278 million in 1990 to 413 million in 2015 (World Bank, 2015). Part of the increase in the number of poor across Africa is due to personal circumstances, and the other part is due to population growth (decrease in infant mortality rate and increase in life expectancy). In the first quarter of 2019, the World Bank published an expected increase in poverty of 90% by 2030 (World Bank, 2019), not knowing that the pandemic outbreak of COVID-19 would exacerbate poverty in African countries beginning in the second quarter of 2020. Since the start of the COVID pandemic, estimations have been that an additional 27 million people in Sub-Saharan Africa would be pushed into extreme poverty due to loss of income from state lock-down orders to contain the virus (World Bank, August 26, 2020 report). That number is now estimated by the African Development Bank to be 49.2 million people by 2022 (ADB, Annual African Economic Outlook Report 2020).

The poverty rate in Kenya specifically decreased in 2019 from 43% to 36% from 2015 to 2019 (World Bank, 2019). Great efforts by USAID, the World Bank, NGOs, foundations, and social enterprises can be credited with this success, but the success was largely in rural Kenya. In urban Nairobi, the number of those living in poverty appears to have grown. The COVID pandemic introduced a new variable into poverty rates, making it difficult to discern comparative data. It is worth noting that at the poverty line of $5.50 per day, Kenya and most of Africa have a poverty rate of 86.5%[13,14]. There has been discussion in the development sector that the poverty line should be raised to $3.20/day as a realistic amount needed to reach a satisfactory level of consumption (Hickel, 2018 Center for Global Development). The extreme poverty marker of $1.90/day set in 2011[15] has recently been acknowledged as too low for human well-being.

### 2.3.2. Statistical Significance of the Informal Settlements

Nairobi is the capital of Kenya. It is the epicenter of over 12 informal settlements. This research is focused on the informal settlement of Mukuru, selected for its size and accessibility. Reviewing the statistics from the 2019 census in Kenya, the population of Nairobi is confirmed at approximately 4.4 million people[16]. As seen in Figure 2.1, a map borrowed from an African news source[17] and augmented for clarity shows how the Mukuru informal settlement stretches across three Nairobi counties: Embakasi, Makadara, and Starehe. See Figure 2.1.

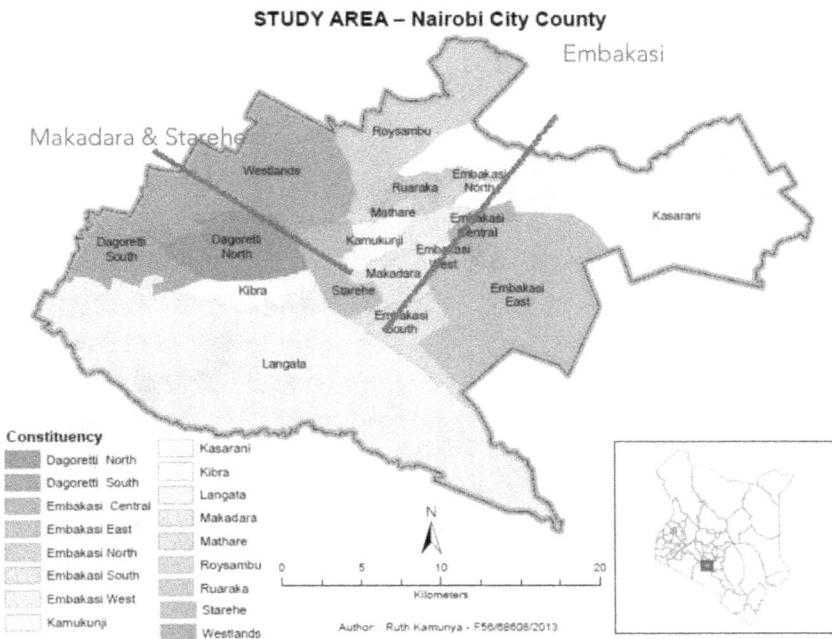

**Figure 2.1.** Nairobi County Map

The population of the three counties is approximately 989,000; 190,000; and 210,000, respectively[18]. The combined county populations make the total population of the Mukuru informal settlement approximately 1.4 million people[19]. The Mukuru population stated in the introduction of this paper (825K) reflects the possibility that some county residents in the three counties may live in dwellings that are not part of the informal settlements. Nevertheless, Mukuru is commonly known as the second-largest informal settlement in Nairobi, which means the population of the largest informal settlement (Kibera) would have to be over 1.4 million.

These two informal settlements together comprise 2.8 million people. If we err on the lower side of the data, the population of the two informal settlements remains over 2 million, and there are several smaller informal settlements in Nairobi that are not counted in this figure. This data supersedes previous public guesstimates[20] regarding the size of the informal settlement population in Nairobi. It supports the unpopular truth that nearly half of Nairobi's population lives in poverty and predominantly in informal settlements. The figure provides an overhead view of Mukuru taken from Google Earth (Figure 2.2) and a flat map from the Muungano Organization that denoted the 30 villages within Mukuru (Figure 2.3).

**Figure 2.2.** Mukuru from Overhead, Google Earth

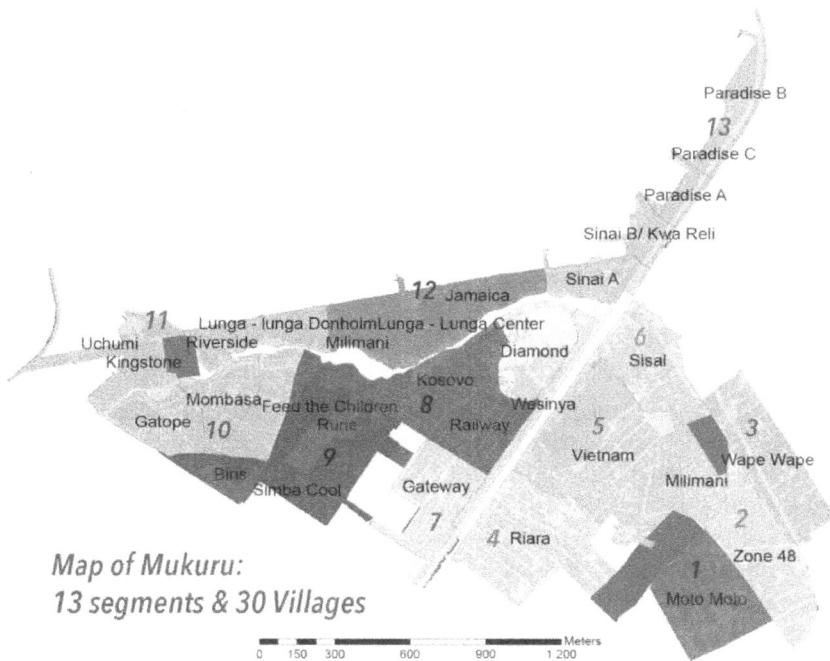

**Figure 2.3.** Mukuru's 30 Villages, Muungano

The census for Nairobi counts 1.49 million households, including informal settlements, which averages three people per household in a population of 4.4 million. Census data shows that 51.3% of Nairobi households have dwellings with iron roofing. The dominant material for wall construction is concrete (40.3%), and the dominant flooring material is concrete at 62.5%[21]. Concrete floors are considered the first step towards a better standard of living. To afford concrete walls is more difficult to achieve. Therefore, about half of the population of Nairobi live in a home without concrete walls. These statistics represent nearly 40% of dwellings with sub-standard flooring and 60% with sub-standard wall construction across Nairobi. Residents of the informal settlement refer to their homes as mabati, one-room dwellings usually 8 feet x 10 feet and made of corrugated tin. The data thus supports the reality of poverty levels in the city, but it does not go far enough. In Nairobi, census takers have difficulty accessing dwellings in informal settlements as compared to the more accessible modern homes. I have walked across the two largest informal settlements (Mukuru and Kibera), in which dung/mud walls and dirt floors are the norm, not concrete. Yet this is not indicated in the census data, at least not in the volume which I have seen.

In addition to substandard housing, the statistics reveal poverty in terms of access to water and waste disposal (Kenya Census, 2019)[22]. For daily household routines, 28.4% of households get piped water to their plot for drinking, and 22.7% get water piped directly into their dwelling. That leaves 48.9% with no piped water. Regarding human waste disposal, 54.3% of households have main sewer taps for waste (pipes in modern bathrooms), and the rest use covered and uncovered pit latrines. A surprising figure of 0.1% use the open bush for human defecation. This statistic is questionable, given millions of people live in informal settlements without toilets or pit latrines. Most families use the open bush near the river as a toilet. I believe the residents of informal settlements answered some of the census questions, protecting their pride rather than expressing the truth, which has skewed the data.

Regarding food preparation, 67% of Nairobi uses propane gas for cooking, leaving the rest to use fuels that are more pollutants, such as paraffin, firewood, and charcoal. With 33% of Nairobi households using dirty fuels to cook, it adds another dimension of poverty related to the continual exposure to gases that are hazardous to respiratory health[23]. Furthermore, using pollutants to cook increases the risk of death by fires. Although census data also shows that 96.5% of Nairobi households have electricity, this statistic does not reveal that residents of informal settlements connect illegally to electrical wires across city grids. When one of these wires has a fault, it can cause uncontrollable fires in the informal settlements (Aiyabei and Ohdiambo, 2020). Overall, the census does not present a true picture of the realities of poverty in Nairobi. Instead, it plays a role in decreasing the urgency for effective poverty reduction by masking the numbers of slum dwellers.

Residents of Mukuru have multiple issues that add to and exacerbate living in poverty. The illegal and unsafe electrical taps from city lines are often controlled by cartels who charge exorbitant rates for access (Lagan, 2014). What little funds or assets residents have left are spent on meeting necessities like food, school fees, and rent. Residents in informal settlements use modern technology regularly; these are tools that development professionals could integrate into poverty reduction programs. More than half of Kenya's population from age three[24] and above (69%) own a mobile phone. Suffice it to say that many of the poor leapfrogged past the modernization step of putting telecom wiring through walls because they never had enough money to acquire homes with actual walls, and wireless technology became readily accessible and affordable. Development programs have used cell phone technology as an approach to poverty reduction efforts but could do more[25].

Another technological approach to poverty reduction is through television programs. Surprisingly, 68.7% of households in the census indicate that they own a functional television (Kenya Census, 2019). Households with or without walls find value in television for entertainment and news, even when it means paying for electricity taps through illegal connections. Having a television indicates preferences for receiving information and sheds light on the spending capacity of residents in informal settlements. The government of Kenya places public service announcements on television. However, other development programs could find television to be an effective alternative to communicate with hard-to-reach communities like Mukuru.

The census data also shows trained skills acquired (KNBS Table 2.7, p.160). The number of Kenyans trained in business (commerce, accounting, finance, marketing, admin, management, insurance, hotel management, tourism) is 779,621. Similarly, 740,605 are trained as educators (in science, arts, management, and economics). There are 307,699 trained in engineering (electrical, mechanical, chemical, aeronautical, bio-systems), most of which are male, and 114,973 trained in interdisciplinary studies (urban planning, cultural & gender studies, project management, human resources). Other categories with more than 87,000 trained are computer science, agriculture, health, and journalism (KNBS Vol IV, Table 2.7, 160). The number of trained Kenyans may demonstrate a compilation of natural talent, education gained at local universities and other post-secondary training programs, and/or the positive impact of government or development programs. The fact that residents of the informal settlements are included in these training statistics means that development programs could call upon talents within the informal settlement community to solve some of its issues[26]. These trainings have also prepared the way for future foreign direct investment (FDI) and public-private partnerships (PPPs) for informal settlements.

Over the three sub-counties (Embakasi, Makadara, and Starehe) in Nairobi that encompass Mukuru, approximately 573K residents of informal settlements are actively working out of 1.3 million (Kenya Census, 2019)[27]. Work may not necessarily mean a steady job; instead, it may consist of gigs or odd jobs that end within a day or a week. This statistic counts workers from age 5+[28] and indicates that one-third of the Mukuru informal settlement population is employed. Working children aged five are likely left at home because their parents cannot afford school fees.

The census measured homeownership uniquely according to categories of land tenure. Dwellings in the Mukuru informal settlement are 5.8% owned with tenured land[29] 53.23% of the dwellings are purchased without land, 29.2% are constructed without land title, and 17.66% of the dwellings are inherited without land title[30]. Households renting by mode of tenure-ship are 4.7% through government leases, 3.9% county government, 2.9% parastatal (having some political authority), 8.1% private companies, 79.1% individuals, and .05% from NGOs[31]. This data supports the idea that the informal settlement population rent their dwellings but do not own the land on which they live. Some have managed to obtain land tenure from the government (5.8%), though the majority are paying rent to individuals (79.1%) who claim to own the land legally. This is relevant to poverty reduction because, for example, an organization that seeks to build safer structures in informal settlements may have difficulties regarding unsupported claims of ownership for the permanent structures built. Considering the statistic that 79.1% of land in Mukuru is privately owned, a buy-out from the local government or a Public-Private Partnership (PPP) could resolve many, if not all, issues of land tenure.

In closing, the census statistics are included in this research to reveal the depths of poverty in the informal settlement (living conditions) and how development may be able to better serve informal settlement residents through their skills and use of technology. These factors are helpful in compiling a clearer picture of poverty for the development industry and the use of foreign aid. The takeaway is that out of 4.4 million people, close to half live in informal settlements without closed roofs, flooring, or piped water. Approximately half of the population uses pit latrines, a statistic that is difficult to believe, seeing that the informal settlements have little to no land for placing latrines for 2.5 million people. The good news is that 57% no longer cook on open flames, and 97% have electricity (not necessarily legal and safely wired). The shocking news is that 80% are paying rent to someone who may or may not own the property they inhabit, leaving the majority of residents vulnerable to expulsion and exploitation. The Kenyan 2019 statistics demonstrate the large-scale funding needed to make a positive impact on poverty in informal settlements. This cannot be accomplished by small non-profits and NGOs or one-off projects.

From Nairobi's census count of 4.4 million (NASA, 2016 report)[32], the population is most dense on 6% of the land occupied by approximately 2.5 million residents of informal settlements. If we know where the density of Nairobi's poor live, and foreign aid has been targeted to reduce poverty since the 1960s, aside from COVID-19, why has there been so little poverty reduction in the informal settlements? Some might argue that the vast majority of foreign aid was initially aimed at rural poverty. My question is, why? There has been strong evidence of poverty in urban areas, beginning with migration to cities post-independence. Moreover, the exported model of Rostow's stages of economic growth failed in rural areas where agriculture was expected to take off. It may be the case that poverty reduction efforts in rural areas signify the low-hanging fruit; rural communities are more accessible than urban informal settlements.

The World Bank measures global poverty through household surveys (World Bank Group, 2019). That, in and of itself, is problematic to gather accurate data on informal settlements. Residents have no "registered" home to speak of; they erect shanties on non-tenured land (Kibera Facts & Information online 2020). Retrieving data is logistically challenging without engaging help from within the community. The Kenyan National Bureau of Statistics census uses this method to count the informal settlement population and marginal communities on the outskirts of the country (KNBS, 2019). World Bank data remains questionable despite the bank's call for better data during its strategic planning (Madavo et al., 2000 IMF). Geospatial information and other remote sensing technologies are currently being incorporated into the count, but further improvements are warranted.

The Bank gets data from country management teams and other official sources such as country reports (World Bank[33]). The bank also uses data from Pew and Afrobarometer, as noted in many of their publications under graphs, charts and in bank publication bibliographies. The data deficit on informal settlements is because Pew and Afrobarometer collect data from households that have electricity, piped water, and sewage systems[34,35]. Pew's datasets are more on global attitudes and trends, of which the most recent is from Spring 2019[36]. Afrobarometer collected data in Kenya from only 1600 households on average that are located within easy walking distance of a post office, school, police station, and health clinic (Afrobarometer[37]). The relevance is that the sample groups do not reflect reality for 50% of the population of Kenya who live in informal settlements because dwellings in the informal settlements do not have electricity, piped water or sewage systems.

### 2.3.3. Significance to Human Aid

Extreme poverty is increasing, regardless of aid money allocations, manpower, programmatic planning, and local human resources. Poverty reduction and aid programs began in the 1960s. Billions of dollars in US foreign aid have been given to African states[38]. The US Congress appropriates the funds for development agencies of the US government to address a wide variety of human development needs, including food security, education, job training, democracy and good governance, and much more. Existing research on why foreign aid and poverty reduction programs have failed suggests systemic problems within organizations, such as bureaucracy, critique of salaries being too low or too high, limitations on how to service clients, insufficient accountability, and inadequate incentives to succeed. This book moves beyond organizational systems to focus on people and solutions to regain lost ground in poverty reduction.

USAID has worked in Kenya since 1962,[39] providing over 50 years of service primarily to the lower-middle class in Nairobi and addressing extreme rural poverty. USAID uses a wide range of contract services and collaborates with local businesses. When locals are used in development aid, shared cultural norms reduce communication gaps that can mislead outsiders regarding the viability of a program. For example, USAID supported Sanergy of Nairobi, a local business that offers waste-removal services and low-cost latrines to parts of the informal settlements (USAID, 2013). In this case, regardless of US bureaucracy and lack of lived experience, the job gets done. The downfall of the Sanergy example is that the business was not scaled up to reach all the informal settlement population. Smaller NGOs and businesses, whether local or foreign, make even less impact than the USAID-Sanergy example, leaving stakeholders and supporters wondering why they continue to donate. Producing significant impact in informal settlements cannot be achieved by NGOs; it takes large organizations working with NGOs, the government, and the private sector together to use a different approach to poverty reduction.

Still, resources and collaborations are not the full solution. There are unspoken interests that even the residents of informal settlements do not realize are vital to success until a program is already underway. Organizations are meeting metrics, while the poor are struggling to meet short-term needs, neither being successful in the long-term eradication of extreme poverty. A deficit of data on residents of the informal settlements is additive to the disconnect.

If the goal of foreign aid is to empower beneficiaries with "the capacity to take ownership of development processes" (US Department of State, 2016:14FAM 243.3-1), we are not offering the kinds of development locals wish to own. For example, between 2009 and 2015, the UN in partnership with the Kenyan government, built new apartments (KENSUP Program) for the informal settlement community of Kibera (Kiti, 2015; Ngunjiri, 2018). Locals from Kibera benefited from training and employment to build the structures themselves. The UN hoped that the Kenyan government would continue to construct more units using trained Kibera residents, thereby allowing them to earn income. However, at completion, some residents of informal settlements moved into the new housing, while others did not wish to move. Some accepted the new housing as an asset to sub-let while they remained in their mabati.

There are rumors of some who received the new home, moved into it, and vacated shortly thereafter. Others made claims that the government raised the rent from $10 to $15/month just before move-in, a 50% increase that was untimely and unreasonable to request (Ngunjiri, 2018). Development professionals may consider the description "unreasonable" to be a subjective statement. However, it is more than a hardship for people earning $1.90/day or less to become capable of paying 50% higher rent over a period of a month with no additional income. Some residents of informal settlements earn less than $1.90/day, and their earnings are inconsistent. Many who live in the informal settlement noticed that foreign nationals (Sudanese and Ethiopians) and the Kenyan middle class were moving into the new homes instead of Kibera residents. Pushed out by the city's increasing rents, the outsiders could afford the rent, and Kibera residents made a profit subletting their units while they remained in the informal settlement. Statements from residents about the problems of the KENSUP housing development are below.

### Reference to government corruption:

"I thought I was going to be evacuated to a better home, [but] things changed," says one resident, Benson K.

"My house's number was changed and since then we were told things had changed. Our rent fee was increased from $10 to $15 every month and if I d'n' t pay that amount, I was threatened that I'd find my things moved out of my house." Citylimits.org (May 2, 2018) Comment anonymous

### Reference to tenants 'not' from the informal settlement:

"I was here when these well-constructed houses were being built. We were told that our shanty houses were going to be demolished. We were to move from these smaller houses to well-constructed houses. However, those well-constructed houses are already full, and I can even see Sudanese, and Ethiopians." Ctilimits.org (2018) Comment anonymous

### Reference to lack of neighborhood advantages:

"This means I can get to the market a lot easier, and the transport drops me just in front of my stall," she says. But because some shacks were removed to make space for development, she now has fewer customers living nearby. Pumiza, Fihlani. BBC News (2015)

The KENSUP project failed due to a mixture of issues. Aside from those issues, moving is known as one of the top stressors in life (Healthy UH Hospitals)[40]. Intellectually, a new housing unit sounds like a promising idea. Psychologically, one must consider the impact of leaving neighbors who may have helped you through difficulties in life or being moved away from convenient and friendly local vendors. The reality of leaving the home where your parents and grandparents were born is not easy. Also, informal settlements provide social networks of support where there are none with the government. The small 5x8 foot mabati that many residents of informal settlements live in is home (Ngunjiri, 2018), where neighborhood shops and stalls crowd narrow corridors, offering anyone the chance to open a stall with just a table – something that was not allowed at the new KENSUP apartments. There are intangible social benefits within the informal settlement that make it unique. The failure of KENSUP (Candiracci, 2007) indicates that programs with the best intentions are not sustainable without appropriate measures in place for success. The disconnect between service delivery and the needs of the residents of informal settlements must be addressed, which I hope to identify and evaluate through my research with a new theory for successful development in the informal settlement of Mukuru and potentially other urban informal settlements in Nairobi and across the continent.

**2.3.4. Significance to Inclusive Development**

Amidst the debate on how best to reduce poverty, inclusiveness has taken high priority. Although development organizations have tried to address all levels of poverty, research shows that some groups remain marginalized (Kristalina Georgieva, 2020). Women and girls are considered a marginalized group, and when coupled with living in an informal settlement or having HIV, they are further marginalized through cultural stigma and having less access to services. Realizing this, USAID launched an initiative in 2017 to integrate inclusiveness into its development programs. All USAID poverty reduction programs were restructured to look for marginalized identities that were missing, including refugees, climate migrants, the disabled, the LGBT, and those who live in obscure[41] locations like the informal settlements (USAID-ADS, 2017: Ch.205). The World Bank followed suit and sought to increase involvement with Civil Society Organizations that reach the marginalized across all social dimensions (Axel Van Trottenburg, 2020). Inclusive development also strives to partner with new organizations instead of working exclusively with USAID's traditional partners (USAID-ADS, 2017: Ch.205). From the highest levels at the Bureau of Policy, Planning, and Learning to the Country Mission offices of USAID, Inclusive Development is being prioritized, yet clear metrics have yet to be specified or quantified.

The Kenyan Government launched the "Big 4 Agenda" in May 2019. The government intends to become more inclusive to its citizens by addressing the creation of jobs through enhanced manufacturing, universal healthcare, food security and nutrition, and affordable housing. However, informal settlements are not officially recognized by the Kenyan government. Therefore, little to no public services are offered to residents. The lack of public service rights was noted first-hand during a visit where a fire broke out, killing 14 people, as I watched two fire- trucks drive by and offer no help. The only Big 4 Agenda item explicitly offered to all Kenyans is universal health care. In attempting to solve any problem of international relations, it is important to recognize that sovereign governments must find value in including their own people. No amount of development aid or human development programs can force local governments to make policy changes to help their poor citizens, even when the U.S. urges countries to do so.

### 2.3.5. Significance to US State Interests

In recent years, the U.S. government has had a heightened interest in investing in Kenya, including addressing issues in informal settlements. While other governments have helped Kenya to develop, the U.S. has a renewed interest in investing in infrastructure and military partnerships like AFRICOM. The current Kenyan-US trade deal, to be signed by April 2024, put issues such as the informal settlements on the table since 70% of Nairobi's workforce lives in slums. (KIPPRA, 2023).

Infrastructure improves trade, but Foreign Direct Investment (FDI) is less attractive in cities with poor infrastructure, weak governance, and poor urban planning, giving rise to informal settlements that house a large percentage of residents. For an investor, great poverty means an elevated risk of political and economic instability. However, infrastructure can be posited as helping the informal settlements if the projects provide jobs. While the benefits of infrastructure programs may not serve the poor as quickly as a well-planned poverty reduction program that creates immediate jobs, the African Union (AU) and the National Partnership for Africa's Development (NEPAD) both seek to ensure economic benefits flow to the community level where infrastructure programs have been initiated[42].

Firstly, the U.S. renewed interest in Africa was the result of China's 1990 long-term strategy to build a closer alliance with Africa, launched aggressively in 2013 through the Belt and Road initiative (Yun Sun, 2014), an initiative to connect all countries on the African continent via rail, bridges, and roads. The program continues today and offers what Africa needs most to enter the global trade market: hard infrastructure, including roads, ports, energy, dams, airports, internet connection, and more. Additionally, African leaders need (or want) cash. Loans from China do not require the economic restructuring often required by the IMF (Yun Sun, 2014). Chinese loan conditions are often easier for African governments to understand and negotiate. As China's Belt and Road program grew, America took notice and aggressively began to pursue new partnerships with African countries.

The new partnerships between America and Africa came in the form of trade pacts and investment acts. In 2000, the Clinton administration launched the African Growth and Opportunities Act (AGOA) to open more trade between African countries and the U.S. AGOA has provided eligible sub-Saharan African countries the opportunity to export 6800 kinds of products to the U.S. duty-free (USTR.gov)[43]. In 2014, when the Obama White House announced the Doing Business in Africa (DBIA) Campaign (WH Fact Sheet, 2014)[44], the intention was to strengthen U.S.-Africa relations through commercial trade and investment opportunities. U.S. exports went up 40% and increased U.S. jobs by 250,000 (WH Fact Sheet, 2014). In 2014, U.S. investments totaled $7 billion under the Power Africa initiative (WH Fact Sheet, 2014), and by 2019, totaled nearly $14 billion (https://www.usaid.gov/powerafrica). Other major USG initiatives launched since 2010 include Power Africa, focused on expanding access to affordable energy, and Prosper Africa, focused on inclusive economic growth. However, I am unable to find out how many jobs these initiatives created for Africans.

Secondly, in 2018, Senator Bob Corker (R-TN) sponsored a bill (S.2463) that passed and was made into law on October 5th, 2018, the Better Utilization of Investment Leading to Development Act (BUILD). It signaled a new push to designate Africa as a focus in foreign policy for U.S. investment. The BUILD Act transformed the Overseas Private Investment Corporation (OPIC) into a new agency, the U.S. International Development Finance Corporation (DFC)[45]. BUILD increases the DFC's spending limit on investments in Africa from $29 billion under OPIC to $60 billion. This is a seven-year limit. The aim is to increase foreign direct investment (FDI) from the private sector into Africa with U.S. government backing, a move that simultaneously contributes to U.S. national security interests. Once U.S. companies are in Africa, the DFC can continually invest in them, an incentive not available in the past. Apart from fine-tuning the scoring of how the investments should be accounted for on the federal budget, African states with the most stability, such as Kenya, are poised for an increase in U.S. investments. As of March 2020, the DFC approved nearly $900 million in global development projects, including a $5 million loan to Twiga Foods in Kenya to improve food security (DFC, 2020).

Lastly, the Prosper Africa Act of 2019, led by the Trump Administration, continues the legacy of trade support to Africa by connecting buyers with suppliers and investment opportunities to the private sector (Prosper Africa, DFC.gov)[46]. However, using a top-down approach will not alleviate poverty to the requirements of the UNSDGs by 2030. Well-funded organizations will need to support Africa from the bottom up. The Power Africa initiative had the opportunity to include local hiring across the African continent as well as in-country manufacturing of solar panels, but it did not[47]. The goal was to provide electricity to off-grid Africa and expand on-grid components in place, a multi-dimensional project with 19 partners[48]. The project created access to electricity for nearly 17 million homes to reduce poverty[49]. Had the program offered one job per every 10 homes it served, 1.7 million people in Africa would be lifted out of extreme poverty by the fact that they would be earning more than $1.90/day. These people are likely to have families, and the total impact could have been as high as 5.1 million people in Africa lifted out of extreme poverty, fortified with income for improved nutrition, medicine as needed, housing improvements, and education fees.

Kenya is considered one of Africa's rising countries[50]. It is home to large NGOs, a UN resident representative that oversees WHO operations under UNDP, the UN Environmental Organization, World Bank offices, and the World Food Program, all of which often partner with the Kenyan government and USAID. Expatriates in Kenya enjoy a lifestyle with top restaurants, cafes, western shops, art, and film festivals. US and other foreign investments in Kenya are primarily in infrastructure and high-end urban development (iglus.org). Yet, the informal settlements remain and may soon become a negative focus for public opinion. Finding a way to improve the livelihoods of residents of informal settlements is not only a humanitarian effort but also likely to help attract future foreign investors. To reiterate, the African Union (AU) and the National Partnership for Africa's Development (NEPAD) both seek to ensure economic benefits flow to the communities where infrastructure programs have been initiated[51], but trickle-down models do not address the needs of abject poverty in a timely manner. Investors visiting Nairobi will no doubt drive through areas of abject poverty and potentially form negative impressions of the city during their visit. In the words of one resident:

"..and now they (government) are building skyscrapers with observation decks, how will the visitors think, when they'll see the slums, yet Nairobi city is vibrant?? The govt needs to style up and convert Kibera from that horrible & shaggy environs, to a city within a City. Citylimits.org (2018) Comment by Samuel Mutinda

All these factors make addressing the informal settlements of Nairobi and other African countries a priority for U.S. interests and support the relevance of this research. It represents a series of events that led the U.S. to increase engagement in the development of Africa as a whole, including Kenya. Many development professionals from the organizations that fund poverty reduction programs may not be inclined to visit informal settlements to communicate directly with residents. Direct communication is farmed out to local organizations that are restricted to the instructions given to them by the program funder. Funder-direct communication with residents would serve well to avoid misunderstanding of needs. However, funder safety is a likely concern.

The informal settlements are not a place for anyone to visit on their own. Mzungu (whites) are outsiders unless accompanied by friends who are residents of informal settlements. There are few to no public community centers for gatherings. Instead, there is a dizzying array of narrow dirt pathways crowded with local vendors, stray animals, and 34abati. Streams of polluted water intersect the dirt paths. A slow and curious walking pace, in addition to phenotype, distinguishes one as an outsider. Walking at a steady pace towards a decided destination signals to others that you are in the informal settlement for a purposeful reason. Development professionals are outsiders and have valid safety concerns. Using locations such as schools, local NGO offices, or meeting spots that are not located in informal settlements is common but excludes aid providers from engaging with the people they wish to serve.

I can attest to personally taking a Deputy Director of a large aid organization on his first trip to one of Nairobi's informal settlements in 2019. I arranged security and chose to take him to a smaller informal settlement that had easy in-and-out access for my driver's van. Nearly fifty neighborhood onlookers appeared, of which I sent thirty-five away to make the visit less of a spectacle. This is a common issue when mzungu visit the informal settlements, relevant to this research because unwanted attention can lead to safety and security issues for outsiders.

With little to no communication about the livelihoods in the informal settlements, development professionals lack data to work with other than their own perceptions of what kinds of programs should be developed to help the residents of informal settlements. Having no data or lived experience rules out development based on the human-centered model. Moreover, if poverty in Africa increases as expected (90% by 2030 per World Bank, 2019), these issues will be exacerbated. The research I propose is relevant not only to bridging the communication gap between development professionals and residents of informal settlements but also for U.S. interests.

### 2.3.6. Significance Revealed by COVID-19

Scientific research has linked population growth, poverty, and encroachments into animal habitats for human living space as key factors to disease transmission (Population Matters[52]; UNEP[53]). The COVID-19 death toll worldwide as of the close of 2020 stood at nearly 1.8 million deaths (Mortality Analysis, 2020[54]). According to epidemiology experts, more incidents of viral outbreaks are likely to occur as humans remain hungry enough to eat bushmeat. Our immune systems are not well-equipped to fight off diseases that jump from animals to human beings. Poverty costs lives, not only of the poor.

At risk are cities filled with citizens that have nutritional deficiencies affecting physical and mental development, particularly in children, as well as insufficient Water and Sanitation Hygiene (WASH) solutions. As demonstrated by COVID-19, such vulnerability leads to the spread of disease around the world. No more is poverty "their problem" but a problem for the world. Other life predicaments lead to a society of illness and a sense of hopelessness that sap civic and economic viability; (1) stress leads to spousal and child abuse, depression, (2) lack of income leads to homelessness outside of the informal settlement and into city streets, (3) homelessness contributes to drug addiction which fills city hospitals at a great cost for countries pursuing universal health-care, (4) anger and resentment from being marginalized can lead to violence and civil unrest, (5) desperation for income can lead to joining terror groups such as ISIS or Boko Haram. It does not pay to ignore poverty.

The relevance of this work became heightened at the onset of the COVID-19 pandemic. The disease has demanded that we think faster, smarter, more practically, and more inclusively. COVID-19 has interrupted development programs around the world, leaving professionals scrambling for new ways to reduce poverty and achieve sustainability before the next catastrophic event arrives. From food insecurity to climate migration and lack of basic services, all these issues stem from extreme poverty. They are exacerbated easily by social and political changes in the global system. COVID-19 has demonstrated that we are all intricately linked at levels of State and society in general, and poverty pulls us all down. The Center for Disease Control categorizes certain meats (bushmeat)[55] as not safe for consumption (CDC, 2018). Bushmeat includes bat and monkey meat, commonly eaten in the Congo (Muyembe-Tamfun et al., 2012). One of the world's most dangerous outbreaks, Ebola[56], was spread by zoonotic transfer from animal to human being[57] potentially through the ingestion of bushmeat (CDC, 2018). The COVID-19 pandemic was also spread by zoonotic transfer and has killed over 6 million people[58] globally. Like in the Congo, bushmeat in China (particularly bats) is the likely culprit of the disease (Aguirre et al., 2020). One wonders if the habit of eating bushmeat could have originated from demand due to hunger and cheaply acquired food. Bats can be captured in large numbers and are easily sold at markets cheaply and with minimal processing (Mildenstein et al., 2016).

As COVID-19 cases and deaths were recorded around the world, the World Bank and IMF took the stance to protect lives first[59] from a humanitarian perspective versus improving livelihoods with increased income. IMF is now fostering long-term solutions for health infrastructure, including social safety nets to provide funding when shutdowns occur in future pandemics. At the World Bank Spring Meetings in March 2020, IMF Managing Director Kristalina Georgieva addressed the difficulty of people living in informal settlements regarding their inability to social distance[60]. She further stated that $100 billion in lending was already approved to help low-income countries. She pointed out that this figure was three times more than what was needed during the 2008 financial crisis. Of the $100 billion in COVID-19 relief, half will go to Africa, and of that, Kenya received $50 million[61]. As inferred within the research question of my work, money for programs is not the problem for reducing poverty. Further analysis of the effectiveness of past strategies is detailed in the literature review.

If residents of informal settlements live in tight quarters where social distancing is impossible, how can development help prepare the informal settlements for future virus assaults? Living in high density with no running water or waste system for fecal sanitation, a virus like COVID-19 can spread rapidly, causing a humanitarian crisis. Furthermore, with no planned communication network to reach people who live in informal settlements, the inadequacy of development programs lay bare for all to see. Though there were fewer COVID-19 deaths in slums than expected, the likely answer is that people who travel internationally or work with travelers are the 30% of Nairobi residents who do not live in slums.

As a final note to confirm the relevance of this research, the lack of social protection for slum residents during the COVID-19 pandemic led to the need for more financial savings tools for residents. Local government's lack of social safety nets is one of many areas that development planning should embrace to strengthen self-reliance in informal settlements.

## Chapter 2 - Key points

### Context & History:

- Population, Kenya's Independence, scope and setting

- Theoretical premise based on Freire

- Research question, hypothesis, significance

- Pre-colonial, post-colonial, and modernization (Rostow's stages)

- Aid and the business of State-building (MDGs evolution to SDGs)

- Rural to Urban migration to land near dumpsites

- Emotional bond with land

- 2019 Kenya Census

- The disconnect between development professionals and their client

- AGOA, DBIA Campaign, BUILD Act, Power Africa, NEPAD

- COVID-19 revelations

**Chapter 2 - Experiential exercise in political and economic ideology**

1) You have just been elected the President of Kenya. Choose your cabinet based on tribal supporters who are like-minded (you can have up to 22 members). Your five closest cabinet members are the ministers of agriculture, industry, defense, planning, and governance. You prize yourself as spearheading the economy. Western countries have agreed to send money in the form of international aid as part of reparation for colonization. You have a decent salary for the first time in your life, and you are accepted on the global stage with your prior oppressor.

2) Knowing your people have been re-directed in terms of speaking the local language, expressing local customs, and being made to think less of themselves in terms of race, you choose not to address these issues. Your economic policy is to keep food costs as low as possible by fixing agriculture prices and controlling imports and exports. Balancing your economy is a constant juggling act. Your cabinet is focused on not being poor again, and collecting rent for favors is common, but you turn your eye because you are afraid of being poor again.

3) With your good efforts to balance the economy and never let Kenyans go hungry, you fail. Foreign direct investment never happened, aid took the place of industry, and no investment was made in your largest asset – the population. With half of your population living in unplanned areas of the capital city, you have one chance to lift your country out of this hole. What would you choose:

   A. Take a multi-million-dollar loan from the Chinese to create roads, bridges, and the infrastructure you need to foster international trade

   B. Wait for western countries to offer loans under stringent conditions

   C. Allow your country to remain on a stagnant path

   After you make your choice, reflect on the identity of other heads of state on the continent of Africa, particularly those who are land-locked, with depleted resources and tribal rivalries. Take 15 minutes to briefly write out your decision-making process as if you were the President writing in your personal journal.

## Chapter 2 - Discussion questions

1) When Kenya gained its independence, why do you think it did not create allies with other countries on the continent?

2) If inter and intra-cultural communication deficits lead to poverty, how can the deficit be avoided?

3) What thoughts do you have about Rostow's stages of growth? Are they feasible for every country? What parts of the stages have the strongest chance of success or failure?

4) According to Ivan Illich, Scott, and others, modernization reduces tools for conviviality, i.e., it takes away jobs. What does Illich say about the constant expansion of industrial tools in terms of public interest? What alternative modes for a post-industrial age does Illich recommend? What weapons of the weak are being used by people who live in informal settlements?

5) Why do you think people in Western countries have less attachment to land? Are there exceptions to this commonality? Is the detachment to land an effect of wanting something better? Is the attachment to land due to a lack of having any other asset? What cultural, economic, spiritual, and/or philosophical factors play a role in attachment to land?

6) The research in this book is significant to the cannon in many ways. Considering a cross-disciplinary approach, what other significance can be revealed from the research?

### Notes

[1] According to World Population Review confirms the Word Bank definition of low-income countries as nations that have a per capita national income (GGN) of less than $1,026.00 - https://worldpopulationreview.com/country- rankings/low-income-countries

[2] The term informal settlement is defined in this work as an unplanned, ungoverned urban area where there is no infrastructure or residential zoning, and residents do not have any legally binding claim on the land they occupy. Informal settlement, slum, and slum community will be used interchangeably throughout the research and are defined a second time in the list of industry terminology. Some readers may feel uneasy about the use of the term "slum" in that it sounds offensive. However, others find it odd to use any other term. Most importantly, the people who live in informal settlements openly express that they live in the slums and have no shame or uneasy feeling about living there. This issue is further addressed at the end of this section.

[3] Kikuyu is the largest ethnic group in Kenya.

4 Kenya gained independence in 1963 and the government allocated land for industrial use on the fringes of Nairobi. Landowners like Mr. Ruben were the early investors looking to make great sums of money and acquire political favor. Within 10 years, the area became a dumping site for nearby industries. The best History of Mukuru can be found in a report by the University of California, Berkley, published in August 2014 and listed in the bibliography of this research.

5 The World Poverty Clock is continually updated in real time. While most references have a fixed year attached to data, this statistical clock changes before, after, and during the time one is viewing the data. It can be accessed at worldpoverty.io

6 The critical consciousness of women was discussed on 12/22020 by Sybil Chidiac, Sr. Program Officer of the Gates Foundation for Gender Equality. Her quote serves as an example of the importance of critical consciousness in poverty reduction. "Women need critical consciousness to begin accessing markets and services through savings groups." Critical consciousness addresses societal and economic barriers for women and the collectives help with overall financial status.

7 I was born and raised in Compton, California.

8 Note that development professionals fighting poverty in Kenya include locals with lived experience. However, the locals are not the ones who design poverty reduction programs The foreign professionals design the programs and pay the local professionals to implement them. The disconnect is between Mukuru residents and the foreign professionals who design poverty reduction programs.

9 The timeline of ancient Egypt is carefully organized by the Institute of Egyptian Art and Archeology at the University of Memphis. Researchers for the institute follow the scholarship of the late Dr. William Murnane and the chronologies of Rolf Krauss and Detlef Franke. The institute serves as an online resource for archaeology majors and general scholars. https://www.memphis.edu/egypt/resources/timeline.php

10 Poverty reduction efforts before the Millennium Development Goals were primarily those of state-building, security for the US, promoting good governance and trade, and other interventions that were not human-centered.

11 The Muungano Alliance report of 2017 is used heavily as a reference. Extensive research conducted within the informal settlement is rare. There are short articles written and published about the living conditions in Mukuru, but not of academic or scientific quality. Muungano Alliance has worked directly with residents of Mukuru for 20 years, and partnered with worked with UC Berkeley, Strathmore University, and the University of Manchester Global Development Institute to produce a comprehensive research report on issues of extreme poverty in Mukuru. The research of Muungano has been presented to the Kenyan government and accepted as valid. It is the first and only piece of research that quantifies and qualifies the issues and needs within Mukuru.

12 According to UN-Habitat, 53.6% of sub-Saharan Africans lived in slums in 2018, https://data.worldbank.org/indicator/EN.POP.SLUM.UR.ZS?locations=ZG

13 Earning $5.50/day has been quantified as an amount to provide adequate consumption for well-being; nutrition vs scrap food, safe clean shelter vs lean-to shelters, etc. (<ahref='https://www.macrotrends.net/countries/KEN/kenya/poverty-rat e'>Kenya Poverty Rate 1992-2020</a>. www.macrotrends.net. Retrieved 2020-10-31).

14 https://www.worldbank.org/en/news/press-release/2018/10/17/nearly-half-the-wor ld-lives-on-less-than-550-a-day

[15] A World Bank publication noted that in 2008, $1.25/day was the poverty line for developing countries, upgraded to $1.90/day using 2011 prices. There is significant data on this in the World Bank publications noted in the bibliography, as well as this Q&A page on the World Bank website https://www.worldbank.org/en/topic/poverty/brief/global-poverty-line-faq

[16] Actual population is 4.397,073 - Kenya National Bureau of Statistics (KNBS), December 2019, Vol I, Table 2.7, 38, Distribution of Population by Land Area and Population Density by Sub-county

[17] Tuko is a news source and digital platform that provides news on Kenya politics, world affairs, business, and cultural affairs. The map is identical to that of the Kenya Census, 2019, but colorized to show the counties and sub-counties. The original author of the map on Tuki is Ruth Kamunya, with news story by Venic Nyanchama, 2018. https://www.tuko.co.ke/285791-list-nairobi-county-wards.html

[18] Actual populations are Embakasi 988.808, Makadara 189,536, and Starehe 210,423 people. KNBS Vol I, Table 2.5, 20 Distribution of Population by Sub-counties.

[19] Actual population 1.388,767 - KNBS Vol I, Table 2.5, 20 Distribution of Population by Sex and Sub-county.

[20] Various non-profit and community organizations have attempted to count the total number of residents in the informal settlements of Nairobi. Varied totals can be found in the news, research articles, and UN reports. To undertake an accurate count requires funding and social capital to navigate the maze of settlement dwellings.

[21] Kenya National Bureau of Statistics (KNBS), December 2019, Vol IV, 10-13, Distribution of Population by Socio-Economic Characteristics.

[22] All of the information in the following paragraphs that denote percentages and other statistics are taken diretly from the Kenya Census, 2019.

[23] The Development Industry refers to different layers of poverty as multi-dimensional poverty.

[24] The age seems unusual, however the Kenya census data on the use of technology is collected based on activities of age 3+. If there is an error in the starting age of 3, it is printed this way in the Kenya Census.

[25] Development programs by social entrepreneurs and some governments send cash to the poor directly through mobile phone systems. However, there are applications in health, education, advocacy and other areas that could be used in human and economic development.

[26] Residents of the informal settlements make up a large portion of three Nairobi counties. The total population of Nairobi is approximately 4.5 million people, the density of which live on 6% of the land which are the informal settlements. Census statistics include residents of the informal settlements in data regarding total number of citizens trained in a particular skill.

[27] The continued writings with statistical data are all taken from the Kenya Census, 2019.

[28] Statistics from the Kenya Census count workers from age 5+. This is an indication of children being used to contribute to household income, something that crosses the western line of abusing child labor. On the other hand, when there is not enough income to feed a family, and the selling of tomatoes near home can be managed by a 5-year-old, the predicament and decision to allow a child to help the family becomes questionable.

29 These residents of informal settlements represent the small percentage that have manage to purchase their plots from the government, as see in KNBS Vol IV, Table 2.7, 160, Main Training Acquired in all of Kenya KNBS Vol IV, 251, Tenured land status of main dwelling unit.

30 KNBS Vol IV, Table 2.11a, 258 Distribution of households owning the main dwelling by mode of acquisition (purchased-constructed-inherited).

31 KNBS Vol IV, Table 2.11b, 264 Distribution of households renting provided with main dwelling by a provider - mode of tenure-ship.

32 https://www.worldbank.org/en/region/afr/coronavirus

33 https://data.worldbank.org/about explains where the bulk of their data originates

34 https://www.pewresearch.org/methods/2019/07/16/video-how-is-polling-done-aroun d-the-world/ explains that Pew gathers data from households that can be found by street address or GPS-enabled tablets. Mabati in the informal settlement cannot be accessed by GPS.

35 https://www.afrobarometer.org/data/kenya-round-8-data-2019 - This link is for the most recent dataset. After downloading, the initial questions confirm that survey takers have piped water and live within easy walking distance to a post office, school, police station, and health clinic. The informal settlements are away from public services. Previous datasets follow the same protocol of surveying residents who live near public services.

36 https://www.pewresearch.org/global/kenya/ - This link is for the most recent Pew dataset from Nairobi, Kenya where global attitudes and trends are key topics.

37 See footnote 20.

38 https://world101.cfr.org/rotw/africa/economics#foreign-aid-reliance-varies-by-coun try – This link provides a breakdown of foreign aid by country in sub-Saharan Africa.

39 USAID history report on Kenya states that the US government trained Kenya's first generation of leaders. https://www.usaid.gov/kenya/history

40 https://www.uhhospitals.org/Healthy-at-UH/articles/2015/07/the-top-5-most-stress ful-life-events

41 The existance of the slum is obscure in that the outer edges that are visible to street traffic are not indicative of the depth of poverty within the slum. Driving a short distance into Mukuru reveals paths to the left and right for pedestrian only access leading to hundreds of thousands of mabati that make up the informal settlement.

42 https://www.nepad.org

43 US Trade Representative office, retrieved at https://ustr.gov/issue-areas/trade-develo pment/preference- programs/african-growth-and-opportunity-act-agoa

44 The Obama Administration Press Release is archived at https://obamawhitehouse. archives.gov/the-press- office/2014/08/05/fact-sheet-doing-business-africa-campaign

45 https://www.congress.gov/bill/115th-congress/senate-bill/2463

46 The Development Finance Corporation handles investments under Prosper Africa, https://prosperafrica.dfc.gov

47 Power Africa did develop an energy generation project in Zambia (https://www.usaid. gov/powerafrica/zambia) and in South Africa (https://www.usaid.gov/powerafrica/south-africa).

48 The partners are mostly large banks as seen here: https://www.usaid.gov/power africa/toolbox

[49] Power Africa was formed to create US jobs and fulfill the mission of bringing light to areas in Africa without electricity. https://www.usaid.gov/sites/default/files/documents/power-africa-fact-sheet.pdf

[50] https://www.worldbank.org/en/country/kenya/overview Kenya has made significant political and economic reforms including a new constitution in 2010. Economic growth was at 5.7%, one of the fastest growing economies in sub-Saharan Africa pre-COVID-19.

[51] https://www.nepad.org

[52] March 13, 2020, report on the dangers of population growth and diseases, https://populationmatters.org/news/2020/03/13/population-growth-and-environmental-destruction-fuel-deadly-diseases

[53] Prevention of zoonotic disease transmission from animals to humans has been studied by the UN - https://www.unenvironment.org/news-and-stories/statements/preventing-next-pandemic-zoonotic-diseases-and-how- break-chain

[54] This mortality analysis is retrieved from coronavirus.jhu.edu

[55] The CDC refers to "bushmeat" as raw or minimally processed meant from wild animals that pose risk of communicable disease. See https://www.cdc.gov/importation/bushmeat.html

[56] WHO published key facts about the Ebola Virus, including how it is transmitted. The virus spreads from wild animals to humans, including fruit bats, chimpanzees, gorillas, monkeys, forest antelope and porcupines via direct contact with bodily fluids including ingestion of animal meat – a common and economical practice in the region.

[57] This is confirmed by a World Health Organization global study on the origins of SARS-CoV-2 published March 30, 2021. The full reference can be found in the bibliography.

[58] This statistic comes from Our World in Data accessed on March 26, 2022 at https://ourworldindata.org/explorers/coronavirus-data-explorer

[59] Information from IMF Spring Meetings April 23, 2020. Kristalina Georgieva, Managing Director, IMF on podcast with Neil Ferguson, Head of Department of Infectious Disease Epidemiology, Imperial College, London and Azra Ghani, Chair of Infectious Disease Epidemiology, School of Public Health, Imperial College, London - https://www.imf.org/en/News/Podcasts/All-Podcasts/2020/04/23/MD-Epidemiologists

[60] In the CSO 2020 World Bank/IMF Spring Meetings, Kristalina Georgieva recognized the difficulties for residents of informal settlements to practice social discancing. See more at https://www.worldbank.org/en/news/feature/2020/06/10/covid-19-turns-spotlight-on-slums

[61] See more at https://www.worldbank.org/en/news/press-release/2020/04/02/kenya-receives-50-million-world-bank-group-support-to-address-covid-19-pandemic

# Theory

This review is focused on poverty reduction, development, and critical consciousness as a tool to evaluate what residents of Mukuru think about their predicament and the best ways to move on the journey to self-reliance. What the residents think are effective poverty reduction programs may be different than what development professionals think. Considering past and current oppressors, residents of informal settlements may submissively agree to accept whatever programs are offered to them. This disconnect may be the missing link to achieving a greater impact in poverty reduction for the informal settlements. Let us begin with a key theory by Paulo Freire on critical consciousness, followed by supportive theory organized into three themes:

1.  *Development and ethnographic literature*

2.  *Socio-political and hermeneutic literature*

3.  *Critical conscious research*

Following the three themes, the point of the literature and theoretical review is to share the work of a theologian whose work is multi-disciplinary and helps this research uncover communication barriers that may be negatively affecting human-centered development. In doing so, additional literature selected supports socio-political hermeneutics, which is important for evaluating how people interpret information received in communication. Finally, I review experiments conducted to test communication and critical consciousness. The experiments applied Freirean principles, as do I in my work. The results of these experiments are discussed by scholars. Overall, the collective body of work points to a correlation between communication and human agency being improved when critical consciousness is raised.

## Freire and critical consciousness

Paulo Freire uses the term "conscientizacao" in Pedagogy of the Oppressed (1970) to explain the process by which people begin to understand their predicament in life and find long-term solutions. This book draws from Freire's theory of critical consciousness. Although Freire's theory was created for use in an educational setting, the basis of his theory is applicable to residents of Mukuru in the self-assessment of their situations living in poverty. From self-assessment and communication with development professionals comes a better understanding of salient needs in the informal community and the creation of better programs to reduce extreme poverty. The theory calls for a progression of critical thought about poverty issues and gives value to lived experiences[62] that contribute to the reduction of poverty in innovative ways. Freirean praxis connects naiveté with actuality to bridge the knowledge gaps.

Freire writes about banked knowledge and the co-creation of knowledge (Freire, 1970). Banked knowledge is knowledge forced upon a student hierarchically (the teacher knows all, the student knows nothing), with the expectation that the student will end her studies well-educated to handle her daily life. Co-creation of knowledge is a praxis where the student and teacher are in a dialectical relationship, teaching and learning from each other, including life experience as relevant to a subject (Brown, 2013). Traditional[63] foreign aid programs are much like the banked knowledge model, whereby professional practitioners in the sector develop the programs with learned knowledge but little to no first-hand knowledge about living in poverty. Recipients of aid follow along with the program regardless of whether they have input in developing it.

Recipients will not refuse help; rather, they walk a delicate line between hoping the program will work and knowing that it will likely fail due to the lack of incorporating lived realities. Recipients speaking up about their true needs may jeopardize the program, so instead, they accept the program as is and bank the knowledge gained for potential use later.

The banked knowledge model is the opposite of the participatory model that development professionals seek to achieve, i.e., place-based, human-centered development. Human-centered development is meant to engage the people in need of aid as active participants in the development of programs that serve them. Recipients of aid should not be considered subjects but full participants. They are counted on to discern whether programs are suitable for the "place" they live and if programs address their "central human needs."

Placed-based, human-centered development is a form of co-created knowledge (Cernea, 1991). However, the model is missing the most crucial factor, the development of critical consciousness that fosters the co-creation of knowledge. Freire saw this gap and identified why it is important; one must understand the issues related to her problem before she is able to contribute the best knowledge towards a solution. This is the essence of critical consciousness, having an awareness of the elements that contribute to the perpetuity of a situation. Critical consciousness is not an imposition of Western ideology onto non-Westerners. It is an awareness of issues related to one's position, condition, or situation.

To reiterate, Freirean theory fosters critical consciousness in the poor through a praxis of equality between teacher and student. This book uses the theory as a tool of development to bridge conscious understandings between development professionals and residents of informal settlements. Overall, Freire believed people take responsibility for themselves as a result of praxis, dialogics, and knowing they can remake themselves and their situation. This approach inevitably leads to political consciousness, usually putting participants in conflict with the governing status quo. Freirean key points are the following:

- Conscientizacao (critical consciousness) is a pathway for individuals and communities to develop critical understandings of their social reality through reflection, examining the root cause of oppression, and action to change their situation.

- Freirean principles are likened to those of Socrates, "know thyself."

- Freirean methods of education are "elenctic," whereby ideas and concepts are inductively obtained by conversation and reflection through dialogics.

- Freirean "problem-posing" refers to a praxis that emphasizes critical thinking for the purpose of liberation.

- Freirean curriculum = praxis; a continual model of interaction, reflection, action, and evaluation of outcomes at the end of the dialogue.

According to Freire (Freire, 1970), the development of critical consciousness comes from a collective of thoughts based on beliefs about yourself and your situation. Freire explains that subjectivism is a phenomenon in which humans create their own oppressive reality, and psychologism is the self-reflection necessary to change that reality. He adds that sectarianism is when false truths quash human agency, false truths that must be shattered by radicalization/actual truths. To reiterate the four stages towards conscientizacao:

1. **Subjectivism:** when beliefs of success are no longer supportable, and one lives under an oppressive reality that he/she is the problem.

2. **Sectarianism:** false consciousness of being part of a losing sect or group, and nothing can be done to change that.

3. **Psychologism:** the turning point, awakening, or interruption of consciousness that helps a person or group confront their reality and begin analysis of how to improve it for the long term.

4. **Radicalization:** new thought that leads to action, innovation, and positive outcomes.

These themes are useful in the promotion and evaluation of awareness among Mukuru residents. Their awareness and beliefs about poverty are essential to their journey towards self-reliance. At the same time, it is important to acknowledge that one's beliefs are not necessarily rational or testable. Beliefs are not necessarily discussed but followed. Often, group beliefs are not challenged; hence, they gain increased support and diffusion to others. Therefore, what one person or group of residents may believe about their predicament can spread and become a belief or value held by the whole community. For example, the late James Brown taught US Blacks in 1968 to "Say it Loud, I'm Black and I'm Proud," which permeated the collective consciousness of 22 million Black Americans[64] and raised the consciousness of non-Blacks around the world about the importance of self-worth. This is critical for development professionals to understand in terms of impact.

For some who are reading this and concerned that raising one's consciousness is a condescending notion, consider that white Americans also experience cycles of consciousness-raising. Whites have recently become "racially awake," whereby they acknowledge and understand their privilege[65], unconscious bias, and "color-blind racism" (Bonilla-Silva, 2018). Likewise, the critical consciousness of Black Americans has recently been raised to see the "structural racism" in US institutions[66] that disempower Blacks in America, including a recent effort by legitimate congressmen to disenfranchise the most fundamental right, the right to vote. Institutional racism is also exemplified in the US health sector, where Medicaid sets income limits that are likely to force low-income earners not to earn more income, lest they be removed from the program with the inability to pay for private health insurance. There is no mid-step or affordable healthcare option to entice low-income earners to leave the Medicaid program. In terms of creating better international development programs for poverty reduction, no number of training sessions can change your station if the structure does not provide a bridge to cross the extreme poverty gap. Policies, practices, and institutions must change. Innovative self-help measures must be formulated by the community and fostered by the development sector. We all must become aware of the elements pertaining to our life station that hold us back or give us the power to make effective changes for the marginalized. Consciousness raising is a process of awakening that should not be stigmatized as condescending or negative.

Freire's approach allows for lived experiences to be used as teaching tools. In Brazil, dialogue about life in the favelas (slums) was used to help favelados (poor) learn how to read. For Mukuru residents, this approach may help them understand broader issues of economics, politics, and issues that impede their journey to self-reliance. From this comes clarification of needs, and better programs can be developed for extreme poverty reduction.

The progression through stages of consciousness falls in no set order, though subjectivism and sectarianism are generally the first. As dialogue or contemplation continues, psychologism becomes central, leading to ideas for effective change – radicalization. This interdisciplinary praxis is evidenced across the fields of education, psychology, political science, and more. In psychology, Freirean psychologism is exemplified in overcoming alcoholism through self-reflection. In education, sectarianism is exemplified in students moving beyond the belief that they cannot succeed because of their race. In political science, radicalization is exemplified in the use of human agency. Critical consciousness and critical theory[67] boiled down, is an emancipatory social science via discourse and reflection.

The differences between the various pieces of literature in this review are the approaches to build, measure, or evaluate critical consciousness. Freire's theory builds critical consciousness through a grass-roots effort to educate the poor. Critical consciousness represents a horizontal, self-managed approach to poverty reduction from the bottom up. This grass-roots approach is likely the best path to foster a pathway toward programs that communities want to own and can succeed in their implementation. Other scholars have cited the work of Freire, noted extensively in the literature review.

### 3.1. Theme One - Development and Ethnographic Work

Michael Cernea was one of the first to write about human-centered development in Putting People First (1991). He found that an inclusionary approach to development improves the effectiveness and outcomes of aid programs. His work also revealed a variety of issues such as education, health, access to markets, and fresh water, all of which play a role in increasing or decreasing one's poverty. Cernea is pro-inclusion of communities in program planning to co-create the program. Similarly, a UNESCO think-piece emphasized the ethics of human-centered development as opposed to projecting outsider perspectives on cultural and place-based issues of poverty. The think piece is short, with little information about its ethnographic roots; however, it ties directly into Cernea's work. Both works support my research and demonstrate the importance of shared knowledge with the community being served, even in difficult places like informal settlements.

The Millennium Development Goals (MDGs)[68] were derived from development professionals undertaking ethnographic research between the 1990s and 2015[69]. They did not, however, encompass the breadth of poverty variables revealed through Cernea's work. Using Cernea's multi-dimensional measures of poverty, decent work reduces economic poverty, while affordable clean energy reduces poverty of health and educational poverty (electricity for school-aged children). Irresponsible production and consumption of food add to poverty, as do countries without infrastructure or policies counteractive to creating industry and manufacturing. Poverty variables such as climate change and clean oceans exacerbate agricultural issues and food security. All these variables affect household security (Cernea, 1991). Cernea's people-centered ideology was supported by the UNDP Administrators Report (2010) titled "People-centered Development: Empowered lives. Resilient nations." The report begins by acknowledging research in the late 1980s that there is no automatic correlation between economic growth (income) and human development in terms of overall well-being. The report from the 1980s and the work of Cernea in 1991 laid the foundation for updating the MDG to 17 SDGs targeting poverty from a variety of directions other than income, including Community-led Development.

The most recent data published by USAID (Center for Innovation and Impact Brief 2018) identifies human-centered development as the most effective with the greatest impact and central to development programs[70]. Cernea's work identified the importance of engagement with the poor, something that has needed improvement in informal settlements. The most current literature about how poverty is measured and the importance of engagement with poor communities is from the World Bank (Hickel, 2018), (World Bank, 2019), (World Bank, 2018).

Cernea opened the door for more scholarship in place-based, human-centered development. Cernea's foundational work revealed the importance of people-centered development and a novelty approach to poverty, framing the need in development for an inclusionary approach484848 to improve outcomes in the effectiveness of aid programs. However, he did not account for hermeneutics, the differences between development professionals and the poor regarding perceptions of poverty and the effectiveness of programs. This research adds the missing piece to Cernea's work.

***

Much literature has been written from the mid-1990s to mid-2000s, including the work of Robert Huggins and Piers Thompson, "Culture and Place-Based Development" (2015), Todes et al., "Spatial inequalities and policies in South Africa: Place-based or people-centered?" (2018), and Osteros-Rozas et al., "Participatory Scenario Planning in Place-based Social-Ecological Research" (2015). Huggins and Piers discuss cultural factors that are not present in the evaluation of economic development. They consider this a "divorcing" from social places that are essential to development success (Huggins and Piers, 2015). In their research, development is approached with a broader sense of the role of culture in long-term sustainability. Todes et al. (2018) compound the importance of place-based and people-centered development using South African spatial inequalities as the core of their research (Todes et al., 2018). The research in South Africa looks at spatial rebalancing and redistributing economic activity or "realizing the economic potential of less-developed areas" within cities (Todes et al., 2018). When working with less-developed areas, human-centered development, by nature of how program ideas are manifested, is likely to be more successful because of how program ideas are manifested (Todes and Turok, 2016).

The work of Todes et al. echoes that of Freire and is relevant in that aid spent in marginal locations can be wasted if planning is not human-centered and place-based. Todes et al. note that horizontal alignment (within the community) is necessary for change to be sustainable (Todes et al., 2018). In the case of development programs, horizontal alignment happens when communities are on the same page as development teams. Critical consciousness from within the community is needed for this to happen and for effective change to take place. This theoretical approach can be applied to residents of informal settlements for more effective programming and positive impact.

*** 

Traditional poverty reduction programs are meant to help the poor; however, they were largely created by Western professionals who often have little to no lived experience of poverty (Oteros-Rozas et al., 2015). Oteros-Rozas et al. (2015) analyze 23 case studies in various places around the world, where focus groups discuss drivers of change regarding natural conservation. Everyone in the groups has lived experience of natural habitat erosion. While different than groups discussing poverty reduction, understanding how people in various places approach the development of programs is what connects the Oteros-Rozas et al. research to this research. Individuals within the groups must develop a broad consciousness to understand the breadth of the problems that contribute to the issue. From this broad consciousness comes a more effective solution to the problem.

In each of the 23 cases of the Oteros-Rozas et al. study, researchers led focus groups that created scenarios of drivers of change based on group norms vs. the norms of the researcher. The process was intended to stimulate "creative thinking and raising awareness" for the purpose of creating outcomes or a "set of narratives and plausible scenarios" (Oteros-Rozas et al., 2015). The focus group methodology included open and closed questions plus a survey (Oteros-Rozas et al.,2015). Focus groups as a mode of measure were chosen because groups "generate social learning and knowledge integration among multiple stakeholders" (Oteros-Rozas et al., 2015). The results were that half the cases created five primary scenarios as drivers of change according to group norms that include social issues, demographics, governance, and economic and market conditions (Oteros-Rozas et al., 2015). The approach to using focus groups for the Mukuru slum residents follows the ideology of Oteros-Rozas to stimulate creative thinking and raise awareness of issues in the informal settlements.

There is a coterie of scholars, including Lancaster (2006), Rodney (1982), Scott (1985), Gendzier (1985), and Carothers (2004), who write about the modernization period and the inevitability that foreign aid will produce dependency on aid. Their work has created considerable understanding within the field of development and foreign aid. These scholars and field workers have determined that development aid, while under the guise of good intentions, can destroy local economies. Note that Carol Lancaster was the former Deputy Administrator of the US Agency for International Development (USAID).

In Foreign Aid: Diplomacy, Development, Domestic Politics (2006), Lancaster's work helps us to understand the various uses of aid to achieve goals other than poverty reduction. Aid paves the way for diplomacy, democracy, and American values to be instilled abroad. It also provides a security advantage for the United States as well as a capitalistic advantage. Lancaster reminds us that aid is a "public expenditure of significant size" that occurs each year (Lancaster, 2006). Aid is riddled with public and private interests, considering it began as a form of Cold War diplomacy, not altruism. To think political agendas are not reflected in foreign aid is naïve (Lancaster, 2006).

Aid is used to expand state exports and joint ventures in building air and seaports – commercial aid for state interests and trade. The UK recently shifted its aid program from a poverty priority to promoting UK trade[71]. Moreover, aid is used for military joint training to manage conflict areas – security aid (Lancaster, 2006). These are two of the three goals of foreign aid, as noted on the US State Department website (state.gov). Aid can also be used culturally by supporting or opposing the use of local languages to advantage selected ethnic groups or to bolster one religion over another in recipient countries (think Muslim vs Christian religion). Finally, aid is used economically to promote financial stability and spread democratic, capitalistic principles (Lancaster, 2006).

Some positions are morally questionable (Gendzier, 1985), nevertheless integrated into the norms of foreign aid. Gendzier writes about early modernization producing "militarized knowledge" (Gendzier, 1985) for national security, such as the MIT scholars who were CIA-funded. She points out that early development missions in Latin America were counterinsurgency missions with ethical issues. Gendzier further points out that development was fear-driven and that conservative beliefs were projected on the "under-developed" societies of the global south (Gendzier, 1985). Last, Gendzier lays bare the information about development theory being formulated based on "cultural deficiencies" that posit development approaches of the west to be superior and justified (Gendzier, 1985). When such impressions are part of development, whether intentional or not, it undermines sovereign identity. An example outside of development is US women in the 1940s who had little sense of agency because of what they were told about their capabilities. It was not until WWII, when women were asked to work in place of conscripted soldiers, that some women discovered their ability. Though there were women who knew their capabilities, there were many who believed they were incapable until called upon to be capable. This example mirrors the disconnect that I believe is occurring in today's development across Africa.

*** 

A paper by Kenyan scholar Japheth Muli, "Social Entrepreneurship, Theory and Evidence" (2019), exemplifies how aid has successfully influenced norms in the financial sector of countries in Africa. Muli writes about the most capitalistic principle, entrepreneurship, and how it helps achieve sustainability for non-profits to continue helping people in the long-term (Muli, 2019). Muli finds that social entrepreneurship is most successful when backed by faith-based organizations, a common thread that I see in micro-entrepreneurs who live in informal settlements of Nairobi. Muli also heads one of the largest financial savings organizations in Africa, Hand in Hand International. His contribution to the literature review is valued not so much to show how aid has informed the financial sector in Africa but to demonstrate how African states have managed to make Western financial models work for Africans. The critically conscious element of understanding how western financial systems can be tweaked in African ways bridged the disconnect and eased the push-back on using Western financial models to reduce poverty.

Galistcheva adds to this train of thought in the article "The Role of Small-Scale Industries in Achieving Sustainable Development; The experience of India." (Galistcheva, Mgimo University Journal, 2020). Like the work of Muli, Galistcheva shares the fact that small-scale businesses in India are successful at decreasing unemployment for youth and women (Galistcheva, 2020). By looking at micro-business data from the National Bank for Agricultural and Rural Development (NABARD) in India, he analyzed and confirmed the positive impact of entrepreneurship and banking. Galistcheva also found acute social problems were addressed through micro-businesses, such as "poverty, famine, undernourishment and food insecurity, lack of quality education, gender inequality and the empowerment of women." (Galistcheva, 2020). Muli and Galistcheva's research supports development through entrepreneurship. The work of Galistcheva also plays a role in my research, as informal settlements are bustling with entrepreneurial small businesses that exemplify the essence of capitalism and democratic values.

***

In James C. Scott's Weapons of the Weak (1985), Scott demonstrates how the poor in rural Southeast Asia use human agency against industrialization and modernization efforts imposed by the government in rice fields. He lived for three years in a small Malaysian village, where he wrote ethnographically about the "symptoms of development" (Scott, 1985). Scott chronicles the cultural aspects that changed during industrialization and modernization in the rice fields. He does so specifically to understand the class consciousness of the village (Scott, 1985). In understanding the class consciousness of the village, Scott evaluates how the poorest of the poor use "soft weapons" or "weapons of the weak" as a form of resistance to modernization (Scott, 1985). Scott is a critic of development and offers examples of burnt tractors and sugar in petrol tanks of any machinery supplied by the government (Scott, 1985). These "everyday forms of resistance" are more powerful and authentic than Marxism, which depends on a well-planned revolution (Scott, 1985). In Mukuru, weapons of the week are demonstrated by the sheer nature of remaining in their habitat on government-owned land. Another example of defiance is a refusal to obtain proper business licenses[72]. Street vendors line the various entrances to Mukuru, selling food, meat, goods and services. Owners feel lucky to have saved enough money to start a business and snub the institutional process of filing paperwork for a business license, even when they have amassed the fees needed for business registration. The action is a near dare for government officials to visit the informal settlement and shut down businesses without a license, a dare that occasionally results in business mabati being bulldozed.

Scott also identifies the struggle between the stratified classes of poor: the peasants and the "extractionists" who own land, laborers, offer loans, collect rents, and pay taxes (Scott, 1985). In my research, the peasants represent the residents of the informal settlements, and the extractionists represent the middle class of Kenya. In relation to development, the middle class of Kenya has adopted the "Gendzier foreign aid narrative" of proselytizing that residents of the informal settlements are inferior. This adds to the disconnect in the critical consciousness of Mukuru residents that their authentic ideas for development are not worthwhile. Like Scott's examples of modernization in the rice fields of Asia, the same modernization efforts pushed many rural Kenyans to the city looking for work. The "weapons of the weak" for 2.5 million Kenyans materialized in the form of being "squatters" on land near light industry and dumpsites. This inadvertent use of human agency was the catalyst that formed the informal settlements. It makes a statement to government leaders that resident-dwellers are not going away.

Scott's ethnography aligns with the 13+ years I have worked with residents of Mukuru. The time passed in Mukuru off and on equates to nearly three years. His theoretical contribution, the weak have weapons of protest against the government, are seen in the everyday lives of Mukuru residents who operate businesses without licenses, pay no taxes, and thwart development in some instances, i.e., cooking on an open fire.

Walter Rodney's *How Europe Underdeveloped Africa* (1982) spells out how Africa became so poor in the first place. He exposes the economics of colonialism and the growth of modern Europe and the USA based on the back-breaking work of African slaves. Critics may argue that Rodney failed to point out that during the colonial period of the 1700s-1800s, the slave trade was mostly carried out by Arabs from Zanzibar, Egypt, the Gulf Emirates, and Portugal. Yet those nations did not extract the mind, body, and spirit of slaves with the degradation of human self-worth as did Europe and America. In fact, many Gulf states used slavery as a method for anyone who needed to pay off a debt regardless of race[73]. Rodney points out the extraction model used by Western states to pilfer valuable resources from Africa and leave the continent underdeveloped. He adds that "nothing of compensatory value was introduced" (Rodney, 1982). Education was introduced but stripped of all cultural context, not to mention it could only be obtained in a foreign language (English). Moreover, someone too intelligent risked being seen as a threat to colonial power. A public health system was introduced that went against native African medicine practices and, again, was forbidden to slaves.

Rodney states that after colonialization, some rulers of African states were selected as puppet rulers. The result: heads of state do not participate actively nor consciously towards the creation of a new history for Africa (Rodney, l982). I contend the same behavior is synthesized at the community level whereby, for example, residents of informal settlements placate Western development professionals by following along with whatever programs have been developed for them despite not providing long-term sustainability. Neither the leaders nor the residents have a full understanding (critical consciousness) of the elements that add to their predicament of poverty. From this basis, the informal settlements are left with an additional layer of underdevelopment created by heads of state operating as colonialism has taught them – take, take, take.

***

Dambisa Moyo, a global economic strategist born in Zambia, educated at Harvard and Oxford, trained at the World Bank, has over ten years of experience working in London for Goldman Sachs. In Dead Aid (2009), Moyo wrote about the prospects of Africans solving problems "their way." She highlights the resources of the continent, including a robust stock market in Nigeria and Johannesburg. Residents of informal settlements may not own stocks. However, they have demonstrated a resilient entrepreneurial spirit in micro-businesses that serve the community. Moyo elaborates on how aid has not helped Africa's economic growth, nor will it be successful at reducing poverty (Moyo, 2009). Moyo continues with the premise that the aid itself hinders the growth of the continent. The closing words of her book are from an African proverb that aligns with the call to action of my research, "The best time to plant a tree is twenty years ago. The second-best time is now" (Moyo, 2009).

Residents of informal settlements, particularly the youth, embrace starting now with sustainable solutions to reduce poverty. The issue that remains is whether the development sector and government support them with appropriate programs.

African American scholar and anthropologist Marimba Ani brings culture front and center to her work (Yurugu, 1994). Ani focuses on Euro-centric perspectives in development that are not aligned with place-based human-centered design (Ani, Marimba 1994). Ani's work employs Conscientization 101[74] to explain the importance of awakening the consciousness of African people to the influences of European culture "on the formation of modern institutional frameworks."[75] The title of Ani's book, Yurugu, is from a legend about an "incomplete" being rejected by its creator. For purposes of this research, Yurugu does not want to go against any "higher" being for fear of more rejection; residents of the informal settlements do not want to go against any programs that development professionals offer. Ani proposes to build a new consciousness, like Fanon (1963). Ani's method is to reconstitute the seed of culture (asili), fertilize it with "culturally structured thought" or world view (utamawazo), and supporting cultural vital force (utamaroho) to motivate "the collective behavior" of a community (Ani, 1994). This research focuses on Ani's utamawazo, conscious culturally constructed world view.

***

Frantz Fanon (1963) writes specifically about black consciousness. Fanon, a psychiatrist, turned his attention to the mindset of oppression in post-colonial times. This specifically addresses Ani's utamawazo and critical consciousness. According to Fanon, how one thinks about their own agency is strong enough to create sustainable changes economically and politically (Fanon, 1963). Fanon expounds that language can strip or support people of their agency and personal sovereignty (Fanon, 1963). He stated that the "inherent unconsciousness" of impoverished people makes them likely to be excluded from dialogue about planning, policy, and governance (Fanon, 1963). In terms of consciousness, Fanon reminds the reader that the oppressed are educated by the oppressor to believe self-degrading thoughts, for example, "The Algerian is born a criminal" (Fanon, 1963). Fanon conducted research with young Algerians under the age of 10 to find that many showed signs of phobias and were "deeply affected by the slightest reprimands" (Fanon, 1963).

These points are relevant to informal settlers in that they, too, may suffer from similar anxieties. Along the same lines of literature is Marcus Garvey's Emancipation from Mental Slavery (1937), reprinted in 2018. It is a testimony to the psychological oppression born of slavery that impedes an inner dialogue of self-empowerment. This lack of self-empowerment becomes the new inner dialogue when recipients of aid are asked to contribute thoughts about effective development programs by development professionals. The disconnect in learning what is really needed for effective development may need to be fostered in Freirean dialogics.

The mindset of oppression remains in some residents of Mukuru and other informal settlements. However, the youth feel hopeful and ready to exert their agency for change. This is seen in the answers from the research survey.

***

Dialogue at great lengths with the poor is a specialty of Duncan Green of Oxfam. In From Poverty to Power (2008), Green shows the importance of state structure in the long-term sustainability of poverty reduction programs. Green also emphasized the importance of place-based, human-centered perspectives for effective development. How a state is structured can cause the failure of the best-intended poverty reduction programs. (Green, 2008). Green points out that some states are not able to manage development. This literature is pivotal in explaining the role of states in the development process and exemplifies the downfall that occurs when states are not ready to support poverty reduction programs, such as the previously mentioned UN- Habitat KENSUP program in Nairobi's largest informal settlement, Kibera.

In The Field of Cultural Production (1993), Pierre Bourdieu's theory of cultural and social capital highlights the importance of strategies appropriately adapted to social worlds. In other words, the legitimization of programs and the likelihood of success occurs across social capital between what Bourdieu calls the "field" and "habitus" (Bourdieu, 1993). In this case, the field represents the concept of an informal settlement, the place of appropriation held together by actors in their struggle. Habitus represents the concept of being born in an informal settlement or having relevant experience in another type of struggle that gives you social capital amongst the residents. Most Western development workers have little to no habitus in the field; they are not recognized by the community as "one of them." Bourdieu's theory of social and cultural capital has allowed me continuous engagement and access to the slum community three to four times a year, five weeks on average per visit over thirteen years.

Unfortunately, it is also through Bourdieu's theory that some missionaries with bad development ideas have gained cultural capital. They enter poor communities promising the goodness and mercy of a savior and only offer aid to those who agree to believe.

### 3.2. Theme Two - Socio-political and hermeneutic theory

Charles Taylor expresses the importance of individual interpretation through the Hermeneutic Theory in Philosophy and the Human Sciences (1985). People interpret situations in a circumstantial, context-based way that includes shared understandings. Resident dwellers may not view poverty the same as outsiders. For example, with a shared understanding that defecating into a bag or consuming a meal from discarded food at the dump is the norm, partaking in those habits is no longer viewed as dehumanizing. It may be the case that outsiders introduce notions of being poor and create stigmas that were not originally present in the psyche of a community.

Interpretations constructed from shared understandings should play a role in developing the kinds of programs appropriate to reduce poverty for residents of informal settlements. Consciousness and perceptions also bear elements of pluralism, where aid, for example, means one thing to development professionals and something else to the community. Africa's development problems are pluralistic. To some, the problems are an opportunity to provide help. For others, it is an opportunity for states to have their needs met by shipping products and services to the continent for self-interest. How one sees aid and the solution to extreme poverty is relative to one's hermeneutics or perspectives.

Pluralism of poverty takes on the perspective of helping people help themselves, says Steven Koltai in Peace through Entrepreneurship (2016). While some make the poor pay for programs by way of selling them products and services, Koltai writes about the benefits of fostering a start-up culture as another way to reduce extreme poverty. Koltai expands on the idea of entrepreneurship to reduce poverty, which is a quintessential American value that also spreads the principles of democracy and open markets[76]. Many scholars are against the idea of spreading Western values through aid. Koltai, like myself, finds that entrepreneurship comes naturally to the poor. Selling, trading, and buying are a part of survival for most people who live in Mukuru. How income is <u>utilized</u> is where Western values vs. African values come into play.

The title of Koltai's second chapter, "It's all about jobs," points to what he views as the bottom-line solution to reducing poverty and more (Koltai, 2016). Koltai posits not only are jobs created through entrepreneurship, but peace and national security are as well (Koltai, 2016). For example, the desperately unemployed across the African and Middle East North Africa (MENA) regions may be inclined to accept well-paid work from terrorists. In this case, the youth bulge in Africa, seen as a poverty issue, is short-sighted, and the security risks are greater (Koltai, 2016).

Regarding critical consciousness, Koltai's work infers that development professionals lack a broad understanding of issues related to poverty. Government support of entrepreneurs would contribute more effectively to poverty reduction and peace than aid (Koltai, 2016).

***

Ann Mei Chang adds to the literature in Lean Impact (2019) that the U.S. Government (USG) has an approach to poverty that is short-sighted. In concurrence with Lancaster (2006), Chang learned that development programs are created for multiple reasons and not necessarily to end poverty (Chang, 2019). Whether human-centered development is used or not, programs have a lifespan, markers are to be reached, budgets are expended, and poverty remains (Chang, 2019). She refers to "one-off" development programs witnessed in Uganda, Liberia, Zimbabwe, Mongolia, Guatemala, and India that exemplify over-budgeted poverty reduction programs that could have brought many more to levels above the poverty line (Chang, 2019). Chang turned her attention toward the system that produced development programs, as does this research.

Like Koltai, Chang emphasizes that non-profits, social entrepreneurs, and private sector corporations are more inclined to "problem-solve" for a client, whereas the USG may have other goals besides solving the problem at hand (Chang, 2019). Here, as with Koltai, Chang has inadvertently identified one of two possibilities: (1) a lack of critical consciousness in development under the USG, or (2) an intentional consciousness in development under the USG. This leads to a different question in terms of informal settlement communities accepting poverty reduction programs that they already know will be non-fruitful. Could it be that they understand "the system" that Chang writes about? And does the critical consciousness of everyone else in the development sector need to be broadened?

***

William Easterly's "The White Man's Burden" (2006) is about accountability, ineptitude, and the failure of Western aid to reach the poor. As the third piece of literature in this review is about progress not made by development professionals, Easterly calls for academics to offer public service by evaluating development programs and approaches (Easterly, 2006). He exclaims that internal research departments at aid agencies and consultancies do not deviate too far from short-sighted top-down goals (Easterly, 2006). Easterly notes that development professionals never find out if their client is satisfied. The result - there is no way to tell who is doing a good job. Easterly's work addresses the intent of this research, which is to analyze the effectiveness of poverty reduction programs. The critical consciousness element of this research is intended to assure that "effectiveness" is understood equally by the "client" and the "service provider."

Easterly also identifies two types of development professionals, "planners and searchers" (Easterly, 2006). This is important because planners represent how large aid organizations think about effective poverty reduction programs, and searchers represent how smaller non-profits think. Easterly writes that "planners announce good intentions but don't motivate anyone to carry them out; searchers find things that work and feel rewarded" (Easterly, 2006). He goes on to write, "planners determine what to supply; searchers find out what is in demand." And last, "planners at the top lack knowledge of the bottom; searchers find out what the reality is at the bottom" (Easterly, 2006). Easterly's descriptions capture the essence of the development divide but demonstrate how planners who employ critical consciousness as part of their planning can bridge the divide with smaller organizations and the impoverished people they serve.

***

Prahalad takes a different approach to eradicating poverty in The Fortune at the Bottom of the Pyramid (2006). He discusses poverty reduction in terms of access to markets and delivery of products and services (Prahalad, 2006). In this light, Prahalad is confirming that when critical consciousness is fostered to understand the wholeness of poverty economics, the poorest of the poor become enabled to "access markets creatively." This shift opens doors for the poor to buy and sell products at the lowest rung of the economic ladder, supporting entrepreneurship among themselves while supporting the manufacturing of low-cost products domestically (Prahalad, 2006).

In Prahalad's work, critical consciousness plays a further role in the evaluation of what kinds of products are to be made, much like what kinds of poverty reduction programs are really needed. Here also, Bourdieu's notion of habitus or cultural capital comes into play because the ability to access the community with a level of trust is essential to finding out what really matters to the poor (Bourdieu, 1993). Trust is part of and inferred through habitus and belonging (Bourdieu, 1993).

Prahalad provides a good example of the 5.5 million people of India who are amputated each year (Prahalad, 2006). For development aid to make the best decisions on how to serve these clients, development professionals may not know that there is little enthusiasm for an Indian to regain the ability to walk unless he can also regain the ability to squat, work in fields, walk on uneven ground, and walk without shoes (Prahalad, 2006). These abilities are needed for everyday living. An inclusive development program for the amputee to earn income in a persons with disabilities (PWD) cooperative would be insufficient. Critical consciousness dialogics would reveal the inadequacy of the development program and enable alternative planning.

Prahalad shares the results that a request for proposal (RFP) led to a contractor providing a prosthetic for under $30 with the express need for (1) dorsiflexion to allow squatting, (2) transverse rotation for sitting cross-legged, (3) inversion and eversion for walking on uneven ground, and (4) natural look for walking barefoot (Prahalad, 2006). This approach does not have to be unique to developing effective programs that meet the needs of the poor. Critical consciousness can partner with human-centered development to identify what the poor need to become self-sustaining.

***

Jeffrey Sachs is known for his contributions to the literature on poverty reduction. In The End of Poverty (2005), Sachs shares economic ideas on the reduction of extreme poverty around the world. His chief concern is the lack of political will and limited USG spending to eradicate extreme poverty by 2030 (Sachs, 2005). Having spent considerable time with heads of state, village leaders, finance, and health ministers, Sachs has the advantage of understanding poverty from a wide range of vantage points. He has witnessed success according to financial goals being met (hyperinflation, national currencies, cancellation of debt, funds to fight AIDS. His eye is turned toward science, technology, and markets to eradicate poverty, including the preconditions of basic infrastructure to access markets (Sachs, 2005).

Sachs proposes nine steps to end extreme poverty, three that involve strengthening the UN, IMF/World Bank, and redeeming the role of the US in the world (Sachs, 2005). Three more steps include harnessing science for the new industrial revolution, making a plan of action (SDGs), and promoting sustainable development to avoid environmental degradation (Sachs, 2005). The final three steps are making a commitment to end poverty individually, at the NGO community level, and raising the voice of the poor (Sachs, 2005). Sachs's idea of raising the voices of the poor is for the poor to stand up and "champion the end of poverty" to the G20 (Sachs, 2005). Sach's development of Millennium Villages was to mimic self-sustaining communities. However, they were not devised by the poor.

Sachs's work is included in this literature review to exemplify the epitome of what Easterly defines as a "planner" (Easterly, 2006). The planner believes "outsiders have enough knowledge to impose solutions; the affected believes only insiders have enough knowledge to find solutions" (Easterly, 2006). This approach of the "planner" is useless and must be abandoned, as evidenced by the failure of Sachs's work in creating the Millennium Villages. The advent of COVID-19 has revealed that all the planning in the world does not address the needs of the people living in extreme poverty. A different approach is needed, despite efforts to develop based on human-centered approaches. Something is missing, which the research in my book intends to identify. Nevertheless, the goodwill of Sachs is applaudable.

*** 

The work of Amartya Sen, *Collective Choice and Social Welfare* (1970), won the Nobel Prize in Economics and adds to the literature review in terms of social those keywords alone, Sen's work is akin to critical consciousness in terms of collective thinking. Sen writes about the power of unanimity, choice versus ordering, liberalism in decision-making, and the Pareto Principle (Sen, 1970).

The Pareto Principle is a phenomenon in 80% of outcomes come from 20% of causes (Sen, 1970). An example would be that 80% of your profits come from 20% of your products, or 80% of decisions in a meeting are made in 20% of the time allotted for the meeting.

The Pareto Principle is intertwined with liberalism; because people are free to do what they like, distinct alternatives arise that foster bargaining advantages and, or collective choice (Sen, 1970). As in the case of the prisoner's dilemma in international relations, social preferences often lead to outcomes that maintain the status quo. In other words, when two dependent parties are aware that their wellbeing relies on each other, no decisions are made to make any changes that might affect the other. Development professionals and residents of informal settlements have an interdependent relationship where both gain from cooperation. Sen refers to this as the individual welfare function for collective choice (Sen, 1970). Decisions in such cases are made by rational choice because preferences are conditional (Sen, 1970; Bates, 1981), keeping in mind that what is rational to you may not be rational to another. This is an alternative explanation of the communities' unconditional acceptance of poverty reduction programs that do not work and the resistance of development professionals to look deeper for reasons why poverty continues to grow.

***

John Stuart Mill argued for people to have freedom as long as it does not materially hurt others (Sen, 1970; Mill, 1859). Fostering critical consciousness in residents of the informal settlements provides them with human freedoms and capabilities (Sens, 1993). Those freedoms may lead to the end of poverty, purported to be the goal of World Bank[77]. Adam Smith advocated for allowing distant perspectives (Sen, 1970; Smith, 1859) to contribute reason to issues that have become commonly accepted, i.e., poverty reduction programs that do not alleviate poverty. Lest the development would be "captured by the limitations of parochialism and confined reasoning" (Sen 1970). Sen quotes Mill often on people's freedom and their capabilities. For someone to ascribe self-help, they must be aware and understand their issues, i.e., gain critical consciousness about their life issues.

The critical consciousness of the poor is tied to their freedom. This may be hard to see by development professionals caught in Sen's individual welfare function for collective choice, Bate's rational choice, or the prisoner's dilemma. All three exemplify why the poor may accept ineffective programs provided to them; the alternative may lead to having no programs at all. Sen describes five types of freedoms that are the ends and means to development:

(1) political, (2) economic, (3) social, (4) transparency, and (5) security. More importantly, each freedom "advances the capability of a person" (Sen, 1970). While credit is due to the development sector for fostering programs in each of the five areas, there remains work to do so that residents of the informal settlements can shape their own destinies.

***

The Kenyan scholar Ali Mazrui contributed hard-to-find works that are included in this literature review. Those works include The African Condition (1980), Africa's International Relations (1977), and an interview with Mazrui in 2011 that was filed at the Library of Congress. The African Condition is a lecture series that began 10 years after aid started flowing into Kenya. Mazrui's Oxford background in political science amidst the Cold War and Apartheid led to predictions about racism in African states, religion, and ethnic conflicts (Mazrui, 1977).

Mazrui covers a lot of ground regarding various countries across the African continent but taps into "consciencism," a term used by Kwame Nkruma of Ghana (Mazrui, 1980). Consciencism signifies a triad of heritage within Africans: Islamic, Western, and African heritage. This informs critical consciousness that poverty reduction programs are attempting to address varied cultural needs on top of economic needs. Mazrui does not address informal settlements, though his insight on the fate of the post-colonial state warns of violence and tyranny which includes poverty (Mazrui, 1980). He discusses the failed modernization "take-off" period and advocates for a theory of "crash-prevention" instead (Mazrui, 1980).

Mazrui's writings are mostly political, covering the African issues on governance, race, the diaspora, gender relations, and political stability (Mazrui, 2011), not on development and poverty reduction specifically. Nevertheless, he promotes a continental strategy of embracing African heritage, which is why his contributions are included in this literature review. Embracing African heritage includes "ujamaa," a socialist ideology that fosters a system of village cooperatives based on self-help, which is applicable to development in slums.

### 3.3. Theme Three - Critical Consciousness Primary Research

This section draws on previous research conducted by like-minded scholars. All seven have conducted interviews or focus groups based on Freirean theory. The fact that Freirean's theory is based on dialogue makes it evident that focus groups and interviews were appropriate to my research methods. Additional scholars with published research on critical consciousness and agency are Zimmerman (1992), Diemer and Li (2011), Boone et al. (2019), Godfrey and Wolf (2016), and Woods (1987).

These authors use Freirean theory in their research for purposes other than education, as do I. Their publications provide examples of how Freire's theory can be applied to issues related to poverty. They apply Freirean theory to the use of human agency, understanding structural barriers to economic advancement, and their work provides examples of co-creating environmental programs to improve living conditions amongst the poor. These scholars offer empirical data, and some combine Freirean theory with Empowerment theory (PE theory). The results of these studies have shown that people who gather in formal or informal community groups build a better understanding of their life situation, a stronger sense of agency, and mastery over their lives (Zimmerman, 1992); they gain critical consciousness. Diemer and Li (2011) test the development of critical consciousness in marginalized youth, specific to political participation. From survey results, an arrow diagram of contextual antecedents points to social engagement as the critical impetus for the active use of agency. The work ties into the concept of ujamaa, and the community engagement that is lacking to reach residents living in informal settlements.

\*\*\*

Boone et al. (2019) write about how to raise critical consciousness in the struggle against poverty. Boone examines Freire's theory by observing social workers who employ Freirean dialogics in a policy-influencing activity with those living in poverty. After observation, the team holds interviews with the social workers. They determined that three themes are used to stimulate critical consciousness in people who live in poverty:

1. *Reframing poverty as a collective issue,*

2. *Linking experience to injustice, and*

3. *Linking power relationships to poverty.*

Where Boone et al. posit that "…poverty is often framed as a problem of unequal and imbalanced power relationships, resulting in the lack of participation and powerlessness of people living in poverty" (Boone et al., 2019:435), the novelty of my research is that power relationships are altogether removed, so that problem-solving becomes the point of focus.

Freire's co-creation of knowledge through dialogue creates two-way learning and enhances solidarity amongst the poor. When individuals unite and work toward a common goal, measures of agency are increased; "…poverty is often framed as a problem of unequal and imbalanced power relationships, resulting in the lack of participation and powerlessness of people living in poverty" (Boone et al., 2019:435). The research introduces poverty as a collective concern, and those in poverty maintain this perspective when in dialogue about solutions.

The notion of poverty as a collective concern complements Freire's insistence on the co-creation of knowledge. As related to the informal settlements, residents and development professionals must come to a collective concern that is understood and shared as a co-created way forward to reduce extreme poverty. Boone et al. take Freire's ideas further to describe "othering" as a way to separate oneself from issues of poverty and conceptualize those in poverty as adaptable (Boone et al., 2019) – in this case, adaptable to Eurocentric poverty reduction programs. Boone et al. highlight Freire's position concerning the detrimental praxis of structures that facilitate 'us' and 'them' pedagogy, creating a culture of silence and passive compliance. Boone et al. emphasize that this praxis affects both the oppressed and the oppressor (Boone et al., 2019). The work of Boone et al. mimics what can and likely does happen in informal settlements – passive compliance with Western programs offered in the form of aid and self-help.

Godfrey and Wolf (2016) interview low-income immigrants and African Americans in the United States whose critical consciousness is different from people in developing countries because of geopolitical differences. The findings uncover a lack of consciousness regarding the U.S. structural barriers that make it difficult to get out of poverty. While the structural barriers for the focus group to rise from poverty are clearer than those from the U.S., a broader conscious awareness of issues related to poverty remains a necessary step to charting a journey toward self-reliance. The work of Godfrey and Wolf (2016) comes closest to my work in terms of looking at poverty from the point of view of Freire's theory of consciousness. Godfrey and Wolf explore critical consciousness in terms of attributes that impede or promote poverty in low-income minority immigrants to the U.S. (Godfrey and Wolf, 2016). They conducted 19 interviews per group consisting of immigrants from three minority groups. The questions were topical and included economic inequality and daily hardship. The explanations were coded based on Freirean themes and evaluated based on three determinants:

1.  *Subjective explanations attributed to lack of talent or ability,*

2.  *Structural explanations attributed to issues such as low wages and*

3.  *Fatalistic explanations attributed to intangibles, such as bad luck.*

The findings reveal that individual attributes (such as beliefs about themselves) and structural attributions (such as systems of employment or institutionalized racism) deter critical thinking about solutions to poverty. I apply similar themes in my research, which can be found further in the text.

***

In research conducted by Zimmerman et al. (1992), the research team measures interpersonal components (self-analysis of agency) and interactional components (interactions that boost agency) to determine self-efficacy and perceived competence in the poor for the purpose of "decision-making and problem-solving skills necessary to actively engage one's environment" (Zimmerman et al., 1992:708). The authors conducted 916 interviews that included questions about activity in leadership organizations and other community activities in terms of perceived effectiveness, difficulty, and the amount of control they have in those settings (Zimmerman et al., 1992:711-713). The team found that individuals involved in community activities have higher levels of agency than those who are non-participants in their community (Zimmerman et al., 1992:720). The work provides a model for me to follow regarding my research questions on the perceived effectiveness of development programs in informal settlements.

While Zimmerman et al. (1992) measure agency and the development of political economy, Diemer and Li (2011) use Freire's frame of developing critical consciousness to measure political participation in marginalized youth in America. The two conducted research on political agencies through surveys online and by phone. They used structural equation modeling whereby variables were included in the construct of the questions (Diemer and Lie, 2011:1819). Answers were coded by the level of constraint on engagement in social action. Diemer and Lie determined positive development outcomes were relational to critical consciousness. Taking into consideration all the literature, the latter studies use Freire's theory as a basis to formulate their work. These studies exemplify previous work that has been done regarding the use of critical consciousness as a tool to help people in poverty manage their lives. This body of work influenced the methodology for the research in this book.

### 3.4. Development program analysis

Concluding the literature review with public opinion is a non-traditional approach, yet it acts as a form of public literature, adding to the breadth of academic literature presented. If the aim of development is to be human-centered, then thoughts from the public about development programs are essential to ascertain program effectiveness. Table 3.1 offers a summary of a few development programs in Kenya. The summary is intended to provide a brief overview of the wide range of programs provided by the respondents surveyed in this research, serving to provide some empirical support.

The public literature about programs notes that some development projects attempted to include input from the communities they serve, where target populations are invited to engage and co-create programs (Scruggs, 2010)[78]. However, probing questions that caused deeper reflection were not asked. Simple questions were posed in the form of a "wish list," resulting in community "wants" instead of authentic needs. Where large organizations with the capacity for the greatest impact missed the mark, mid-size and smaller organizations with less capacity but stronger inter-cultural communication skills were successful in creating effective programs.

**Table 3.1.** Effective Program Table

Sampling of development programs / E=Effective NE=Non-effective

| E/NE | Program Name | Org. Size and Type | Public Information on effectiveness | Program Intentions |
|---|---|---|---|---|
| NE | **KENSUP - UN Habitat** https://unhabitat.org/ un-habitat-and-kenya-slum-upgrading-programme-kensup | Large Govern-ment | Government communication breakdown + housing attributes not wanted by residents FAILED PROGRAM | new housing for 45K residents |
| NE | **KISIP - World Bank Informal Settlement Development** https://projects.worldbank. org/en/projects-operations/ project-detail/P113542? lang=en | Large Govern-ment | $100 million spent in 2019, with moderately satisfactory results. Funding issued with little to show. FAILED PROGRAM | Cash was distributed to local govt. Marginal infrastructure improvement. |
| E | **KYEOP - Youth Employment Training** http://mis.kyeop.go.ke/live/ register/ | Large Govern-ment | Program applications do not reach the poorest residents. Computer access needed. Dated info on website. PARTIALLY EFFECTIVE | Paid training to 32K with 75% hiring rate after training |
| E | **USAID with local company Sanergy** https://www.usaid.gov/div/ portfolio/s2sanergy | Large Govern-ment | No structure for expansion of this very successful program. PARTIALLY EFFECTIVE | 772 toilets, 779 jobs, removed 7245 metric tons of waste |

| E | **Ruben Center-Mukuru Kwa Ruben** https://www.rubencentre.org | Medium NGO | Multi-dimensional poverty reduction, community, and primary education EFFECTIVE | High impact, 3K daily + 800 students |
|---|---|---|---|---|
| NE | **Hope Worldwide - 4 programs for women and girls** http://www.hopewwkenya.org /index.php/our-work/ success-stories/item/215- moyo-safi-self- help-group- reaps-the-benefits- of-value- chain-development | Medium NGO | Micro-business, loans. NO JOBS AVAILABLE = LOANS CAUSING DEBT | 743 women trained for business & jobs |
| E | Mercy International Association - schools https://www.mercyworld.org/ about/mercy-family/ organisations/mukuru- 271/ | Medium NGO | Primary education, one of the better educational environments in Mukuru EFFECTIVE | Primary education |
| E | **Mukuru SPA - Muungano Alliance** https://www.muungano.net/ muk uru-spa | Medium CBO | Mapping of community services needed EFFECTIVE | 300K people served but only in 1 area of the community |
| E | **BLEP-Better Living** https://www.facebook.com/ Blep Kenya/ | Small CBO | Micro-agriculture serving the immediate community EFFECTIVE | 48 local families served |
| E | **Mukuru Art Center** https://www.facebook.com/ muk uruartclub2010/ | Small CBO | Community Art for idle youth serving the immediate community EFFECTIVE | Painting, sculpting, drawing, design |

Literary conclusions reveal the market value of the poor (Prahalad, 2006) and the importance of building trust and legitimacy in communication (Bordieu,1993) between residents and development professionals. Further literature conclusions emphasize that dialogue between community residents helps raise the level of critical thinking about personal and community issues (Oteros-Rozas et al., 2015; Zimmerman, 1992; Todes et al., 2018).

**Chapter 3 - Key points**

<u>Existing Theory:</u>

- Critical Consciousness and the Co-creation of Knowledge

- Ethnographic

- Socio-political

- Hermeneutics

- Public Opinion/Effective Programs

**Chapter 3 - Case Study in hermeneutics**

*Hermeneutic theory is centered around the methodology of interpretation. The fact that perceptions are different based on perspective opens nearly any statement to scrutiny. Read the scenario below to understand the importance of hermeneutics in extreme poverty reduction.*

A Tanzanian unmarried woman aged 22 years takes her one-year-old child with her to attend an information session about the benefits of Table Banking offered by XYZ Nonprofit. The nonprofit has a diverse staff with offices in the US and Arusha. XYZ also uses local contractors to bridge language and cultural barriers. The information session is a planned intervention and part of a design matrix with the objective of helping women build social safety nets. The Tanzanian woman found out about the session from her neighbor who saw the information on WhatsApp.

After walking three miles to reach the meeting, she is greeted by the Nonprofit coordinator at the door with a cool bottle of water. One-third of the room is filled with Tanzanian women working on their mobile phones with guidance by local contractors. Another third of the women are talking in groups led by an XYZ staff member. The last third of the women are distracted by their children.

*What do you think is happening in each of the three groups?*

Pause here and consider the hermeneutics/perspectives of the women, the NGO staff, the local volunteers, and your own perspective.

Read further to see possible hermeneutic differences:

**The women participants:**

The 22-year-old woman came to the meeting expecting to learn about Table Banking, which would be controlled by XYZ Nonprofit. She and the other women already knew about community Table Banking but were looking to learn about greater security for their savings. Most of the women were expecting a snack or meal since the meeting call time was 5:30 p.m. Some were disappointed that they walked such a long way with their hungry children only to be greeted with water. The hermeneutics of the women included presuppositions about the offering.

**XYZ Nonprofit:**

XYZ Nonprofit staff were excited to offer the best practices of Table Banking and explain the benefits of creating a social safety net autonomously. The staff wanted to empower women with the tools necessary for financial resilience in times of need. XYZ had planned to share a PowerPoint of key benefits and entrepreneurial ways that Table Banking can help women achieve economic stability. However, the presentation was not well received. Afterward, the women gathered in groups to ask specific questions to the staff. The questions to staff were about the possibility of XYZ managing the funds, mostly because e-savings with Mpesa or Airtel safely store up to $ 750 USD in savings on their mobile phones. The hermeneutics of the nonprofit included inaccurate pre-understandings about e-banking and dinner time for locals.

**The local contractors:**

The local contractors were happy to have a well-paying job for the day. They were all women and very familiar with Table Banking at the community level. The contractors were eager to carry out whatever the staff at XYZ Nonprofit requested of them, even when knowledge from their lived experience could have prevented missteps in XYZ's program. The contractors had knowledge of e-savings mechanisms built into systems like Mpesa and Airtel, yet they never critically thought about sharing that knowledge with XYZ staff. Likewise, XYZ staff did not ask the contractors for their opinions about the program. The contractors expressed non-verbal communication with each other. The semiotics expressed a mutual feeling of being happy to have a job for the day regardless of misgivings within the program strategies.

**Hermeneutic Impact:**

1.  The women invested their time and physical energy to attend a meeting that offered no more than an unfruitful gathering. They returned home hungry, tired, and to families still waiting for dinner to be prepared.

2.  XYZ Nonprofit invested their time and physical energy to offer a meeting that did not produce the outcome planned. The intervention in their design matrix failed.

3.  The local contractors invested their time and physical energy to assist at a meeting, were paid well, and went home happy.


**Chapter 3 - Discussion questions**

1)  What steps should be taken to ensure that development practitioners have an accurate perception of needs in communities of poverty? How can practitioners learn about local nuances without having ethnographic knowledge?

2)  Why is it that the local contractor has become the beneficiary in this development program? Do you think this is common? What are the socio-political ramifications of the unintended beneficiary switch? How do practitioners get contractors to become vested deeper in program effectiveness?

3)  Walking three miles to attend a program is a long way. What are some of the reasons programs are located long distances from communities? What are the alternatives? How can practitioners broaden inclusion for the poor that do not live near meeting facilities?

4)  Recent initiatives for childcare have been launched in development by the US. Having childcare available at gatherings like the one in the case study would serve as an introduction to the idea to local women. What is the role of hermeneutics in such an offering? What is the local public opinion on strangers taking care of other people's children?

5)  Considering the opportunity to leverage multiple development initiatives in a single gathering, would offering "nutritional snacks" add confusion to the objectives in the case study? What are the pros and cons? Do you think critical consciousness in communities could be improved through overlapping multiple initiatives?

6)  Considering a cross-disciplinary approach, what other messages could be offered at this gathering to add value to development interventions?

## Notes

[62] Personal knowledge about the world gained through direct, first-hand involvement in everyday events rather than through representations constructed by other people. It may also refer to knowledge of people gained from direct face-to-face interaction rather than through a technological medium. Oxford Reference. https://www.oxfordreference.com/view/10.1093/oi/authority.20110803100109997

[63] By "traditional" I mean ongoing programs that are believed to be human-centered but are not. These programs are based on the belief that programs in education and job training are beneficial to those that live in extreme poverty. If this was the case, then poverty would not be rising.

[64] The actual figure is 22.539,362 million Black Americans from the 1970 US Census (https://www.census.gov/library/publications/1972/dec/pc-s1-13.html).

[65] A scholarly book printed in 2017 by InterVarsity Press in Illinois captures the essence of the white awakening. Written by Daniel Hill, "White Awake" offers an honest look at "What It Means to Be White."

[66] The Urban Institute published a think-piece on structural and institutional racism in 2021 that links to other research on racial disparities, poverty from structural barriers versus personal choices, the widening racial wealth gap, and structural racism in educational systems (https://www.urban.org/features/structural-racism-america). To date, the US federal system allows for the right to vote to be diminished for some citizens. This demonstrates a brazen example of institutional and structural racism.

[67] Critical theory is used narrowly and broadly as noted in the Stanford Encyclopedia of Philosophy. The term is used here to say that the theory of critical consciousness brings freedom through awareness from dialogue and reflection, as discussed here at: https://plato.stanford.edu/entries/critical-theory/

[68] Un-authored. 2012. "Advancing a human centered approach to development: Integrating culture into the global development agenda." A UNESCO think piece.

[69] The Millennium Development Goals were instituted in 2000 with an initial timeline of completion for 2015. Updates of the goals have been pushed back to 2020, and 2030, https://www.un.org/millenniumgoals/bkgd.shtml

[70] The importance of the UN Sustainable Development Goals Knowledge Platform is that poverty shifted to an approach that sought knowledge from those in poverty versus outsider thoughts about poverty.

[71] An article published by DEVEX, a leader in development, explains the UK's restructure of aid towards promoting British expertise to "control how taxpaper's money is spent." The strategy from the UK is to be published at the end of March 2022 (https://www.devex.com/news/new-uk-aid-strategy-will-promote-british-expertise-truss-says-102734).

[72] Alan Sears, scholar from Notre Dame Law School, conducted extensive research in 2016 on businesses in Mukuru's neighboring slum Dandora. He notes the barriers to business entry as well as habits for informal businesses in the slum which include non-registration of businesses. While some business owners do not register because they are not knowledgeable about the registration process, other owners simply don't care. https://klau.nd.edu/assets/331821/searsbarriers.pdf

[73] In Bahrain, the National Museum exhibits a large painting of two slaves with ankles in chains, loading crates onto a ship. One slave was white. When I questioned the white image, the museum docent explained that gulf states were not racist, slavery was instituted as a method to repay debt. I made this trip in 2019.

[74] This online site highlights cultural works of scholars and pro-Africa activists, https://conscientization101.com/video/dr-marimba-ani-the-fundamentals-of-yurugu/

[75] By "traditional," I mean ongoing programs that are believed to be human-centered but are not. These programs are based on the belief that programs in education and job training are beneficial to those who live in extreme poverty. If this was the case, then poverty would not be rising.

[76] This specific information can be found in Koltai, Peace through Entrepreneurship, on page 170.

[77] This active campaign began in 2016, https://www.worldbank.org/en/events/2016/11/08/end-poverty-campaign-panel-discussion

[78] Gregg Scruggs reports directly from Nairobi, Kenya, in an online publication and shares the details of the UN-Habitat program, KENSUP, from an on-the-ground perspective. A traveling journalist who embeds himself with the community, Scruggs shares powerful stories about solutions to urban problems. He won the UN Correspondents Association award for his coverage of global urbanization, writing as a voice of the people for the people.

Chapter 4

# The Inquiry

Influenced by seven previous studies that used Freirean theory[79], two methodologies were chosen for this research: interviews and focus groups. Due to the COVID-19 pandemic, and because this research was reviewed and approved by an Institutional Review Board (IRB), face-to-face research restrictions due to the COVID-19 pandemic did not allow me to be on the ground and led to an alternative approach employing community surveys by phone. The cultural norms of gathering for group discussions unexpectedly prevailed when the surveys got underway. The details of this and other unexpected occurrences will be explained in section 4.1.2 further in the chapter. Allow me to continue in chronological order of how the methodology was planned.

Community surveys were conducted with 500 residents of Mukuru. Interviews were conducted with 100 development professionals who have expertise in programs for residents of informal settlements. For convenience, the research question and hypothesis are reiterated below:

**Research question:**

"Are residents of informal settlements using their knowledge to help development professionals understand what kinds of programs will effectively reduce extreme poverty?"

**Hypothesis:**

Residents of Mukuru are not expressing how they feel about the effectiveness of poverty reduction programs offered by development professionals.

The point of the research is to merge varying perspectives, including those of the Mukuru residents, to foster a solution to abject poverty in Nairobi's informal settlements. To gather information from one source of respondents would provide results from one perspective and be unproductive to this research. The goal is to gain and share knowledge horizontally across agencies, organizations, and the affected community, a process henceforth referred to as the horizontal knowledge spread.

## Sample Size for Interviews and Community Survey

Selecting a sample size can be based on many factors. Small sample sizes are typical for qualitative analysis (Creswell, 1998), though they must be large enough to describe or capture the phenomena of the research question. Additional saturation may or may not add to the body of information ascertained. For interviews, Creswell suggests 20-30 participants (Creswell, 1998).

Pew research, Gallup, and Afrobarometer are well-known data collecting services that publish data from sample sizes as small as 1000 people[80]. Unlike medical studies, the nature of this research does not call for a quantitative format or calculation to be used to justify the sample size needed. This research is a mixed method, blending qualitative and quantitative methods. Hence, the approach taken is to err on sampling a higher number of participants from both the community and professional organizations to support stronger validity and correlation. The number of interviews intended and achieved for the collection was N100. The number of community survey participants intended was N320, but instead, N500 was achieved.

### 4.1. Community Survey

In lieu of conducting traditional focus groups, a computer-aided approach was used to ask 33 questions in open-ended, Likert scale, multiple choice, and rating scale format. Participants from the informal settlement of Mukuru in Nairobi, Kenya, gained access to the mobile survey at the Ruben Center located in the Kwa Ruben area[81] of the settlement. The Ruben Center is a central location for community gatherings and services (school and medical center). Activities are steadily taking place at the center, including programs on weekends, a factor that provided a high likelihood of participants.

A flyer was posted at the Ruben Center in a location where other self-help information is routinely posted. The poster was written in English as a precursor for eligibility to participate, as the survey questions were also written in English. This does not introduce selection bias, as English is widely spoken in Nairobi[82]. In my experience since 2012 working in Mukuru, I have encountered less than 15% of residents who do not speak or understand English. Most of the residents speak, read, and write English at a basic level sufficient to answer the questions of this research.

The survey offered a dialogue box for qualitative answers, in addition to selections based on common answers provided in the pilot study conducted in 2019. The center notified visitors about the research opportunity as they passed through the self-help area, pointing out the location of the flyer where more information could be read. Links for mobile phone surveys were posted on the flyer, as well as information about the research, including directions for participation and informed consent.

A remuneration of 200 Kenyan Shillings ($2.00 USD) was paid to each participant via M-Pesa (mobile pay) from the U.S. using an e-pay application (Sendwave). The first set of answers from the residents provided their mobile numbers for payment. Demographic data in the next set of questions (age, place of residence, daily earnings) helped to qualify the respondents in terms of being over the age of 18 and living in Mukuru. Duplicate inputs could be easily identified by duplicate mobile numbers from the 500 mobile numbers received.

Safeguards for personally identifiable information include the use of first names only, ages with no dates of birth, and the use of non-legal names at the discretion of participants. Electronic files were encrypted through the electronic survey system. Copies of data and images were wiped from device hard drives and saved on external hard drives, locked in an office cabinet located in Washington, DC. Survey platform data is encrypted and password-protected until March 2023, when the data will be erased.

In a setting with no designated director on hand to answer questions, participants often ask each other questions about how to begin the survey or to gain clarity about the questions. Participants are likely to continue doing so throughout the survey when they feel the need to discuss an issue (Afolabi, 2020). With that in mind, staff from the Ruben Center were available if participants needed further assistance.

Participants provided authorization through informed consent to be captured on film or photos for use pertaining to this research. A representative from the Ruben Center agreed to take photos and videos of the participants in unplanned dialogue as they went through the survey. All video and photos were taken from a 6 ft distance per pandemic protocol, and the transfer of video and photos of the sessions were encrypted. The recruitment flyer was originally to remain posted for 2 weeks. However, according to the staff at the Ruben Center, word-of-mouth regarding the research opportunity rapidly increased the sample size, which was achieved within 10 days.

There are arguments for and against qualitative research in terms of the subjectivity and objectivity of the researcher (Ratner, 2002). As an example, the pandemic-induced community survey approach ironically served a greater purpose in reducing Western influences and researcher bias. Besides basic demographic information, the survey consisted of 32 questions about poverty-related issues in general. Freirean-themed variables were purposely added to some of the questions to help in the evaluation of critical consciousness development in the participants. These variables add subjectivism, sectarianism, psychologism, and radicalization prompts to the questions. Examples are:

*Subjectivism:* Do you blame yourself for your economic predicament?

*Sectarianism:* Are your problems because you are part of a certain ethnic group?

*Psychologism:* Can you think of how you got to the point where you are financially?

*Radicalization:* Are you ready to change your predicament?

The survey was written in English, knowing that ethnic dialects are not spoken much in Mukuru; instead, they are used in rural areas[83] where tribal allegiances and rivalries are more likely[84]. Residents of the community do not have a choice of where to live in the settlement.

Although they may prefer to reside with their own ethnic group, they accept whatever space is available to erect a mabati, and intermingle their daily lives with those of different ethnic groups. Allegiance in the informal settlement is to survive. The residents have more of a desire to pull together than to create difficulties based on ethnic rivalry[85]. Over the years, I have been told, "we leave that job [stirring ethnic rivalries] to local politicians."

### 4.1.1. Question categories

The first set of questions for the residents included mobile numbers for payment, age, sex, marital status, place of residence, income, number of children, and number of children (if they had any) that attended school. Participants who reported earning more than $1.90/day did not qualify to have their data included in the analysis and were dropped off the survey. When the data arrived electronically, it was checked for qualifiers (age, residence, and income), and then the payment was sent to M-Pesa mobile accounts using the Sendwave Application.

A COVID-19 question was included to ascertain the heightened urgency of elements needed in poverty reduction programs. Questions about leaders within the community were asked to ascertain the likelihood of the community leading its own development programs. Questions regarding marital status and how income is earned helped identify if participants were receiving remittances or had additional income from spouses. The question about long-term needs versus short-term needs served as a prompt for participants to think critically about sustainable solutions to extreme poverty. Some Western scholars may object to the probing nature of the questions in this research, particularly when participants are asked how they earn income. My reply is that these questions are essential to the research, and participants have the option of exiting the survey at any time.

Moreover, from my experience, residents of the informal settlements are not ashamed or need to keep private the amounts of their earnings. They earn so little, mostly in the same ways: collecting scrap metal or plastics for the local middleman who pays them 19 shillings per kilo (19 cents), washing clothes for the middle class, selling chapati, or carrying bricks at new construction. Those lucky enough to start micro-businesses earn income by selling vegetables, coffee, meat, cereals (dry goods), or offering hair braiding services, each business charging less than $1 for products or services. The residents are not ashamed of what they must do to survive. Their work habits are normalized within the community. From first-hand experience, I have watched over 45 residents gather at 7 a.m. (for five to be selected) to work in knee-high rubbish sorting plastic for recycling.

The question about giving birth at home versus giving birth in the hospital helps to measure the development of health initiatives to curb child mortality and morbidity. Although data on child morbidity is not essential to this research, the data helps to shed light on the health of the next generation living in informal settlements. Questions about school-aged children not enrolled reflect a policy deficit that the Kenyan Government does not provide free public schools nor a mandate that all children attend school. This question points to the poverty of knowledge.

Two of the questions (q.13 and q.14) have sub-questions that asked about foreign aid programs that have been helpful. A list of well-known programs was presented so that respondents could identify programs they were familiar with. See Table 4.1.

**Table 4.1.** Question categories for Community Survey

| CATEGORY | EXAMPLE | PURPOSE |
|---|---|---|
| Demographics | age, gender, marital status | Demographics are essential to understand the dynamics of poverty across gender and age. Marital status is important to identify the potential for additional streams of income. |
| Daily challenges | income, shelter | The top challenges identified provide clarity on the key needs of residents. Other than income, the remaining challenges may provide unexpected insight on drivers of extreme poverty. |
| COVID-19 effects | worsening poverty | The pandemic has worsened poverty globally. It is important to ascertain how it has affected residents of the informal settlements. Answers may lead to the urgency of certain needs over others. |

| | | |
|---|---|---|
| Participation in development programs | program type, effectiveness | This category is key to measuring if well-known development programs are reaching who they are intended to help. This category leads to the need for better accessibility to informal settlements. |
| Community Capital | leaders in the informal settlement | Leaders are needed for sustainability. Questions about community leaders may provide knowledge about the potential for cooperation within the informal settlement. Projects to improve the community need community leaders. |
| Government | voting habits, corruption | Since the government has failed to provide adequate services in informal settlements, questions in this category shed light on whether the residents use human agency to change policy. The questions in this category also prompt answers about corruption and how it affects life in the informal settlement. |
| Dream Program | Unlimited budget to create a sustainable transformation of Mukuru | This question allows residents to share what elements in the community they would like to change, how those elements should be changed, how residents prefer to engage with development professionals, and how their vision of transformation can be sustained. |

The question, "do you consider yourself living in poverty?" was integral to applying Freirean praxis and starting the process of critical consciousness. Other similar questions were posed to prompt sectarian and subjective lines of thinking. See Table 4.2.

**Table 4.2.** Freirean Questions for Community Survey*

(with Freirean Critical Consciousness element)

| CATEGORY | EXAMPLE | PURPOSE |
|---|---|---|
| Subjective/ Sectarianism | Is your financial predicament your own fault? | This category is essential to prompt critical thinking about poverty. Freirean theory will allow for simple evaluations of what the residents say about living in poverty. Self-blame is an example of subjectivism, while ethnicity or being an informal settlement resident is a group (sect) identification that serves as a sectoral self-blame. |
| Psychologism/ Radicalization | How can you create a sustainable livelihood in the informal settlement? | This category is also essential to prompt critical thinking in terms of self-reflection and taking action to change things for the better. Freire's psychologism is identifiable as participants begin to think and reflect on their own situation. Listening to others in a group setting fosters reflection. Evidence of this is commonly seen in a variety of group discussions: academic, work setting, casual discussions, and family interventions. Radicalization questions ask about action steps to make change. |

As with many methodological plans for international research, cultural influences can alter what occurs. The changes that occurred spontaneously in the methodology of this research are the following:

- Participants came in higher-than-expected numbers to share their voices and have their opinions captured in the data. Participants requested assurance from staff at the Ruben Center that they were using the QR codes correctly to answer the research questions.

- Staff at the Ruben center found participants organically discussing the survey questions, forming dialogue in small groups of three, seven, and up to 15 participants.

- The Ruben Center Staff found it more practical to group the participants in tens, oversee the dialogue, and input the data using the QR codes. It saved time from answering individual questions from 500 participants and staved off potential errors in data input.

- As a result, a lively discussion occurred among the participants, further bolstering Freirean dialogic philosophy, captured by video and images.

- The negative impact of this methodological change is that data was input in groups of ten instead of individually, resulting in the inability to compute cross-tabulations from the community survey.

### 4.1.2. Unpredicted occurrences - Community Survey

It is noteworthy to share the cultural differences employed by the Ruben Center staff to attract residents to participate in the survey. With the pandemic thwarting face-to-face recruitment of participants, the Ruben Center played loud music to attract participants. Music was not a planned part of the methodology but, instead, a cultural addition introduced by the facility. Music is a normative tool used in the community to announce new programs or offerings.

As a result, more participants were gained than anticipated, increasing the sample size of community surveys from N330 to N500. Receiving the surveys electronically allowed me to immediately see how many men and women were responding. Being in contact with the Ruben Center several times a day, staff were able to encourage more men or women to participate as needed to maintain a gender balance in the results. We successfully obtained equal male

(N250) and female (N250) resident participants. Video and photos were taken by Ruben Center staff.

As expected, many participants asked each other questions about the issues that were part of the survey. With no person to direct them, they turned to each other. In the video footage, many were soft-spoken, yet there were always a few who spoke their minds in discussions with other residents about certain issues. Thus, despite not being able to hold traditional focus groups due to the pandemic, the community dialogue among themselves with assistance and clarifications from the Ruben Center staff. From the video, the women and men were equally talkative. Older men were the most talkative, the community patriarchs. Additionally, more men than women lowered their masks to speak. Both men and women elected to sit together despite recommendations to stay six feet apart.

## 4.2. Development Professional Interviews

One hundred interviews were chosen to engage in conversation with development professionals who work in Nairobi to ascertain their perspectives on what kinds of programs are successful for resident-dwellers. Interviews provide for a fuller understanding of perspectives, including elaborate qualitative responses and concrete answers that can be coded quantitatively (Gajaweera and Johnson, 2015). Due to pandemic travel restrictions, interviews were conducted from the U.S. via Skype, Zoom, WhatsApp, or telephone. There is literature on research during crises that support using media as an alternative to face-to-face research (Deakin and Wakefield, 2014). Scholars have written about using Zoom and online research tools for ethnographic and qualitative research (Howlett, 2021).

Others have shared the benefits of using online data collection to adapt to conducting quantitative and qualitative research during the pandemic (Torrentira, 2020). More published work addressing these issues was found in the American Psychological Association Journal, The Journal of Service Management, the Qualitative Research Journal, and more sources (Abd. Halim et al., 2018; APA, 2020; Dodds, 2020; Farooq & De Villiers, 2017, Sy et al., 2020, Townsend, et al., 2020). An academic journal, PubMed, published several articles on carrying out qualitative research during a pandemic, inclusive of the difficulties of conducting research on healthcare delivery, including ethical challenges, setting up research teams, and obtaining ethical approval to conduct the research (Vindrola-Padros et al., 2020). Howard University IRB approval confirmed the acceptability of using technology and media for this human research.

After interviews with the development professionals were completed, any printed notes taken during the interview were converted into electronic data and saved on internal and external hard drives that are password-protected, encrypted, and stored in a locked cabinet in Washington, DC.

Interviewees were screened for eligibility using protocol to select a variety of development positions at aid organizations. Organizations were called and asked for direction concerning staff from their project development or project monitoring department that might be willing to volunteer for research on extreme poverty reduction. Lists were compiled of potential interview respondents with email addresses to which invitations to participate were sent.

Organizations contacted include non-profit and community organizations, government professionals, academic institutions, prominent aid organizations, and health organizations. Interviewees were selected based on the attributes listed in Table 4.3.

**Table 4.3.** Development of Professional Interviewee Attributes

| Attribute | Importance |
| --- | --- |
| Interviewees with development program offices in Nairobi to reduce extreme poverty | Important for place-based development, i.e., familiarity with local culture and norms. |
| Interviewees from governmental and non-governmental agencies of various sizes | Political organizations often consider larger urban planning needs, while non-political organizations typically serve based on immediate needs. |
| Interviewees from educational institutions in Kenya | Academic perspectives offer theoretical as well as evidence-based approaches and solutions to poverty. |
| Interviewees from prominent name organizations with large budgets and substantial organizational capacity | Substantial program budgets may or may not benefit the reduction of extreme poverty. Substantial capacity can increase productivity or decrease productivity due to bureaucracy. |
| Interviewees from the medical profession | Multi-dimensional poverty includes poor health. Clinicians and hospitals see patients with conditions that stem from poor hygiene, lack of water, poor nutrition, physical abuse, lack of money for medicine, unattended children, and lack of education. Tapping into interviews from health professionals reveal layers of poverty. |

Preliminary questions asked were about the organization and the demographics of the interviewee, followed by questions about key issues surrounding programs their organization or department has developed to help reduce poverty in the informal settlements. Interviews were conducted via Zoom or phone. Interview sessions had no time limit and were taped if consent was given.

Having five categories of interviewees helps to ensure the external validity of the information provided about poverty reduction in informal settlements. Each category offers a different perspective and approach to extreme poverty reduction. National, city, and local levels within each category serve to provide broader perspectives. Information to reach contacts at the organizations can be publicly found on websites. Potential interviewees can also be found on conference websites as guest speakers.

Over the eight years of working in the informal settlements of Nairobi, Kenya,[86] I have learned that approaches to poverty reduction, organizational structure and goals are key drivers of program development. Table 4.4 gives a further breakdown of the interview categories that were used in this book, written to facilitate the replication of this research.

**Table 4.4.** Development of professional interviewee categories

| Category | Importance | Levels/Examples |
|---|---|---|
| Non-profit/ Community Organizations | Provides insight on foreign aid from a local, place-based perspective. | -National non-profit (Action Aid Kenya) -City non-profit (Napenda Kuishi Trust) -Local community non-profit (Good Hope Community Center) |
| Government workers | Provides insight on complexities of development urban planning, including the use of private and government land. | -National government organization (Kenyan Ministry of Social Services) -City government organization (Nairobi City Council) -Local government organization (Kibera Judiciary Court) |
| Academics | Provides theoretical and evidence-based approaches to poverty reduction across inter-disciplinary fields (development, sociology, agriculture, and economics). | -National University (Nairobi University) -City University (Cooperative University) -Local University (Mt. Kenya University) |
| Prominent Aid Organizations | Provides insight from well-known organizations with significant budgets and capacity. | -National NGO (The Kenyan Red Cross) -City NGO (Pamoja Trust) -Local NGO (Kwetu Home of Peace) |

| Health Organizations | Provides insights on multi-dimensional poverty. | -National (Mater Hospital) -City (Mbagathi Hospital) -Local (Pipeline Health Center) |
|---|---|---|

Questions for the interviews were like those in the community survey, only turned towards development professionals about their perspectives on what causes extreme poverty and how poverty reduction programs should be developed. Some interviewees were Kenyan, and some were expatriates. There were no personal questions regarding income or demographics other than sex and age for the purpose of evaluating any difference of perspectives in their answers. Informed consent was provided through reading the preamble to the research and, or via email to the interviewee.

Questions were asked about the organization where the interviewee works to learn about the focus, i.e., hygiene, sanitation, gender, youth, agriculture, fin-tech (financial technology), entrepreneurship, etc. This information helps explain why organizations approach poverty in certain ways. There were also questions about "traditional" programs and whether they help reduce extreme poverty. In the development industry, traditional programs typically offer education and job training. Innovative programs typically offer entrepreneurship guidance, micro-loans, and tech-savvy ways to reduce poverty, including receiving direct cash. Asking questions about types of programs helps identify what the industry is thinking about approaches to reduce poverty.

Questions about COVID-19 were asked to learn how and if organizations pivoted during the pandemic. Several interviewees from well-known programs were part of the interview sample. Residents of Mukuru were also asked COVID-19-related questions. Having the program type and the name of the organization as part of questions posed to the community residents and development professionals allowed for a direct comparison of effectiveness as perceived by both sets of respondents. Like the resident survey, development professionals were asked how they would create a poverty reduction program for the informal settlements with an unlimited budget. The question does not represent Freirean theory for development professionals, as development professionals are accustomed to radicalization, i.e., the implementation of development programs. However, for the residents, the same question is posed to analyze readiness to radicalize their ideas into action to help themselves.

**Chapter 4 - Key points**

<u>**Surveys and interviews:**</u>

- Researcher positionality

- Accessible location

- Appropriate remuneration

- Adapting to the unpredicted

<u>**Research instruments:**</u>

- Survey

- Interview

**Chapter 4 - Discussion questions**

1) Research conducted inside informal settlements can provide the detailed data needed to design programs that are more effective. What are some of the reasons that thwart this research? How can practitioners circumvent those issues? Is there a greater role for academic researchers in this context?

2) How might research conducted inside informal settlements change the dynamics between local government and local slum-dwellers? Could active research influence the beginning of policy changes to address tenure issues in slums?

3) Why are informal settlements key in reducing extreme poverty? What happens if they are ignored? Who benefits from improved livelihoods in the slums? In what ways?

Men's group led by male Community Leader

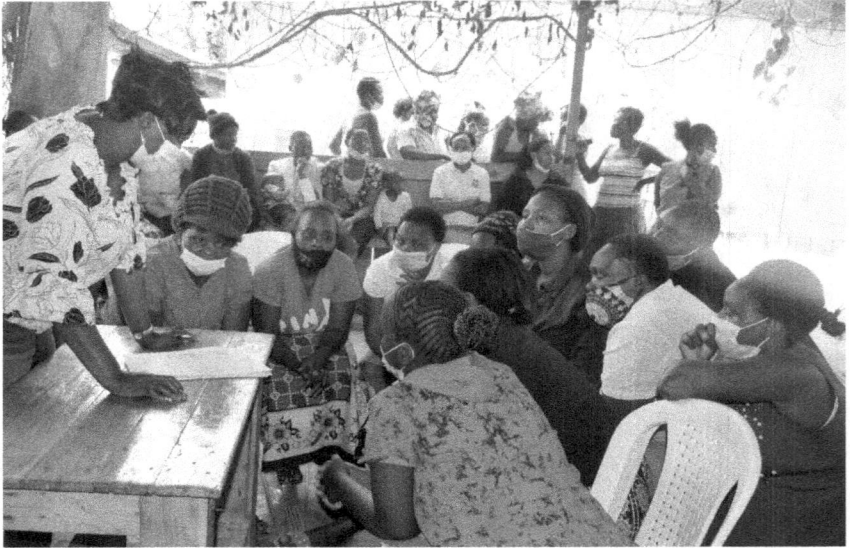

Women's groups led by female Community Leader

# Notes

[79] These studies are discussed in the last section of the literature review. All were conducted using interviews and focus groups. The nature of Freirean theory is dialogue, making this methodology the most appropriate choice to use.

[80] Pew Research done in Nairobi 2020 used a sample of 1003 for a population of 4 million people as shown here: https://www.pewresearch.org/methodology/international-survey-research/international-methodology/all-survey/all-country/all-year
Afrobarometer used a sample size of 1600 in Kenya for a population of 51 million people as shown here: https://www.afrobarometer.org/countries/kenya-0. Gallup used a sample size of 1000-2200 for research in Kenya with a population of 45 million (2008).

[81] Mukuru is divided into two main sections, kwa Ruben and kwa Njenga.

[82] In my travels to work in the informal settlements since 2012, I have rarely encountered anyone who could not speak, read, and write basic English. English is the language taught in schools; Kiswahili is a secondary language. A recent article in The East African written January 2020 stated "Kenya rated second best in English fluency test" in all countries of Africa. This ranking is based on the English Proficiency Index (EPI). More can be read here: https://www.theeastafrican.co.ke/tea/news/east-africa/kenya-rated-second-best-in-english-fluency-test-1435814

[83] This link provides a breakdown from the African Studies Center at the University of Pennsylvania. The groups live in large numbers outside of Nairobi - https://www.africa.upenn.edu/NEH/kethnic.htm

[84] Many of Kenya's ethnic struggles are in rural Rift Valley, as noted here: https://www.crisisgroup.org/africa/horn-africa/kenya/248-kenyas-rift-valley-old-wounds-devolutions-new-anxieties

[85] Informal settlement residents live together regardless of ethnicity. Crime and poverty are the main enemy, not ethnic groups, https://www.globalcommunities.org/node/37446

[86] I began developing and implementing programs to reduce extreme poverty in Mukuru in 2011. Visiting the slum four times a year and spending from 3 weeks to 3 months at a time over ten years provides me collective experience and ethnographic insight into the community. Programs developed were entrepreneurial-based but also included health, agriculture, education, women's groups, youth empowerment, storytelling, and art therapy.

Chapter 5

# Data and Analysis

Analysis was conducted using the Statistical Package for Social Sciences and a thorough review of qualitative data. The findings and analysis are discussed in two sections: (A) Community Surveys and (B) Interviews. Dependent and independent variables are noted, followed by cross-tabulations. Tables are listed within each section for convenient verification of key facts. Appendices A and B provide the full range of frequencies on all questions.

### 5.1. Community Survey Variables

Table 5.1 offers a list of the 14 independent and dependent variables from the Mukuru community survey. Variables with notes in parentheses denote Freirean variables of consciousness, i.e., self-reflection and awareness of deeper factors that may contribute to poverty. Table 5.1 outlines standard variables measured by written responses. All questions were entered into the computational application known as the Statistical Package for the Social Sciences (SPSS) to ascertain the frequencies.

**Table 5.1.** Community Survey variables*

Variables are not listed in any order or combination with dependent variables.

| 14 Independent variables | | 14 Dependent variables |
|---|---|---|
| Age | | Origin in Mukuru |
| Marital Status | | Daily challenges |
| # Of children | | COVID-19 effects on livelihood |
| Home/hospital childbirth | | Earn money how |
| Years in Mukuru | | Cause of poverty (psychologism) |
| Kids not in school | | Rise from poverty possible |
| Community lending | | Long/short-term needs |
| Community leader | | How government helps |

| Government help (sectarianism) | | How government hurts |
|---|---|---|
| Vote | | Why did you vote |
| Self confidence (subjectivism) | | Why didn't you vote |
| Likelihood that job training helps | | Effective program type (psychologism) |
| Issue for you alone? (subjectivism) | | Effective program by name |
| A way out of poverty for residents? *(sectarianism)* | | Dream program (radicalization) |

* Frequencies were calculated in lieu of crosstabulations.

### 5.1.1. Community Survey Findings and Analysis

The frequencies represent 500 participants, of which 100% live in Mukuru. The variables brought forth answers that were analyzed by frequency of mentions. For example, rent may be mentioned 400 times as a key challenge, followed by safe passage and finding shelter. Percentages are also listed as direct calculation of the frequencies.

While some research would summarize the data with fewer details, the profession of development requires detail to fine-tune programs to help the poor. For example, to summarize that half the participants are ages 18-34, it leaves out critical details about child-birth years, teen issues, and family planning. Likewise, to summarize, half the participants are over 34 would omit valuable information needed for adult programming, including health and aging. Because development professionals want and need to know this information, summaries in this book are broken down with salient details.

Additionally, the highest frequencies are presented first within each summary, followed by lower frequencies. This approach is used because funding for development programs is issued where the big numbers are those that indicate the greatest need. Development professionals look for this information to prioritize programming.

A summarized profile of Q2 (question 2) shows that most of the participants are aged 25-34, followed by 33% aged 18-24. Although 96% have children[87], only 54% are married. Further breakdown from Q5 shows 28% have two children, 25% have three, 23% have four children, and 20% have one child. In Q6, 70% of the children were born in a hospital; the rest were born at home.

This data reflects the youth bulge and an increase in births, though overall fertility rates in Kenya are not as high as they were 20 years ago[88]. The fact that more children are born in a hospital shows positive movement in the health sector to reduce child mortality in communities of poverty.

The age breakdown is like that of the Kenya National Bureau of Statistics Census 2019. Ages 25-34 make up the largest population in the census and the sample from this research. The second largest age group from the census and the research sample are aged 18-24. However, it is noteworthy that the largest population in the census is people under the age of 18 (1,538,589), which is not reflected in this research sample. The comparative percentages demonstrate that the research sample has younger participants. This may suggest the need for policies that promote affordable housing, evidenced by the youth bulge living in Nairobi with no place to live except the informal settlements. The youth bulge across all of Africa has been measured and cited as the fastest-growing population around the world (World Bank, 2021). See Table 5.2.

**Table 5.2.** Comparative Age frequencies

(This research vs Kenya Census 2019)

| Census Frequencies | % Total Nairobi age 18+ | Nairobi Population 4.396.828 | Research Frequencies | % Total of N500 | Total responses |
|---|---|---|---|---|---|
| Age 18-24 | 25% | 712,532 | Age 18-24 | 33% | 146 |
| Age 25-34 | 39% | 1,078,818 | Age 25-34 | 44% | 221 |
| Age 35-44 | 21% | 598,948 | Age 35-44 | 21% | 94 |
| Age 45-64 | 14% | 409,466 | Age 45-64 | 2% | 39 |

58,265 population over age 64 (1.3%)

Time living in Mukuru (Q9) is reflected in years, with the greatest number of participants (25%) living in the informal settlement for 3-5 years, followed by 19% (6-10 years), 17% (11-15 years), 13% (16-20 years), and 14% for those living in Mukuru over 20 years. The near evenness of the percentages demonstrates that Mukuru is neither a temporary nor long-term home – instead, it is both. Fifty-five percent of the residents came to live in Mukuru because of ancestors who fled rural areas looking for better life options in the city (Q10). Twenty percent moved to Mukuru as a first step out of the family home. Ten percent moved to Mukuru as the result of an early marriage. In Q11, daily challenges were noted in qualitative and quantitative responses.

Quantitatively, results were computed based on percentages and qualitatively on a number of mentions noted further down in the analysis. The top three challenges were rent (94%), school fees [89](91%), and food (87%). Other challenges include hygiene (79%), health (78%), water (72%), bribes (67%), childcare (64%), safety (56%), transportation (44%), elder care (40%), no spouse (28%), and police brutality (23%)[90]. Instead of collapsing these challenges, they are more impactful and disaggregated. The percentages point to the fact that the challenges are equally important across multidimensional areas of life. For example, with school fees being the second greatest challenge for residents, 57% of the sample confirmed that one or more of their children are kept home due to the inability to pay school fees.

According to the participants, the COVID-19 pandemic lockdowns increased poverty (Q12) in terms of hunger (87%), lack of income (86%), and lack of services open (77%). The pandemic also increased domestic violence (75%), bribery (66%), increased anxiety (54%), no access to a protective mask (58%), increased child abuse (58%), eviction (56%), divorce/separation (48%), small space to quarantine (44%), curfew related police brutality (41%), and bribes to be released from hospital quarantine sites (16%). Notice the difference in percentages of those who complained of increased bribery (66%) versus those who complained of bribery to be released from hospital quarantine sites (16%).

Bribery to be released was prevalent at hospitals in Nairobi and other areas of Kenya, as reported by several journalists during the peak of the pandemic. Some patients were being held for prolonged periods without knowing COVID-19 test results; others, after testing negative, had surpassed the 14-day mandatory quarantine but still were not being released; some desperately needed to work to provide for their families, still more were justifiably held but bribed to pay for hospitalization and food before release[91]. The fact that the residents reported only 16% experiencing such bribes indicates that either residents did not get tested when COVID-19 was suspected and or few chose to seek hospitalization.

The top three ways to earn money each day (Q14) are construction work (39%), collecting plastics or metals[92] for recycling (38%), and washing clothes (35%). The remaining methods include entrepreneurship (31%), cash from non-profit organizations (28%), and spouse contribution (14%), with 1% or less from government disbursements, a steady job, and remittances.

It is noteworthy to reiterate that only 1% of 500 residents of Mukuru identify government disbursements as a source of income, and 0% gain income from remittances. People who are not familiar with developing countries may not realize that local government aid programs are nearly nonexistent in many countries except for the elderly, orphans, and the disabled[93]. Remittances are also not commonly received by people who live in informal settlements. From ten years of on-the-ground experience, most residents do not have relatives who have made it out of Mukuru to earn a steady income or relatives who migrated to a foreign country for work.

Traditional male and female roles for work are blurred in the community. Women in the sample reported taking on construction jobs at the same percentage as men. From qualitative answers, it was made clear that at construction sites, they are performing tasks such as clearing stones, wood, or steel from the work area instead of construction buildings. Men did not report engaging in traditional women's roles, such as washing clothes, yet they reported cooking chapati and selling food for income. Likewise, recycling entails collecting metal remnants and carting them to a location to exchange for cash. This, too, is done by women, carrying less weight to exchange but nevertheless doing a job that Westerners would not expect. It is important to realize that people do what they must to feed their families. See Table 5.3 for a gender breakdown of work habits.

**Table 5.3.** Comparative labor roles per 250 female + 250 male respondents

(Over 80% of the sample follow these work roles)

| Work Role | Female | Male |
| --- | --- | --- |
| Construction | Yes | Yes |
| Washing Clothes | Yes | No |
| Cooking food for sale | Yes | Yes |
| Recycling metal and plastic | Yes | Yes |
| Spousal contribution | Yes | Yes |

The subject matter of the "hustle" is not new regarding communities of poverty. Sudhir Venkatesh, 2008, writes about a poor Black neighborhood on the Southside of Chicago. He explains the hustle of illicit work at home, gangs, illicit preachers, and the underground world of how to survive poverty. Having lived in poverty, I grew up seeing hustling as the ultimate form of entrepreneurship. Males and females in the community find opportunities to sell or trade items that have "fallen off a truck" or items from a container that got "lost" when it was lifted from the shipping dock. Items were vastly different, from electronic gaming devices to Krugerrand coins from Johannesburg or rare pets.

In Mukuru, people are often interrelated in activities of survival. A woman washing clothes might experience an unexpected tear in a garment. Upon returning the garments to the owner, the woman could gain more work if asked to mend the tear or be fired because of the tear. In either case, she wins, as she can peddle the job to her neighbor for a percentage of the neighbor's profit. Venkatesh writes about first-world poverty, including deceitful hustling for the purpose of earning income (Venkatesh, 2008). More importantly, in Chicago and Mukuru, only a subset of residents earn income from deceit. However, a hustle is still a hustle where people do what is needed to survive.

Turning to social/community capital in Q15, 88% are certain that their neighbors will donate or lend money in case of a death or grave illness in the family. In Q16, 74% can identify a person in the community who is considered a leader. These indicators point to a supportive community that has the capacity for compassion despite a dire need for daily survival. It also points to the ability of the community to take ownership and a leadership role in its own development. Residents expound on community capital and cohesion in relation to having the ability to work together for the good of the informal settlement.

> *"Life in Mukuru is interesting because many people living here are equal even though there are those people doing much better than others but still feel comfortable with the life here."*

> *"We have landlords here owning more than 20 houses, but still live here."*

The participants confirmed the ways in which their government provides help (Q23), mostly through providing fresh water (57%), state security or protection from harm (53%), and by providing limited health services (44%). A total of 98.4% of the participants believe that their government has funds to help them (Q22), but their government chooses not to help them as part of corruption (59%), and 28.6% believe that the government does not care about them. The residents of Mukuru know they are being used to gain aid money that never reaches them. The majority of the Mukuru residents want their government to get more involved with their welfare.

> *"Sometimes or most of the time the money intended for poverty reduction in the slum end up being used for other things by the leaders (stolen) or because of corruption only little is left available for use to benefit the community."*

> *"Government to open up [accessible], and create more opportunities is what we want."*

*"The government is not doing enough, and our problems are passed from one government to another. They come during elections to ask for votes, thereafter they go never to come back for any meaningful development."*

In Q25, 93% of the participants voted in the last election (2017) with 86% doing so because they want things to change for the better. Seven percent of the participants did not vote, mostly due to not being registered (Q26). Regarding the effectiveness of job training programs in Q30, 88% of the participants think job training programs are very likely to reduce poverty, 12% likely, and 0% unlikely. Although job training programs are identified as helpful, later in the qualitative answers, the participants specify that there are no jobs being created that align with the training they receive. The community residents agree (485 out of 500) that training and entrepreneurship are key elements needed to reduce extreme poverty.

*"The main cause of poverty in the slum is lack of formal employment. Many residents work as casuals in the industries and the jobs are not granted on a daily basis. The salaries are also very low."*

*"Lack of marketable work skills is a major cause of poverty...most dwellers have attained basic education but not advanced to attract or compete in bigger job market."*

*"Lack of money to start business… as people live hand to mouth and cannot save to start a business."*

The community residents were asked in Q31 about development programs that have been helpful in reducing extreme poverty. Twelve programs well known for their intention to serve the poorest of the poor were part of the survey. Five programs were identified as being helpful: The Ruben Center (61%), Kenya Red Cross (61%), programs that offer pay-toilets and showers (55%), US Agency for International Development (USAID) 50%, and small community-based programs (35%). The remaining seven programs received a minimal amount of mentions as being helpful. Those programs include Save the Children, Muungano Alliance, KYEOP, Sanergy, KENSUP (Kenyan Slum Upgrading Programme), Pamoja Trust, and Mercy Corp. The programs are publicized as helping the poorest of the poor in Africa, yet they have no name recognition in Nairobi's second-largest informal settlement. The question of "why" requires a different research project. Statements from the community participants about a list of key programs that are meant to help the poorest of the poor in Kenya:

*"We have never received help from these aid programs."*

*"These programs are surrounded by corrupt individuals, especially the leadership who are the first people to know about such programs. They determine who is to benefit."*

*"Benefits go to family members and friends of organizations leaders, or people who bribe to be put on the list of beneficiaries."*

### 5.2. Community Survey Freirean variables

The Freirean questions were qualitative, analyzed by reading and grouping the answers according to frequencies. Because of the research restraints due to the COVID-19 pandemic, no group discussions were planned. Nevertheless, four key staff at the research location were apprised of the questionnaire with copies and had received an overview of the questions with me via Zoom in case participants needed clarity. Based on the collaborative culture within the informal settlements, it was expected that participants would speak with each other regarding the qualitative questions; however, it was unexpected that the discussions would become in-depth as shown in video footage. Four staff clarified several of the questions and remained present during participant discussions. They helped input the qualitative answers, some being very lengthy.

In a later inquiry, the staff reported that the questions were taken very seriously by the participants. The issues struck a chord with the residents because the issues concerned their livelihoods. The staff reported that 95% of the participants engaged in discussion on qualitative, and some quantitative questions. While the impediments of the pandemic forced the removal of planned focus groups for this research, the respondents, nevertheless, gathered on their own accord to discuss some of the issues. Table 5.4 outlines Freirean variables and explanations of how the variables relate to critical consciousness.

**Table 5.4.** Community Survey Freirean variables

| Freirean variables | Critical Consciousness | Lacking Critical Consciousness |
|---|---|---|
| Subjectivism (created reality) | No Self-blame | Self-blame |
| Sectarianism (false truth) | No belief in group inferiority | Beliefs of group inferiority |

| Psychologism (self-reflection) | Self-reflection | No Self-reflection |
|---|---|---|
| Radicalization (active truth/agency) | Active solution | No Active solution |

### 5.2.1. Community Survey Freirean Findings and Analysis

Seven Freirean-themed questions served as prompts toward a progression of critical thinking (Freire, 1970). They were analyzed separately from the rest of the data to help evaluate the residents' critical consciousness regarding their predicament in poverty and their ability to move towards thinking deeply about sustainable solutions to poverty. The separate analysis is intended to help development professionals create more effective programs for extreme poverty reduction with direct input from residents of the Mukuru informal settlement.

In Q8, nearly all (91%) of Mukuru residents consider themselves to be living in poverty. There is no misunderstanding of the plight they face daily securing basic human needs. The deeper question in Q17 about what causes poverty (psychologism) revealed three top answers:

1. lack of jobs (92%),

2. corruption/bribery (60%), and

3. low paying jobs (40%)

In Q20, the question of poverty being an individual problem could be seen as a dead-end question with an obvious answer. People who are despondent due to their predicament often ascribe self-blame for their issues, even when others nearby suffer from similar problems. When the residents were asked this question, there was no indication of self-blame for causes of poverty (subjectivism), but 12% ascribed laziness as a possible cause for others who remain living in poverty on the qualitative portion of this question. However, laziness is an indicator ascribed by 12% as the cause of other residents' poverty, not their own.

None take ownership of things that have, or have not, occurred, such as unemployment, lack of plumbing, and other related issues that have caused dysfunction in their lives. They see that poverty is a problem for their settlement, other settlements, and other people. In the qualitative portion of the question, they blame government corruption for their lack. In developed countries where social service programs are available, blame is often placed on the people who do not take advantage of the services and the opportunities offered to rise out of poverty. However, in low-income countries where government-based support programs do not exist, residents indicate they are not at fault for their livelihoods.

Regarding long and short-term needs, the frequencies show cash as their short-term need and job creation as their long-term need. However, some Mukuru residents varied in thoughts worth sharing.

*"In the long-term, people need to be trained on skills and be employed to earn their own money or given business startup kits that are interest free."*

*"Short-term need is [to] ban drugs and cheap alcohol, track, and arrest all those who sell them."*

*"Long-term [we need] government, church and Muslim-based organizations and NGOs to train us on basic education, vocational programs and help us start community projects."*

In qualitative Q17, causes of poverty with no self-blame were bad governance (30%), illness (20%), lack of education (20%), alcoholism and drug abuse (18%), tribalism (9%), and high population (1%). Gender issues, lack of skills, poor infrastructure, reluctance to try, and discrimination are less than 1% of overall mentions. Qualitative answers place the blame for alcoholism and drug abuse on a justified lack of hope instead of self-blame. Unlike someone with the financial ability to indulge in drugs, the residents risk dangerous side effects, including sudden death from the least expensive drugs that can remove their hunger, fear, and pain. The community participants made several statements about what they believe to be the top causes of poverty.

*"Corruption based on tribalism and joblessness."*

*"Corruption, lack of employment, lack of education, poor health facilities, and insecurity." "Disease, corruption, lack of employment, overpopulation."*

*"Corruption, lack of jobs, bad governance, poor salary/pay." "Joblessness, nepotism. Alcoholism is only lost hope."*

*"High population, low income, lack of job opportunities, bribery, coronavirus." "Lack of jobs, no support from government."*

*"Unemployment, reluctance syndrome, bad politics, corruption, drug abuse, financial instability."*

*"Unemployment, lack of capital."*

*"Lack of education, overpopulation, early marriages and pregnancies, and finance."*

Regarding the possibility of a way out of poverty in Q18 (sectarianism), 96% of the participants affirm there is a way out, with only 2% in disagreement and 2% unsure. Deeper reflection from the next questions in the survey revealed that 100% of the participants believe that poverty is not an issue for them alone (subjectivism) and cash is the short-term solution. The top three long-term solutions (psychologism) are:

1.   job creation (92%),

2.   cash to start a business (86%), and

3.   empowerment groups to keep them motivated (28%)

Further solutions are better governance (26%), free public education (26%), better clinics (22%), reduced corruption (14%), and job training (12%). Sponsors, better security, and infrastructure, respectively at less than 1%. In Q28, 77% believe they have what it takes to be successful (radicalization and psychologism), 20% do not, and 3% think they might have what it takes. Ninety-nine percent of the participants believe their government has funds to help reduce poverty in Q22 (sectarianism) and that the government does not utilize those funds (Q24) because of corruption (62%). Thirty percent believe funds are not properly used because the government does not care about the informal settlements (30%). Four percent believe their government does care but is busy, and the remaining 4% believe plans are in the works.

Residents made similar comments when asked to extrapolate the question, "Do you have what it takes to be successful?"

*"I am physically well and in good health with no disability."*

*"I can do any work to earn money to meet the day needs and become successful." "The system is not working, and I cannot get employment."*

*"I have what it takes but do not have education to get any gainful employment that would take me out of the slum."*

In the qualitative questions, critically thinking about what kinds of programs (Q29) would best reduce extreme poverty (critical consciousness question), the participants mentioned advocacy the most (813 mentions). This number reflects some participants mentioning advocacy more than once. The second and third most mentioned types of programs were job training (485 mentions) and entrepreneurship (454 mentions), which tied with mentions of hygiene-related programs.

The remaining mentions were education (444), housing (438), cash (426), gender equality (423), health (420), child-care (408), savings groups (382), urban micro-farming (348), substance abuse (284), and climate/environmental issues (272). Note that the number of mentions reflects the urgency for certain types of programs over others. As an example, if someone is homeless and has not eaten in five days, they are likely to mention needing food far more than they may mention needing shelter. Regarding the effectiveness of poverty reduction programs, the community residents shared a disconnect between program offerings and what is needed on a practical level.

*"Poverty reduction in this slum may take much more time to achieve and this is because the government and other NGOs bring programs for [us] but do not consult the people." "They bring projects [that are] not relevant to the needs of the people."*

The final question (Q32) is about developing a "dream program" to transform the informal settlement (radicalization). The top three elements identified by the community to include in a dream program are:

1.  Health clinics (93%) tied with free public schools

2.  Pay toilets/showers (88%)

3.  Electricity (84%)

This finding confirms the importance of health and education as approaches to poverty reduction prescribed by those in extreme poverty. Hunger is not a top issue for the residents, although nutritional food intake to benefit health and boost the ability to learn may not be an element of consideration for the residents.

Nine more elements with frequencies above 70% are home upgrading in the informal settlement (80%), concrete paths for passage and emergencies (79%), and piped water/plumbing (78%). These elements of the dream program reflect a need for secure housing and the capability to practice safe hygiene (Water, Sanitation and Hygiene, known as WASH programs). Installation of these elements would benefit idle residents looking for work if a practical training program were developed specifically to address these needs.

*"Job creation and training, quality education, housing, health and hygiene programs, safe pathways to help fight fires, legal electricity connection as opposed to the illegal ones that cause fires every other week, clean energy."*

Further elements for a dream program include child care (74%), social empowerment/advocacy/savings groups (74%), an easy business license process, safe cook stoves, and community vegetable plots (71%). These reflect the higher ambitions of the residents once foundational needs are met. Entrepreneurship and socialization are also elements that foster innovation and economic growth, as discussed in the literature review on modernization approaches.

The remaining four elements of a dream program are identified as care for elders and persons with disabilities (65%), and internet access and community guards for safety (55%). For a community to have lived for decades without such services, these are nearly last on the list of needs, yet not exclusively last. It is also noteworthy that due to illness and lack of health systems for the poor, many residents of the informal settlement do not achieve old age.

Last on the list of essential elements to include in a dream program is the creation of new housing away from the informal settlement (35%). This is important because the UN-built housing for Kenya's largest informal settlement (Kibera) in a project known as KINSUP, failed to meet its objective to re-locate residents to better, affordable housing[94]. Additions to the wish list from the qualitative answers include centers within the informal settlement for services (family planning, domestic abuse, loans, drug rehabilitation, hospital 24/7, nutritional education, job and life skills training, import/export of commerce for inter-continental trade, and community projects, and for the Kenyan Government to become more involved with their welfare.

The "Dream Program" is the collection of thoughts from the community on what types of programs are best to help them rise out of extreme poverty. These comments represent critical elements of aid programs that are currently not reaching intended clients.

*"I would make income generating programs that include Merry-go-rounds ....money collected or generated here would be channeled back to individuals whereby the group constitution compels members either to start a small-scale business for self-sustainability."*

*"We would begin with skills training for public needs, i.e., masonry, art, carpentry, hairdressing, and offer workshops and seminars. The next step – create companies to open employment to improve infrastructure*

*and proper sanitation, i.e., public toilets and drainage systems. Employment needed to increase food and water supply through access to cooperatives that forward the people's petitions."*

*"Partnerships with potential organizations that influence selection of [government] leadership."*

*"Modern housing, manufacturing companies to employ people, health programs, improve roads, education, training for skills, improve security and increase food production."*

*"Programs that are not led by external organizations. Programs with financial structure to suit the fragile and irregular income streams of slum dwellers. Some micro-financing programs have high interest rates and heavily penalize people when payments are missed."*

*"No job training! Training in sectors where there are no jobs or where one cannot make a living wage and enough to support advancement is wasted programming dollars."*

*"Advocacy like Transparency International."*

### 5.2.2. On critical consciousness

The Freirean-theme questions revealed that subjectivism and sectarianism are not issues for residents of the Mukuru informal settlement. This is important because attitudes of self-defeat will not produce sustainable programs. The Mukuru residents place no blame on themselves personally, nor as a sect of society, for their predicament in poverty. One hundred percent of the residents think poverty is not an issue just for them, and 96% believe there is a way out of poverty for the community. Development professionals can feel confident that subjective depression or self-prescribed blame for living in the informal settlement is not a barrier to the residents' determination to succeed.

The last question for both development professionals and community residents, referred to as the "dream program," is a question that requires a description of elements needed to reduce extreme poverty with no budgetary limits. Development professionals noted the following elements in order of importance:

1. Savings groups

2. Entrepreneurship

3. Skills training

4. Health

5. WASH (Water and Sanitation Hygiene)

6. Housing

7. Gender issues

8. Comprehensive Millennium Villages (UNHCR refugee villages)

9. Policy changes on land tenure

10. Education

11. Micro-finance

The Freirean-themed question falls under the final stage of critical consciousness, radicalization, which asks, "What should we do" to fix the problem? Having answered what works and what does not work to reduce extreme poverty, the community residents offer four key problems that urgently need to be addressed:

1) basic human rights,

2) housing improvements,

3) social support, and

4) economic support

### 5.2.3. Basic Human Rights

Mukuru residents identify the need for 24-hour clinics as the top element to ensure that basic human rights are met. The clinics that currently exist are poorly staffed, and their pharmacies issue expired medicines, similar medicines, or the wrong medicine – all of which can be fatal.

*"People get sick in the night and do not have means to take to hospitals outside the slum due to security issues or some delay."*

*"Emergencies like assault, labour [childbirth], happens in the night and the community needs to be secure in terms of health care anytime to alleviate sufferings."*

*"Care is essential in any place, but especially the slums, we are overpopulated and prone to disease outbreak."*

Additions to basic human rights are free public education with free uniforms. As noted previously, many parents send one child to school while their siblings wait for the next semester to attend school. This creates a time gap whereby children age out due to embarrassment and ridicule by other students. Many prefer to drop out completely by grade five.

*"The kids that stay home due to lack of school fees, some of them stay idle while they move around in the slum."*

*"Some of they engage in antisocial behavior such as drug use, alcohol and even premarital sex and rape and begging."*

*"Some spend time collecting plastics, scrap metals to sell. Some join boda-boda and carwash business."*

WASH is essential as a human right to access water for health and hygiene. Mabati in the informal settlements do not have piped water. There is no infrastructure to support it. Water containers are kept and used in strict portions for drinking, cooking, cloth bathing, and washing hair. Pay toilets and showers are few and too far away to use for human excretions. Lines are long, and the number of people using a stall counter-act the reason to pay for the service – cleanliness.

*"Lack of water means cholera and typhoid."*

*"We must make open defecation or help ourselves in plastic bags for flying toilets. More pay-toilets can give us privacy and cleanliness in our surroundings."*

*"The pay-showers improve life, give us privacy and safety to not wait until night to bathe, cost is 10 shillings."*

*"You can make income with pay-toilets and showers through ownership or cleaning them."*

### 5.2.4. Housing Improvements

The residents identify electricity, housing upgrades, and concrete paths for easy access to mabati dwellings as their second priority. No differentiation is made between gaining electricity by traditional wiring or solar power, even though the wires contribute to fire danger in the informal settlement. The residents prefer upgrades to their mabati in the informal settlement (402 mentions) versus re-location out of the community (179 mentions). Concrete paths are expressed as a need for main passageways into the community and for access to put out fires, etc.

> *"We want the slum to be more secure with permanent structures and paths."*

> *"Minimize the risk of fire consuming all the mabati, and a path of escape."*

> *"Rain creates muddy passageways and mabati structures slip and fall. Upgrading for safety and navigation of the slum can improve our lives."*

> *"I don't have gumboots, I cannot go out if it rains."*

### 5.2.5. Social Support

The third tier of elements that community residents identify as necessary for effective development and reduction of extreme poverty include care for those left at home. This includes children, elders, and persons with disabilities.

> *"In the slums there are limited facilities that care for children, elders, or the disabled. Most of the time when I am looking for work, I leave my children alone at home without care. They go hungry until I am back."*

> *"Sometimes they become victims of abuse for example they are sexually abused, raped, beaten or sometimes they get lost."*

> *"The disabled are neglected, abused or abandoned by some families."*

> *"For the disabled, stigma and discrimination is there. They need a care centre and for the elderly to avoid maltreatment and suffering."*

Creating social groups was identified as important in terms of community empowerment. The residents describe community vegetable gardens, savings groups, and a block patrol for safety within the informal settlement.

> *"The groups give us a place to talk freely in security."*

> *"We can do merry-go-round to start small scale businesses like vegetable kiosk and mandazi baking."*

*"Empowerment groups to increase our capacity and talk about issues to support each other in business and life skills. Groups can teach us about reporting systems in table-banking and how to resolve problems."*

*"We can get to know each other very well in women's groups."*

*"Community protection groups can enhance the security among ourselves and families including children's safety."*

*"If gardens are community owned, everybody can have access to utilize the produce from them to improve food security. But this is not sustainable because of space and large population in the slum."*

Access to the internet was noted next to last, with new housing away from the informal settlement dead last. Internet access is not viewed as an essential need in the community. Informal work does not call for sending emails or research on the web. From my experience, using Facebook or social media is considered a luxury, as many mobile phones used in Mukuru are basic.

Issues of safety and access to knowledge are important for everyone. The COVID-19 pandemic moved some Nairobi schools online, and education in Mukuru was interrupted because residents do not have access to the internet. Though residents do not see the need for internet access, it may be the case that they do not know what they are missing in terms of access and empowerment. One of the development professionals made this point at the end of the interview:

*"Mukuru needs internet to connect to the world for safety and to learn what is happening. They do not realize the information they are missing in terms of new [pandemic] cases and how the world was treating Covid."*

### 5.2.6. Economic Support

While income is rudimentary to reducing extreme poverty, the issue was set aside and relegated to one key element – a business license. In earlier questions, job creation was the answer residents gave as the way to reduce poverty, yet after further survey questions that progressed the Freirean stages of critical thinking, residents concluded that having access to a business license was the primary means of economic support they need. Job creation does not lose its importance, though it is dependent on factors that one cannot control herself. Having a business license puts fate in the hands of the license owner. Having access to a business license at a reasonable cost without a lengthy application and extensive delays was expressed as a key economic need by 71% of the residents.

> *"People collect rent for you to do business near them, but they don't own the land. When government demolishes your stall, you have no recourse."*

> *"Business permits are timely and costly...sometime back you would pay someone to make it fast for you."*

> *Concluding this analysis, one answer stands alone with the highest number of mentions as being necessary for economic sustainability: advocacy.*

> *"We have no voice in the slum."*

> *"To air out issues we need people or rights-based programs to speak for us."*

> *"Some are not even aware of rights and do not have knowledge of issues affecting them. They need people with knowledge to speak on their behalf to be able to change the story of their lives."*

With 813 mentions, advocacy was mentioned more than once by over half of the Mukuru residents as essential for reducing extreme poverty in the informal settlements, hence the work of this book, to advocate for those who are being left behind.

Table 5.5 offers a quick glance at the highest frequencies and percentages of all variables in the Community Survey.

**Table 5.5.** Community Survey Highest Frequencies

|   | VARIABLE | HIGHEST FREQUENCY | PERCENTAGE |
|---|----------|-------------------|------------|
| 1 | Age | 221 (age 25-34) | 44% |
| 2 | Marital Status | 272 (married) | 54% |
| 3 | Number of children | 126 (2 children) | 25% |
| 4 | Children born where? | 336 (in hospital) | 67% |
| 5 | Mukuru Resident | 500 | 100% |
| 6 | Time in Mukuru | 100 (6-10 years) | 20% |
| 7 | Arrived in Mukuru, how | 209 (ancestor rural migration) | 41% |

| 8 | Daily Challenge | 473 rent / 456 school fees | 94% / 91% |
| 9 | Covid-19 increased poverty | 436 hunger | 87% |
| 10 | Cannot pay school fees | 289 cannot pay | 57% |
| 11 | Earn money how | 197 construction | 39% |
| 12 | Community lending | 433 yes | 86% |
| 13 | Community leader | 373 yes | 74% |
| 14 | How does the government help | 289 fresh water | 57% |
| 15 | Voted last election | 466 yes | 93% |
| 16 | Why vote | 433 for positive change | 86% |
| 17 | Why not vote | 24 not registered | 0.04% |
| 18 | Effective poverty programs | 500 advocacy | 100% |
| 19 | Name of effective programs | 474 Ruben Ctr/309 Red Cross | 94% / 61% |
| 20 | Job training helpful | 440 very likely | 88% |

## 5.3. Interview variables

The interview variables were similar to the community survey variables. This was done intentionally to provide a comparable set of answers to questions in both instruments. The interview data and tables are included in this section to help summarize the information. See Appendix A.2 for the full interview questionnaire. See Table 5.6 for a list of interview variables.

**Table 5.6.** Interview variables

Variables are not listed in any order or combination with dependent variables.

| 13 Independent variables | | 9 Dependent variables |
| --- | --- | --- |
| Age (Q1) | | Time allocation (Q10) |
| Sex (Q2) | | Definition of informal settlements (Q12) |
| Years of experience (Q3) | | COVID-19 effects on programs (Q16) |

| | | |
|---|---|---|
| Position held (Q9a) | | The belief that traditional programs reach informal settlements (Q15) |
| Organization focus (Q8) | | The belief that traditional programs are effective in informal settlements (Q14) |
| Organization location (Q5) | | Effective programs by type/strategy (Q20) |
| Organization type (Q6) | | Effective programs by name (Q19) * |
| Organization size (Q7) | | Belief in certain elements needed for a Dream program (Q23) |
| Years at the organization (Q9) | | Effective program categories (Q21) * |
| Programs in informal settlements (Q11) | | |
| Program restraints (Q13) | | |
| Aid likely to reduce poverty (Q17) * | | |
| Programs use human-centered development (Q22) | | |

*Likert scale variables

Organization name (Q4) and Familiar programs (Q18) are not being used as a variable

### 5.3.1. Interview findings and analysis

Beginning with demographics in Q2, the interviewees were 41% female and 37% male, totaling 78% and leaving 22% of the interviewees, noting the irrelevance of the question as related to poverty reduction. Most of the sample participants are between the ages (Q1) of 35 and 44 (40%). This age group, being the largest, may reflect low turnover in the aid profession during the years 2000-2010. The sample may also reflect the importance of the study that a high number of experienced professionals chose to volunteer. The next dominant age groups were 18- 24 (19%), 25-34 (18%), and 45-54 (16%).

The frequencies for the number of years of experience (Q3) in the development profession were 1-5 years (45%), 6-10 years (26%), 11-15 years (17%), and 16 years+ (15%). The fact that 45% of the sample have 1-5 years of experience conflicts with the premise of high job retention during the early 2000s. Instead, it may point to the industry hiring what I refer to as "new thought," which includes innovative thinkers from interdisciplinary fields, including academia, to tackle the rising rates of poverty that began in 1990. Because of population growth in Africa, "More people are poor today than in 1990." (World Bank, 2016). Overall, 71% of the development professionals interviewed have up to 10 years of experience in extreme poverty reduction.

Seventy-two percent of the interviewees work for development organizations based in Kenya (Q4). Twelve and fifteen percent have headquarters in the U.S. and other locations, respectively (Q5). Fifty-three percent of those interviewed work for NGOs or nonprofit organizations, while 18% are in government, 17% in education/training organizations, and 11% are community organizations (Q6). Based on the number of employees (Q7), 23% of the organizations have 11-50 employees and 21% have 51-200. Seventeen percent have 1-10 employees and 13% have 201-500. Only 1% of the organizations have 1000 or more employees, while 61% work for organizations with a workforce of up to 200 staff.

The focuses of the organizations (Q8) are 26% training, 24% education, 16% health, and 12% financial services. However, 79% of the organizations report being multi-focused across the sectors in addition to women and gender equality, entrepreneurship, agriculture, housing, trauma and peacebuilding, leadership, and drug rehabilitation. Of the 79% of multi-focused organizations, none of them create jobs to put cash in the pockets of the extremely poor residents they serve:

> *"My organization covers agriculture, health, women gender issues, and advocacy."*

> *"I work on trainings, education, health, entrepreneurship, women and gender issues, and advocacy programs."*

> *"We develop a multidimensional poverty index and a women's empowerment index." "Women and gender issues, trauma counseling, and peace building."*

> *Others noted work across the following areas:*

> *"Agriculture, Health, women gender issues advocacy."*

> *"Training health, Gender and women issues, Advocacy Agriculture environmental."*

*"Training education, Agriculture, Health, Entrepreneurship, Environmental, housing, women and gender issues, and advocacy."*

*"Loans, Trainings, health, Agriculture, Entrepreneurship, Environmental."*

*"Training, Education, Agriculture, Health entrepreneurship, Housing, women gender issues." "Education. Entrepreneurship, health. Gender/ women issues."*

Eighty-three percent of the interviewees have worked for up to 10 years for the organization where they are currently employed (Q9), however, 51% of this group have only worked 1-5 years at their current job. This, again, may reflect an influx of "new thought" from development professionals entering the field or a likely reflection of the project life cycle. Thirty-three are in positions (Q10) to mobilize the communities they serve, lead training, and coordinate fieldwork. Twenty-eight percent are in positions of management where monitoring and evaluation are key elements of their work, in addition to program development, analysis, and coordination. Twenty-three percent work in technical positions dedicated to information technology (IT), engineering (water, waste), finance (loans), and legal advocacy. And 10% are in medical positions or health and/or nutrition, with the remaining 6% divided between work in research and administration for the organization. These findings demonstrate a solid sample that includes predominantly those who are in positions that work directly with people who live in extreme poverty (61%).

Forty-six percent of those interviewed spend their time (Q10) mostly in the office, 24% spend their time in the field, and 30% split their time equally between the office and the field. For 78% of the interviewees, the field is the informal settlements (Q11), with 22% working in other impoverished areas of Nairobi, a likely reflection of university and hospital interviewees. It is important, however, to note that many in the sample spend 54% of their time working directly with residents in the field. The sample of development professionals interviewed are well qualified to speak on the effectiveness of programs intended to help residents.

All of those interviewed describe the informal settlements (Q12) as unplanned areas where occupancy is not legal, basic infrastructure is lacking, and overcrowding of those living below the poverty line is common. This finding follows the descriptive term "unplanned urban development," as noted in the literature review of this book regarding the legality of land use in and around the informal settlement of Mukuru. The descriptions are accurate according to the history of how the informal settlements began in the 1960s when Kenya gained independence from colonizers, the details of which are also outlined in the contextual background and literature review of this book. Interviews with development professionals revealed these descriptions of the informal settlement:

*"Settlements in areas where there is no legal occupancy and the housing is not in compliance with current planning and building regulations as stipulated by the government."*

*"Unplanned structures that are temporary in nature and people living in the settlement earn very little income and lack basic social amenities like toilets clean water, and electricity."*

*"Mabati structures often overcrowded with lack of water, food and have poor hygiene."*

*"Geographical area that hosts people who live below the poverty line characterized by poor living conditions, insecurity, limited services among other [things]."*

*"Semi-permanent structures that are overcrowded with poor social amenities." "Unpleasant settlement with living difficulties where people struggle to meet their needs." "Disorganized structures of the socio-economically deprived."*

*"Involves people living in areas they neither have ownership nor security of tenure."*

*"Areas of residence not recognized by the government. No proper services provided."*

Sixty-six percent of the development professionals state they have no restraints (Q13) on where to operate or development programs, while 34% are restricted from helping residents resolve issues within the settlement unless land tenure issues are resolved by the government. However, services can be offered outside of the settlement. Some organizations may not wish to engage in projects that include housing, plumbing, or electricity as permanent improvements that go against government law. Comments from professionals who attest to constraints include:

*"[We] Strictly deal with people inside their catchment area, only in catholic based institutions." "[We] Cannot help unless government agrees to land tenure issues."*

*"[Restriction when there are not] Enough finances to address various needs that come up outside the budget proposals."*

Fifty-one percent of the development professionals have the opinion that traditional programs (education and training) do reach those living in the informal settlements (Q15) and 62% believe the programs are helpful. Thirty-eight percent are less convinced that such programs reach informal communities, and 24% feel that traditional programs are not helpful to residents. The nay-sayers note that COVID-19 has revealed the programs are insufficient and have not reached (Q15) the poorest of the poor. Analysis of more COVID-19-related questions can be found in Table 4.10.

While 44% of the development professionals have the opinion that aid is likely to reduce poverty in the informal settlements (Q17), 56% believe aid is not likely to reduce poverty in the informal settlements. This position is common, as today's experts continually debate the success of old approaches versus innovative approaches to poverty reduction that embrace technology, direct cash, and self-help programs that build resilience and self-sustainability in poor communities. The end date to reach poverty reduction goals set by development leadership at state-backed agencies has been pushed back to 2050. The Millennium Development Goals (MDGs) began in 2000 with a goal date of 2015[95]. Unsuccessful, the MDGs evolved into the Sustainable Development Goals (SDGs) that continued to refine the agenda in 2015, with the goal date of 2020 pushed to 2030[96]. This finding substantiates the need for a real change of approach in extreme poverty reduction, not only to reach the UN SDGs but for the sake of improving the lives and livelihoods of the poor. Statements about effective programs from development professionals:

*"Education and sanitation programs have the highest success rate. Sanergy is a social enterprise that seems to be doing a great job in the slums. Hearing success stories from girls and boys that have accessed quality education is always a big transformation. The secret is a program that creates longer term transformation. Micro-loans when managed effectively have also been successful."*

*"One that focuses on land tenure and affordable housing to give urban dwellers a decent place to buy and sell a home. This includes access to water and sanitation services. When people have a home base, they invest in themselves and their communities. The program would focus heavily on sustainability to ensure that communities are sustainable after the program has finished."*

A lesser amount of development professionals (20%) feel aid is very likely to reduce poverty in the informal settlements. Twenty-four percent believe aid is neither likely nor unlikely to reduce poverty, and the remaining 12% believe aid to be unlikely (8%) and very unlikely (4%) to reduce poverty. By organization or program name (Q18), 28% of the interviewees are familiar with the program elements of KENSUP, 27% with KYEOP, 18% with the Ruben Center, 6% with micro-loans, and less than 2% with Save the Children, Mercy Corp, SHOFCO, Muungano, and Sanergy. The professionals believe the Ruben Center (81%) and KYEOP (60%) are very likely, and likely respectively, to help reduce poverty in the informal settlements respectively (Q19). This may reflect a lack of knowledge about program elements versus program name. KENSUP and KISIP programs are seen as neither likely nor unlikely to help reduce poverty in the informal settlements, while Mercy Corp., Save the Children, and Muungano are viewed as unlikely to help residents. Of these programs, development professionals expressed the following:

> *"They are likely to reduce poverty. However, they need to invest in accountability."*

> *"They all are likely to reduce poverty since that's their objective. Nevertheless, they must implement sustainable programs."*

> *"Blended programs are better. More effective."*

> *"Not very sure. If only resources can be put to proper use."*

> *"Informal settlements need concerted efforts from all stakeholders to help reduce poverty in the slums."*

> *"Informal settlement programs are rarely effective: In many cases, the people living there have over time adapted to being there and hence relocating them to what would be modern houses would totally disrupt what they are familiar with."*

Based on program type (Q20) and best strategies (Q21), the top three areas viewed as most effective are education (59%), training (49%), and entrepreneurship (37%). Gender, youth, health, and micro-loans are viewed as effective at 23%, 20%, 19%, and 15% respectively. In terms of the likelihood of reducing poverty, development professionals rate entrepreneurship the highest at 66% very likely, followed by health programs at 64% very likely, education 54% very likely, and training 42% very likely. Development professionals had this to say about the types of programs with the best strategies for reducing extreme poverty:

*"Training and education for entrepreneurship."*

*"Programs that target capacity building with local talent. Opening up opportunities for seed capital for micro enterprise development."*

*"Improvement of opportunities to generate income which will directly improve the standards of living of the people."*

*"Skills training for youth with loans and grants for business start-ups and education." "Education and training for improved shelter and water."*

*"Offering skills, knowledge, business grants that will ensure they are self-reliant."*

*"Household income generating activities, life skills development, talent development for entrepreneurship, linkages to loans and grants through micro-finance."*

*"Entrepreneurship, skills training." "Entrepreneurship, training and education, health."*

*"Loan/cash, entrepreneurship, education and training on skills of job market, health." "Creating job opportunities, trainings, provisions of education, entrepreneurship."*

Ninety-nine percent of the development professionals use a place-based, human-centered development approach in programs (Q22). This highlights the acceptance and inclusion of Michael Cernea's work in the early 1980s discussed in the literature review, a significant degree of consensus on development approaches. Place-based, human-centered development has been widely integrated into development programs as an important approach to poverty reduction and is affirmed by 99% of the sample interviewed.

*"Programs conceived outside the country is less effective. Programs must be designed to be financially sustainable. Funding targets and policies must change. In housing to date, they do not provide housing the people want. Locally conceived solutions seem to get the least funding but are the most positively received by those in need."*

*"Blended programs that work collaboratively with and are regularly informed by the local population. Ones that take into account the communities' priorities and works collaboratively to address those priorities."*

*"Effectiveness comes from programs based on human-centered approaches and working with communities to address the underlying cause of vulnerability and add to dignity."*

With an unlimited budget (Q23), the professionals would create a "dream program" that includes four top elements measured for importance by a number of mentions.

1. Education (30%),

2. Health (23%)

3. Entrepreneurship/finance (23%)

4. Practical skills training (14%)

Following the top four, development professionals list policy issues regarding land tenure and housing (11%) as a fifth element to include, followed by WASH, gender issues, and food security (8%). The least mentioned program elements are youth-specific programs, leadership, mentorship, and drug abuse programs. These figures match up with what the development professionals expressed in Q8 regarding programs most likely to help people who live in informal settlements: education (55%), health (64%), and entrepreneurship (67%). Though not in the same order of importance, the professionals identified the same program elements in Q8 and Q23 as beneficial to reducing extreme poverty. A reason for the difference in order of importance may have to do with the capabilities and ease of constructing programs within the framework of the current programmatic level. The development professionals mentioned specific program elements listed in order of importance:

*"Health, education, training, water, gender equality, advocacy."*

*"Health, education, housing, youth empowerment, gender equality, advocacy." "Health, education, training, advocacy, entrepreneurship."*

*"Women's empowerment, micro-loans for business start-up, quality education, access roads."*

Finally, there were several quotes from development professionals about what to include in a dream program:

*"Comprehensive Millennium Village program"*

*"Programs that are not "free aid" ...corruption plays a big role in this, benefit from riding the backs of the poor. Well-paid aid workers write reports, collect data. Once the donors go, most programs crumble."*

*"Build on the approach UNHCR is taking in refugee camps: health and hygiene, competence building, and micro-entrepreneurship. Each of these has tested programs to address issues. A big and perhaps first step is to clarify the legal status of the slums with host governments because programs need a legal basis to make lasting change."*

*"One that blends grants, debt, convertible notes, equity and tech assistance to social enterprises who collaborate with communities and address different parts of the entire value chain of a communities ' priorities."*

*"Wow, that is a thesis in itself. I would create a fund with interest free loans for the community and income improving/sustaining programs. It would not just value financial returns but would have some metric that valued wider and more qualitative impact as a return, i.e., a community space, a school, a training program in life skills. We could even ask the community to value some of these things to know which areas to support."*

*"Domestic workers are often drop-outs with no literacy. I would equip them with additive skills like babysitting, basic first aid, home hygiene, cooking, and operation of common appliances. I would also have different options for those with a higher level of literacy such as driving skills. Graduation would be connected to jobs through a tech platform with decent working terms that would include micro-medical, micro-savings, and a pension. Accumulated savings could lead to entrepreneurship over time."*

*"A wholistic, cross/cutting program that links these 5 priorities: 1) food security, 2) safe living conditions, 3) healthcare with access to reproductive care, 4) EDUCATION, and 5) access to livelihood opportunities."*

*"A dream program would include vocational and artisan skills with an integrated platform for employment or entrepreneurship. In brief, I would onboard slum residents into various courses including domestic work."*

*"Ones that are not top-down vertical. Need comprehensive look at links between sectors."*

*"I don't think it's about programs, it's about approaches. The most effective ones should look to address the underlying cause of poverty and exclusion."*

*"Low interest loans, capacity building for business skills, talent building, structural improvements-free toilets, more education institutes, youth employment initiatives, encouraging people to venture into rural activities to decongest the slums and remove mentality of urban is better than the village, cash transfers to those who need it-elderly-disabled-total orphans."*

Table 5.7 offers a quick glance at the highest frequencies and percentages of all questions asked of the development professionals. This is offered to help readers in the development sector quickly see the age, organization type, and other variables that make up the most significant part of the interview sample. This table is relevant for identifying where funding is needed to improve programmatic efforts. Note, at the end of the table, entrepreneurship in a "dream program" is 100% agreed upon as necessary to reduce extreme poverty.

**Table 5.7.** Interview Question Highest Frequencies

| VARIABLE | HIGHEST FREQUENCY | PERCENTAGE |
|---|---|---|
| Female | | 41% |
| Male | | 37% |
| Age | ages 18-44 | 59% |
| Years of Experience | up to 10 years | 71% |
| Organization HQ | Based in Kenya | 72% |
| Organization type | NGO/Nonprofit | 53% |
| Organization size | up to 200 staff | 61% |
| Organization focus | multi-focus | 79% |

| Time at the organization | Up to 10 years | 83% |
|---|---|---|
| Job Description | mobilize-train-manage | 61% |
| Time allocation | mostly in the office | 46% |
| Field location | informal settlements | 78% |
| Definition of informal settlement | unplanned area | 100% |
| Restrictions on where to run programs | none | 66% |
| Traditional programs reach resident-dwellers | yes | 51% |
| Traditional programs help resident-dwellers | yes | 62% |
| COVID-19 says programs do not work | yes | 38% |
| COVID-19 affected their programs | yes | 100% |
| Aid reduces poverty in informal settlements | very likely | 20% |
| Familiar programs | KENSUP and KYEOP | 55% |
| Most likely to help resident-dwellers | KYEOP | 60% |
| Most effective program types | Education | 59% |
| Most likely program to reduce extreme poverty | Entrepreneurship | 66% |
| Uses HC development | yes | 99% |
| Dream Program | Entrepreneurship | 100% |

### 5.3.2. Categories of Organizations and Professionals

It is noteworthy to highlight the benefits of setting a methodology to gain data from distinct categories of organizations and development professionals. As a result, perspectives were gained from a broad range of professionals working in different areas of development. Five categories of organizations were selected as part of the methodology: government, prominent aid organizations, development academics, health professionals who serve the informal settlement, and multi-dimensional CSO/nonprofit organizations. The number of years of experience in development was one of the interview questions, important to help validate the weight of their perspectives.

Of the 100 professionals interviewed, the highest number were from CSOs/Nonprofits (30) and prominent aid organizations (23), followed by development professionals in academia (19) and government professionals

(10). A complete table of organization names, categories, and the number of years of experience of each interviewee can be found in Table 5.8:

**Table 5.8.** Disaggregation of Interviewees

Government

| INTERVIEW # | CATEGORY: GOVERNMENT | YEARS of EXPERIENCE |
|---|---|---|
| 1 | Kenyan Ministry of Health | 24 |
| 2 | Kenyan Ministry of Education | 4 |
| 3 | Kenyan Refugee Secretariat | 5 |
| 4 | Danish Refugee Council | 19 |
| 5 | Kenyan Ministry of Interior | 8 |
| 6 | Nairobi City Council | 6 |
| 7 | Judiciary Kibera Law Courts | 5 |
| 8 | Kenyan Population Council | 15 |
| 9 | Kenyan Ministry of Gender & Social Services | 15 |
| 10 | EU Delegation to Kenya | 1 |

Prominent Aid Organizations (23)

| INTERVIEW # | CATEGORY: PROMINENT AID ORGANIZATION | YEARS of EXPERIENCE |
|---|---|---|
| 1, 2 | Kenyan Red Cross (2) | 11, 5 |
| 3 | World Vision | 14 |
| 4 | The Rotary Club Kenya | 7 |
| 5 | The Homeless Org. Kenya | 8 |
| 6 | KYEOP-World Bank | 3 |
| 7 | Kwetu Home of Peace | 18 |
| 8 | RTI International | 8 |
| 9 | Pamoja Trust | 2 |
| 10 | Street Families Rehabilitation Trust Fund | 14 |
| 11 | UN Habitat | 25 |
| 12 | UNHCR | 20 |
| 13, 14 | Plan International (2) | 6, 6 |

| 15 | Mukuru Slum Development Project | 9 |
|---|---|---|
| 16 | Hope Worldwide | 5 |
| 17 | Compassion International | 6 |
| 18 | HROC Friends Peace Teams | 2 |
| 19, 20 | USAID (2) | 30, 21 |
| 21 | Global Alliance Africa | 19 |
| 22 | UNaids.org | 12 |
| 23 | Center for Global Development | 5 |

Academics (19)

| INTERVIEW # | CATEGORY: ACADEMICS | YEARS of EXPERIENCE |
|---|---|---|
| 1, 2 | Pwani University (2) | 19, 3 |
| 3, 4 | Nairobi University (2) | 2,3 |
| 5 | Cooperative University | 2 |
| 6, 7 | Mt.Kenya University (2) | 2,2 |
| 8 | Joe University of Nairobi | 3 |
| 9 | Kisii University | 4 |
| 10, 11 | Kenyatta Ag & Tech University (2) | 4, 3 |
| 12 | Wayland Baptist University | 4 |
| 13 | Daystar University | 2 |
| 14, 15 | Strathmore University Kenya (2) | 2, 2 |
| 16 | Masinde Muliro University | 4 |
| 17 | Kibera Salem Academy | 7 |
| 18 | University of Maryland Kenya | 8 |
| 19 | Jua Kali Artisan University | 1 |

Health (9)

| INTERVIEW # | CATEGORY: HEALTH | YEARS of EXPERIENCE |
|---|---|---|
| 1, 2 | AMREF Health Kenya (2) | 4, 12 |
| 3, 4 | Mater Hospital (2) | 10,15 |
| 5 | Kitengela Medical Center | 10 |

| 6 | Mbagathi Hospital | 10 |
|---|---|---|
| 7 | Ilara Health | 10 |
| 8 | Pipeline Health Center | 14 |
| 9 | Safari Doctors | 4 |

CSO/Nonprofits (30)

| INTERVIEW # | CATEGORY: NON-PROFITS | YEARS of EXPERIENCE |
|---|---|---|
| 1 | Mukuru Promotion Centre | 2 |
| 2 | Mwalimu Kingi Madzo Investment | 16 |
| 3 | Kenya Institute of Management | 5 |
| 4 | Mothers2Mothers | 20 |
| 5 | Kounkuey Design Initiative (KDI) | 13 |
| 6 | The Lutheran Church | 15 |
| 7 | Good Hope Community Center | 12 |
| 8 | Mennonite Center | 8 |
| 9 | Good Neighbors Int'l | 5 |
| 10 | St. John's Community | 12 |
| 11 | PCEA Eastleigh | 8 |
| 12 | Action Aid Kenya | 7 |
| 13 | Life Song Kenya | 5 |
| 14 | Kwangu Kwako | 8 |
| 15 | Mathare Community Initiative | 4 |
| 16 | Group for Transcultural Relations | 3 |
| 17 | Caritas Nairobi | 13 |
| 18 | Call Africa | 4 |
| 19 | Napenda Kuishi Trust | 10 |
| 20 | Homeless of Nairobi | 9 |
| 21 | New Life Mwangaza Rehabilitation Center | 4 |
| 22 | Tugutuke Youth | 4 |
| 23 | AVP Trust | 7 |
| 24 | Inua Jamii | 3 |

| 25 | KISPED | 3 |
| 26 | Agape Model Solutions | 4 |
| 27 | Jitegemee Kenya Pamoja | 5 |
| 28 | Mukuru Land Mawe Resource Centre | 6 |
| 29 | Mukuru Promotion Center | 1 |
| 30 | Volunteers Oversees | 20 |

Interviewees who asked for their organization name not be listed (9)

| INTERVIEW # | CATEGORY: as noted | YEARS of EXPERIENCE |
| --- | --- | --- |
| 1 | Kenyan Government | 17 |
| 2, 3 | US Bilateral Organization (2) | 4,15 |
| 4 | US Private Sector Aid Organization | 10 |
| 5 | US Investment Assurance Organization | 10 |
| 6, 7 | US Multilateral Financial Organization (2) | 3, 17 |
| 8 | US Development Organization | 14 |
| 9 | US Government | 20 |

## 5.4. Interview cross-tabulations

As previously seen in Table 5.6, the following are the independent and dependent variables among development experts that were used in the cross-tabulations. Cross-tabulations were not calculated on variables from the residents of Mukuru because of the qualitative and unanimous nature of their answers. A list of all variables is provided along with the corresponding question number (Q1=question 1):

*Independent:* age (Q1), gender (Q2), years of experience in development (Q3), organization focus (Q8), organization location (Q5), organization category (Q6), organization size (Q7), years at organization (Q9), programs in the informal settlement (Q11), program restraints (Q13), belief that aid reduces poverty (Q17), program uses human-centered development (Q22).

*Dependent:* time allocation in office versus fieldwork (Q10), effective programs in informal settlements (Q14), programs that reach the informal settlements (Q15), effective types of programs (Q20).

To expand the correlations, some independent variables were used as dependent variables, such as variables that are "beliefs." A belief cannot stand on its own as an independent variable because beliefs change. A belief can stand on its own if it is accepted as truth.

*Cross-use:* belief that aid reduces poverty (Q17), belief that a program is effective in the informal settlement (Q14), belief that a program reaches the informal settlements (Q15), belief in effective program categories (Q21).

Three questions from the survey were not used in cross-tabulations, instead they were used to create word clouds that reveal emphasis: Job title (Q9a), Description of the informal settlements (Q12), Covid effects on programs (Q16), Elements of a "Dream Program" (Q23).

The interview cross-tabulations revealed two significances and one that comes close to being significant.

### The first significant cross-tabulation is:

- Q7 (staff size) x Q10 (office vs field)

Staff size and allocation of time spent in the office versus in the field demonstrates that the larger the staff size, the less time spent working in the field. Organizations with 500+ staff spend little to no time working in the field, which means they are not interfacing with their clients (people in need). See Table 5.9a and calculations:

**Table 5.9a.** Interview cross-tabulation Q7 x Q10

Staff size x time allocation in the field vs. office (0.001 significance)

| Organization Staff Size | Office Work | Field Work | Equal time | Total |
|---|---|---|---|---|
| 11-50 | 26% | 39% | 35% | 100% |
| 501-1000 | 100% | 0% | 0% | 100% |
| 1001-3000 | 80% | 0% | 20% | 100% |

p<.001; Chi=19.4; df=4; N=490

### The second significant cross-tabulation is:

- Q11 (program in informal settlement) x Q10 (office vs field)

The calculations demonstrate that development professionals with programs in the community spend more time in the field as compared to those working on extreme poverty without programs in the informal settlement. However, having programs in the informal settlement still dictates the need for both office and fieldwork or an equal split of time. This is expected when one considers the logistics of running a program for residents of informal settlements. There are no city-identified walkways to enter the informal settlement, only narrow dirt paths. There are few physical buildings or meeting spaces in the community to engage with clients. Time in the field would be limited for any development professional servicing the informal settlement. Still, programs intended to help residents of the community require professionals to enter and work within the informal settlement. See Table 5.9b.

**Table 5.9b.** Interview cross-tabulation Q11 x Q10

Program in informal settlement x Q.10-time allocation in office vs field (.001 significance)

| Program in informal settlement | Mostly office | Mostly field | Equal Split | Total |
|---|---|---|---|---|
| Yes | 36% | 28% | 36% | 100% |
| No | 82% | 9% | 9% | 100% |

p<.001; Chi=14.5; df=2; N=500

## The final cross-tabulation demonstrates marginal significance:

- Q11 (program in informal settlement) x Q7 (org size)

The calculations show that the larger the organization's staff size, the less program work is planned in the informal settlement. Initially, this finding appears ironic in that the larger organizations typically have the budget and capacity to make the greatest impact on poverty reduction.

Although this may be true, it is customary for larger organizations to contract out their program work to smaller organizations that are more familiar with informal settlements. In essence, programs developed at large organizations are often actualized by smaller organizations[97]. Table 5.9c illustrates that 43% of organizations with large staff sizes do not run programs in the informal settlement. However, this may reflect the procurement process. No additional questions were significant.

**Table 5.9c.** Interview cross tabulation Q11 x Q7

Program in informal settlement x size of organization (.012 significance)

| Program in informal settlement | Org Staff Size | | | | | | | |
|---|---|---|---|---|---|---|---|---|
| | 1-10 | 11-50 | 51-200 | 201-500 | 501-1000 | 1001-3000 | 3001-5000 | Total |
| Yes | 19% | 28% | 22% | 13% | 0% | 5% | 13% | 100% |
| No | 9% | 5% | 19% | 14% | 5% | 5% | 43% | 100% |

p<.001; Chi=16.4; df=6; N=490

After going through all the data, the cross-tabulations that were expected to yield significance but did not include the following:

- Years of experience (Independent) x effective strategies (Dependent)

- Organization focus (Independent) x most effective type of program (Dependent)

- Staff size (Independent) x effective strategies (Dependent)

- Staff size (Independent) x allocation of time/office vs field (Dependent)

One might expect that development professionals with more total years of experience would know the best strategies to reduce poverty. In other areas, professionals with the most experience add to solving issues with successful strategies. For example, in the sector of trade, professionals with more years of experience might know how to solve issues pertaining to securing trade through financial factoring. In poverty reduction, the industry continues to struggle to achieve its goals after 60 years of aid. Looking at organizations with a specific focus, the data show no program more effective than another. Yet, financial programs like Give Directly may have hidden success not shown in these results and in need of further inquiry.

Turning to issues that might impede progress, small staff size could be a deterrent to operationalizing effective strategies in poverty reduction programs. It is natural to think that a large staff has a greater capacity for effectiveness, though this was not the case. Organizations with a staff size of 3,000 reaped no greater results in effective programming than those with a staff size of 30. Likewise, organizations with large or small staff sizes allocate their work time fairly the same, with only slightly more time in the office than in the field. This finding nullifies the thought that large organizations never do fieldwork.

My analysis is that development professionals view extreme poverty reduction programs similarly, regardless of organization staff size or other variables perceived as differentiators. Years of experience matter in terms of knowledge gained but not in terms of implementing the most effective strategies. When the focus of an organization is on one area of poverty reduction, it does not blind those professionals to the effectiveness of programs focused on something different. Development professionals from large organizations are using the same strategies as those from small organizations, only with differences in how their time is allocated (office vs. field).

### 5.5. COVID-19 Questions Survey and Interview Responses

No cross-tabulations were done on COVID-19 issues related to extreme poverty. The questions were qualitative and produced brief answers that were generally the same. Mostly, all programs were severely interrupted or stopped completely regardless of staff size, years of experience, or any other variable. Instead, a word cloud was produced to show the most prominent and frequent answers to the question.

It is because of the global pandemic that truths about the severe vulnerability of the marginalized were brought to light[98]. Amidst the pandemic, an aerial view of the informal settlements provides sobering clarity that living in a valley of tightly positioned mud and rusted tin shacks is like living in a petri dish for the corona virus[99]. Issues of density are only the start. Sanitation, clean water, and waste processing are non-existent. Living spaces are small, making quarantine impossible for a family member who contracts the virus. Income at less than $1.90/day does not allow for the purchase of masks and hand sanitizer, nor does it allow for missing a day of work.

The pandemic lockdowns interrupted the daily hustle necessary to earn income, which led to increased hunger and domestic violence[100], and curfew violations, which can be deadly[101] in African states. Migratory issues began as residents were evicted[102] from their mabati and forced to flee to rural areas to rejoin distant family or friends for a simpler life[103]. Rural villagers rejected many as "corona refugees" who would kill the villagers, particularly the elderly.

Initially, tests for COVID-19 in Kenya cost up to 10,000 KES ($100)[104], making it moot for resident-dwellers to get tested. In cases where residents were tested by non-profit health workers, testing positive led to stigma and isolation[105]. In cases where residents were caught after curfew and rounded up by police, bribes were necessary for people to be released from detention-like facilities, followed by stigma in the community. Many nonprofit services were limited or paused due to the risk of infection or interruptions in service delivery[106]. The need for self-help was apparent[107] and weaknesses in the largest and most financially robust aid programs were exposed.

When the community survey asked how COVID-19 affected lives (Q12), their answers demonstrated such poverty reduction program deficits. The top three answers from the residents were hunger (436 mentions), no income (434 mentions) and program services closed (388 mentions). Programs across the spectrum of types of aid and types of organizations, including well-funded programs, were not prepared to offer continual aid to their clients.

> *"The government should come up with programs that provide food for people, especially in the slum during this COVID-19 period to save lives and alleviate suffering."*

When the development professionals were asked if traditional poverty reduction programs helped people living in the informal settlements (Q1), 62% said yes. When asked if they believed that traditional programs reach those living in the informal settlements (Q2), 51% said yes. Specific to COVID-19, development professionals who answered "no" had more to share:

> "Covid has shown us that traditional programs are not good enough to reduce extreme poverty."

> "Covid says traditional programs don't work."

> "Covid increases dependency syndrome."

> "Covid has taught us that traditional programs are insufficient." "Not all programs reach [the slums], only some."

> "Not all the programs. This is why most of the people still remain poor." "A lot of people still languish in poverty."

When the development professionals were asked in Q16 how COVID-19 affected their programs and program recipients, analysis revealed that the pandemic affected 100% of program work. Professionals reported staff reduction due to contracting the virus, cutbacks in fieldwork, and the inability to provide service to their clients in informal settlements. Others noted the inability of their clients to visit centers for services due to state-mandated movement restraints.

*"COVID-19, especially the second wave, has created fear in everyone. Staff have found themselves contracting the disease in the line of duty. Management has minimized its field activities and take precautions for its staff. Reaching out to the most needy has been reduced in the frequency it used to be done earlier on."*

*"Patients [are] not visiting health facilities due to fear of Covid diagnosis, reduced income, fear of contracting the virus, shortage of staff due to quarantine of exposed staff."*

*"Big impact is not running programs the usual way face to face, but now virtual. This is not effective."*

*"Due to restricted movement, it was difficult to reach the people in slums with services of home visits. Clients missed appointments at the HIV clinic, poor clinic attendance and reduced number of clients [led to] pay cuts and unplanned unpaid leaves."*

*"Field staff were affected; 2 tested positive but recovered. Running of the program became expensive because of the additional cost of unplanned activities due to Covid, i.e., cost of masks, sanitizers, and hand washing detergents."*

*"It has limited our medical camp programs where we usually bring doctors to the Slums for a day or two to attend to various medical challenges."*

*"Restraints in visiting our clients due to containment measures and lockdowns, loss of income by many beneficiaries, increased food shortages, insecurity, increased gender-based violence."*

*"Many children on the streets in search of food and space, loss of income in the slums, rising insecurity, police brutality."*

*"Micro-loan payments stopped, default."*

*"Education programs completely stopped. Digital divide. No tech tools or reliable internet."*

*"Yes. Program had to shut down, recipients lost any gains made. Kenyan government offered no help. Sold off some of the donated PPE to Tanzania. No accountability."*

*"Workers stuck home in lockdown with no means of income. Government gave no financial support, landlords insisted on rent regardless of the pandemic, banks offered no reprise to landlords."*

*"Curfew has shortened the day given that some of our programs operate even at night. Loss of income and businesses has led to extreme hunger and suffering."*

*"Fear of stigma and discrimination, patients hiding Covid-like symptoms such as coughing. Fear to be associated with Covid-19."*

*"Increased poverty leading to teenage pregnancies, drug abuse, early marriages. Increased crime in the slums, reduced contact with people."*

*"Drug and substance abuse increased, containment measures reduced contact with beneficiaries, job losses led to mental health issues leading to domestic violence and even suicide, crime rate has gone up."*

*"Reduced accessibility for services due to restricted covid measures, reduced uptake of services, Increased expenditure due to taking care of things that were not initially budgeted, for example masks and sanitizers."*

*"Accessing the informal settlement due to fear of infection limited our operations in the Slums." "Our programs are directly given to people in terms of food, shelter, Healthcare and Education. Due containment measures and the safety of our field officers, we scaled down operations and do believe that many may have missed out on our services."*

One development professional had a unique experience, a testimony to the sustainability of development programs using information technology (IT) to reduce extreme poverty:

*"We experienced no problem [during COVID] because we are fully digital program – cash disbursements. However, we have incurred late payments in loans."*

A key finding of post-COVID-19 analysis is services to help the extremely poor need to be located within the community. For the informal settlements to be less vulnerable, focal points within the community must be created for the distribution of services. The poor will need to become micro-entrepreneurs to take on some of these services themselves through non-profit/government funding or basic grants. The use of cash is becoming increasingly obsolete in informal settlements, as digital payments have been used since 2010. Additionally, digital payments protect residents from the physical theft of paper cash and provide development professionals with a way to send messages and provide cash without being present. Table 5.10 offers a quick glance at the top poverty issues increased by COVID-19. Note that the first three issues are the foundation for the five that follow.

**Table 5.10.** Top COVID-19 poverty issues

| Issue | # of mentions |
|---|---|
| 1. Hunger | 436 |
| 2. No income | 434 |
| 3. Commerce and services closed | 388 |
| 4. Domestic Violence | 378 |
| 5. Bribery | 331 |
| 6. No PPE | 294 |
| 7. Eviction | 281 |
| 8. Child Abuse | 281 |

## Chapter 5 - Key points

### Variables:

- Survey variables + findings and analysis
- Survey Freirean variables + findings and analysis
- Interview variables + findings and analysis
- Cross-tabulations
- COVID-19 data

## Chapter 5 - Discussion questions

### Community Survey

1) Which cross-tabulation results surprised you? What would you have expected to find in the results?

2)  What differences could be revealed if the data were disaggregated by sex? What would your hypothesis be in terms of the critical consciousness questions?

3)  If you could add more questions, would they be Freirean-based or regular, and what would they be? Write five questions and identify the added independent or dependent variables.

4)  How would you cross-tabulate the new variables? Create a chart.

5)  There were only a few COVID-19 questions to not detract from pre-pandemic issues of poverty. Write 10 additional questions on pandemic-induced poverty and identify the variables and potential cross-tabulations you would apply.

## Interviews

1)  Considering a cross-disciplinary approach, what other questions would you add to the interviews with development professionals?

2)  If you could ask more questions concerning COVID-19 program disruptions and revelations, what would they be? Write 10 additional questions.

3)  Do you think Freirean-based questions posed to development professionals would reveal new insights? Does the disconnect between development professionals and their clients require fostering critical consciousness in both parties? Why or why not?

4)  What kinds of questions could be added to discern between vested professionals and those who are local contractors with the sole intent of doing what they are told to get paid? Write five discernment questions.

### Notes

[87] This percentage, although remarkable, is common for informal settlements where idle time and life hardship often lead to gender-based violence, teen pregnancy, and child marriages that are not legal. A random sample taken in another part of the slum, or a different Nairobi slum would likely reveal the same percentage.

[88] Fertility rates in Kenya were 3.416 births per woman in 2020, a 1.5% decline from 2019 (3.468 births per woman). This data is macrotrends based on the Kenyan Census (https://www.macrotrends.net/countries/KEN/kenya/fertility-rate).

[89] A total of 441 participants has school-aged children.

[90] The fact that only 23% of the respondent's report police brutality as an issue indicates that the response set of the survey is stable. A response set is the human tendency to "respond in a manner that is unrelated to the content of the instrument" (Hui and Triandis, 1985). Simplified, it means to choose answers that acquiesce, have directional bias, or limit a participants response range due to fatigue or to compliment the respondent or the instrument. The Instability of response sets is discussed in detail in an article by Hui and Triandis listed in the bibliography.

[91] Reports by Transparency International, The Kenya Star, and the New York Times tell of prison-like conditions under quarantine in various countries across Africa including Kenya. Citizens experience difficulty getting out of quarantine and into hospitals for care. The references and links are in the bibliography.

[92] Women and men reported carrying scrap metals for recycling. The metals are carried on a rolling cart, on which the women are not able to pull as much metal as men, nevertheless they engage in this method of earning money because there are few alternatives.

[93] The Kenyan Government provides mobile cash disbursements for the elderly over age 65 and living in extreme poverty, disabled citizens, and orphans who are registered in the state system through the Ministry of ICT. A link to the Kenya Government ICT page is provided in the bibliography of this research.

[94] The KINSUP program was discussed in an earlier section of this book that shared a review of existing programs. Ratings of successful programs in the surveys of both the community residents and development professionals also reveal the inadequacies of the KINSUP program. There is much literature on outcomes of relocating the poor outside of their customary neighborhoods, however it is not the focus of this book. Some of the literature includes that of Roland Fryer Jr. and Robert Sampson from Harvard, Steven Levitt from the University of Chicago, Heather Schwartz from RAND Corporation, with the most popular work by Jens Ludwig from the University of Chicago, MTO Program, published in the American Economics Review (May, 2013).

[95] The MDG End Poverty dates can be found on the UN.org website at https://www.un.org/millenniumgoals/bkgd.shtml

[96] The UN.org agenda for the SDG's notes that the goals were not advancing at the rate required to meet needs by 2020 and were therefore pushed back to deliver goals by 2030 (https://www.un.org/sustainabledevelopment/development-agenda/).

[97] USAID is the world's largest AID organization, directed by the US State Department. Requests for proposals are sent out by Country Mission offices to invite local organizations to bid to carry out programs to reduce extreme poverty. The process is published in the US, locally in-country, and is part of USAID's procurement. More information about procurement awards, tenders, and notices can be found here USAID Procurement Announcements.

[98] In April 2020, the IMF published in-depth research on the impact of COVID-19 on Sub-Saharan Africa. The research team, led by Kothari and Fang, compared the Ebola outbreak in West Africa to the large-spread vulnerability across the continent, including cumulative effects on markets and the health sector in Africa.

[99] An article from the GlobalDashboard.org confirms firsthand knowledge that the tight quarters that are indicative in the informal settlements are the perfect place for a virus to spread. Additionally, neighbors live back-to-back in housing with no running water or toilet facilities.

[100] Like the data in this research from residents of Mukuru and Development Professionals, articles in Reuters continually reported a rise in violence against women and girls during the pandemic.

[101] In March 2020, Al Jazeera reported excessive force used by Kenya Police, beating commuters with batons and whips for missing curfew. Human rights groups such as Amnesty International and others joined together in a statement aimed at Kenya's Interior Minister.

[102] In defiance of a court order, Kenyan authorities demolished the homes 7000 residents in slums. They were evicted, without notice, despite the COVID-19 pandemic. This report was published by VOA News, May 19, 2020. On August 9, 2020, another 8000 homes were demolished amidst ongoing pandemic and mandatory curfews.

[103] Paradoxically, some residents of the slums began an exodus back to rural areas in hope of staving off financial ruin due to the pandemic. Landlords insisted on rent, regardless of the world being on shutdown.

[104] The Nairobi Hospital published testing rates beginning ranging from 6500-10,000 Kenyan Shillings ($65-$100 USD) on their website and Facebook page.

[105] An organization from the University of North Dakota, KFGO reported voluntary testing in Kenya's largest slum– Kibera where being found positive resulted in negative stigma within the informal settlement.

[106] The April 2020 regional outlook by IMF reports probability of food insecurity and interruptions in service from NGOs, as reported by the development professionals and slum dwellers in this research.

[107] Residents of Mukuru and other slums realized they were on their own and shifted toward using their own human agency to help themselves; from making masks to selling home-made hand sanitizer. An article from thenation.com expands on this.

Chapter 6

# Conclusion

The conclusions reveal six themes that encompass key issues revealed as important for effective poverty reduction in informal settlements. The data from residents and development professionals align in terms of these key issues. The data does not align in terms of approaches to resolving these key issues. Taking different approaches toward improvement is common. It is through communication that those differences are better understood and the consensus is formed.

The difference with extreme poverty is that lives are at stake, and communication has been difficult due to social, cultural, economic, and political factors that foster docile appeasement from the historically oppressed.

## The conclusion is divided into five parts:

6.1.     Six key takeaways

6.2.     Results on critical consciousness

6.3.     New theory

6.4.     Recommendations

6.5.     Future research

### 6.1. Six Key Takeaways

#### *Takeaway #1 - Job Creation*

Experienced development professionals from organizations with knowledge of joblessness in informal settlements are hired to develop programs that reduce poverty. Their answer to joblessness is to offer training to improve the residents' skills. If extreme poverty is measured by the World Bank standard of earning less than $1.90/day, the direct approach to extreme poverty reduction is creating jobs that earn more than $1.90/day. Development professionals are not creating jobs and, therefore, not creating programs that reduce extreme poverty.

## *Takeaway #2 – Program Reach*

Quantitative data from the community survey and the interviews reveal that residents of Mukuru are not effectively reached by many of the largest aid organizations that claim to service the poorest of the poor. The lack of services in the informal settlement is not new, as 49% of the community residents do not recognize the names of prominent aid organizations. These residents have lived in Mukuru for up to 20 years, and another 14% have been residents of Mukuru for 20+ years.

Not only are the largest aid organizations not known to residents of Mukuru, but they also are not known to approximately 75% of the local development professionals who work in the informal settlement. In some cases, the reason may be due to the trickle-down structure of how aid funds move, for example, from USAID and on to non-profits or private sector development firms that further partner with local organizations. In other cases, for example, Save the Children, direct dealings with children in the informal settlement are not happening. These organizations are likely helping the moderately poor through systems like schools or churches. How do we reach the SDGs if the largest aid organizations are not able to reduce extreme poverty? Whose responsibility is it to reach the SDGs? Should country governments commit more to partnerships? Or are both sides slipping between doing good and serving state interests?

Regardless of how these questions are answered, there should be a way forward to address all needs of charitable and state interests. However, the void of program presence in informal settlements is not the way forward. A refined strategy is needed, founded on the ideology that people must be led to develop themselves.

When the Mukuru resident survey asked about programs that have helped reduce poverty, only 70 out of 500 (or 14%) confirmed receiving help from Save the Children, and 1 out of 500 from Mercy Corp (.002%). The programs with an effective rating by Mukuru residents are USAID (250 received assistance), the Kenya Red Cross (309 received assistance), and The Ruben Center (474 received assistance). When development professionals were provided with the same names of programs intended to reduce extreme poverty that were shared with Mukuru residents, the development professionals, only 29% of development professionals were familiar with KENSUP (one of the largest recent undertakings in informal settlement housing), and 27% were familiar with KYEOP, a World Bank program that offers paid train-to-work opportunities for the poor. In terms of the likelihood of helping reduce poverty, 60% of the development professionals believed that the KYEOP program would be likely to successfully reduce poverty in the informal settlements since it is a World Bank program. When analyzed together, only 33 out of 500 Mukuru residents reported having received beneficial help from KYEOP.

When residents were asked to provide names of organizations and effective programs that do reach them, Mukuru residents named The Ruben Center and the Kenya Red Cross. While most residents interviewed live near the Ruben Center and would be expected to list it as effective at poverty reduction, the residents do not live near the offices of the Kenyan Red Cross. This fact points to The Red Cross making strides to reach all the poor, including those in hard-to-reach areas like informal settlements.

The bottom line is that many poverty reduction programs intended to help the poorest of the poor are not reaching their clients. Part of the issue could be a lack of program continuity or name recognition by Mukuru residents due to the trickle-down operations through sub-contractors. Because some Mukuru residents have lived in the informal settlement for 20 years, one would think that names of the most powerful aid organizations would be known or at least heard of. Even if poverty reduction programs are being carried out under the names of local CSOs instead of well-known organizations like Save the Children, these programs are thought to be helping - but are not.

### *Takeaway #3 - Human-centered Development*

The critical daily challenges for Mukuru residents are paying rent, school fees, and buying food. The development professionals in Nairobi believe residents need income-producing programs for effective poverty reduction. The disconnect between program intent and the actuality of results speaks to something occurring between the initial funding aid organization and the poor. Development professionals with a decade of experience in Nairobi understand many of the needs of those who live in informal settlements, but the programs provide insufficient impact on the livelihoods of residents. Authentic information from residents about their daily challenges is not making it from the community to the program developers. This is where Freirean theory and dialogue can be helpful. If program development is intended to be human-centered, then dialogue with the affected humans must be included.

### *Takeaway #4 - Program Effectiveness*

To further highlight the disconnect, education has long been considered by development professionals to be a key element of poverty reduction. Though the residents of Mukuru agree that education is necessary to reduce extreme poverty, the approach to education as the main development tool may be off.

The Freirean-themed questions that prompt critical consciousness of poverty issues helped the Mukuru residents express that school fees are the second greatest daily struggle for them. Fifty-seven percent of the participants stated that they must rotate their children in and out of school per semester to afford the fees. Therefore, while development professionals are correct in promoting educational programs K-12, they are missing the element of the education process that keeps their clients in poverty – the school fees. Public schools in Kenya are not completely free. School fees of approximately $220/year must be paid to cover books, exams, and activities in addition to the cost of uniforms (Ministry of Education, 2021/2022). When you earn less than $1.90/day, such fees are exorbitant.

Additionally, recent research conducted in Nigeria shows that post-secondary education does not lead to guaranteed jobs (Gadi, 2020)[108]. Gadi points out that the job market in several African countries does not generally call for post-secondary education. Her research shows that post-secondary education has no significance for personal economic growth or productivity, though it does increase human agency. The takeaway is that Freirean dialogues in this research produced clarifying information about how best to reduce poverty using education as a development program – make it free. After level 12, educational programs in vocational and entrepreneurial skills may prove more effective at reducing poverty than a post-secondary degree.

A similar study in Kenya from the University of Nairobi looked at the status of vocational education in post-secondary education. While middle-level manpower is needed to drive Kenya's economy, interest in adding vocational training into the national curriculum must be embraced as a complement to traditional education (Akala, 2018). The study does not measure the significance of traditional or vocational education against personal economic growth, though it offers insight into the value of gaining life skills and vocational training. Pre-colonial Kenya provided indigenous education and skills for home building, domestic farming, and crafting using natural materials to make tools, baskets, and pottery (Akala, 2018; Simiyu, 2001; Otiende et al., 1992). Skills and training were passed down from parents, siblings, and elders in the community (Akala, 2018; Okaka, 2001). However, the colonial era introduced formal education, and vocational skills in agriculture were relegated to those looked upon for cheap manual labor. Formal education was more attractive, and the perception of vocational education carried a negative perception (Akala, 2018; Bongonko,1992), to the extent that the Kenya Education Commission report of 1964 recommended the abolition of vocational education as part of primary education (Akala, 2018; Republic of Kenya,1964). These facts highlight the mismatch of educational top-down approaches that are intended to help Kenyans earn income and contribute to the economy but lack the much-needed vocational option that would actually allow more of them to do so (Akala, 2018).

To simplify, in the Freirean-themed sessions, residents of Mukuru noted the most frequent type of work they engage in (construction, recycling, and washing clothes). Out of 500 participants, only two confirm receiving remittances from family or friends abroad, and only 24 confirm having a regular job. Innovative development, recycling, and construction together could lead to the building of unique structures within the informal settlements to upgrade housing. Recycling could be developed into a government program with decent wages to curb pollution and reduce greenhouse gases. What began as a job out of desperation could, through public incentives and entrepreneurial effort, decrease extreme poverty and make an environmental impact in urban Nairobi.

Similarly, washing clothes could become a key industry for the informal settlements to serve the needs of the hospitality industry. The development professionals understand that entrepreneurship and skills training for micro-enterprises are essential in program development for the informal settlements, as reflected in their qualitative answers. The lack of a practical strategy for programming appears to be the problem.

### *Takeaway #5 - Human Capital*

The Freirean methods led to new knowledge about community capital. Eighty-eight percent of Mukuru residents affirm their neighbors will contribute money when families are in need because of a grave illness or death. This is not only an indicator of community capital but also of compassion. The ability of someone living in extreme poverty to give a portion of their livelihood to another speaks volumes. Moreover, 74% of Mukuru residents can identify someone in the community they consider a leader. For development, this knowledge adds to the likelihood of cohesion if programs in entrepreneurship were developed specifically for informal settlements. Compassion and leadership are critical to the success of development programs if development programs are to be led from within the community.

Human agency is not lacking in Mukuru. Ninety-three percent of the community residents voted in the 2017 Kenyan election. Eighty-six percent said they voted because they want change. Human agency is not lacking in the informal settlement. Residents were willing to lose a day's income to stand in line to vote in a country where election violence has led to candidates being charged with crimes against humanity. In the face of such danger, Mukuru residents clearly understand the importance of using human agency to support the democratic process. The importance of human agency, leadership, and community capital can be found in the work of Adam Michael Auerbach[109]. His dissertation on development in India's urban informal settlements reveals the aforementioned attributes as key to gaining services in informal settlements. Having leadership, compassion, and human agency translates into community capital that can inspire others in the informal settlement toward cohesion and successful engagement with the government. No matter how little the local government may contribute to a program, the poor find value in knowing their government cares about them.

Aid programs exist because of agreements with local governments. In this light, one can view even the largest aid organizations as subcontractors for governments. Informal settlement residents may feel that foreign aid agencies have better relationships with the Kenyan government than they do themselves. The idea of knowledge sharing to help create a large, government-backed aid agency in Kenya has not been explored. The data suggests that government involvement, no matter how small, may have a positive effect on poverty reduction efforts.

Sixty-two percent of the community residents blame continued poverty on lack of government support and government misuse of funds allocated to help them. The residents reported that lower-level government officials (district managers) must be bribed to gain services.

Nevertheless, 70% of the community residents believe the government of Kenya cares about them. Fifty-seven and forty-four percent are knowledgeable about water and health projects installed by the government specifically for informal settlements.

### *Key Takeaway #6 - Top Causes of Poverty in Mukuru*

The Freirean dialogics brought forth a deeper analysis of extreme poverty and self-reflection (psychologism), resulting in four top causes of poverty according to Mukuru residents:

1.  Lack of jobs
2.  Corruption/nepotism
3.  Low wages
4.  Poor governance

One may think that the lack of jobs and low wages are the same, but they are not. Lack of jobs refers to insufficient industry in the country, while low wages refer to the government-approved wage determinants that range from 141,500 kes/month (140 USD) to 197,800/month (195 USD) for government jobs as of

July 2020 (Salaries & Remuneration Commission, 2020). These pay rates translate to 4.66-6.50 USD/day, low wages[110]. Likewise, one may think corruption/nepotism is the same as poor governance, but it is not. Residents speak of corruption/nepotism as giving jobs to family, friends, and those who will pay a bribe to obtain a job. Residents speak of poor governance in terms of government misuse of aid funds.

Poor infrastructure was nearly last on the list[111]. Residents have become accustomed to not having access to water and plumbing at their mabati and may see it as secondary after having lived without it for generations.

Development professionals are aware that entrepreneurship and job creation are most needed to reduce poverty, yet the top three areas of their program focus are:

1.   Training

2.   Education

3.   Gender equality

The resident's top problem is the lack of jobs, and training serves the need from a program development perspective only. Poverty due to lack of jobs means that emphasis is needed on job creation. As noted in takeaway #4, development professionals are aware that training the poor for jobs that do not exist is ineffective, but they still continue the training. Development programs that focus on education and gender equality are helpful but do not reduce corruption or increase the low wages earned by residents of informal settlements. Freirean dialogics reveal nuances that have fallen through the cracks between development planners, sub-contractors, and the poor.

Freirean theory helps to identify faults in program development intended to be human-centered. A 20-year veteran development professional and critic had this to say after analyzing the data:

> *"Development practitioners see poverty alleviation as a short-term solution of skills/training, while slum-dwellers see a long-term solution of education and health. One of our failures as development practitioners is that we live on the 5-year project cycle of our donors and can't see 20 years into the future. 'What can we do in the next 5 years to fight poverty?' is our limited thought process. I tend to agree with the slum dwellers on this one [that long-term solutions are needed]. Anonymous, 2022*

Development professionals may also be missing the mark on the short-term needs of residents. Cash is needed to alleviate immediate needs. To reiterate, long-term needs are job creation (92%), followed by cash (86%). To earn a living in the informal settlement means being able to hustle, i.e., multi-task selling, trading, or bartering of goods and services to survive each day. These are the skills of an entrepreneur, in this case, working in the informal sector.

Seventy-seven percent of Mukuru residents feel they have what it takes to be successful. Their self-confidence has not been shaken by extreme poverty but anchored by it. The perseverance of generations earning less than $1.90/day is testimony to survival by innovation. Moreover, experiences that thwart radicalization (taking active steps to make change) center around the corruption and bribes necessary to succeed. Given the chance to work a decent job, residents of informal settlements are likely to contribute to their country economically and socially.

Ninety-nine percent of the development professionals interviewed use place-based, human-centered development. Had the Freirean dialogue been integrated into their strategic planning, programs might have been developed to target the needs of informal settlement residents more effectively. With the greatest need of residents being lack of income, only 16% of the development professionals offer programs in direct cash, equitable loans, saving groups, and access to credit or other financial services. This is likened to offering shopping baskets to people who are hungry.

1. Savings groups

2. Entrepreneurship

3. Skills training

4. Health

5. WASH (Water and Sanitation Hygiene)

6. Housing

7. Gender issues

8. Comprehensive Millenium Villages (UNHCR refugee villages)

9. Policy changes on land tenure

10. Education

11. Micro-finance

1.  Basic human rights

2.  Housing improvements

3.  Social support

4.  Economic support

## 6.2. Theory of Extreme Poverty Reduction

Conclusions about Freirean critical consciousness reveal a struggle between agency and appeasement on the part of the residents, backed up by an inhibited mindset explained by the theoretical contributions of Fanon 1963. A new theory is offered as a method to engage informal residents in authentic dialogue. The theory embraces Freirean foundations combined with elements from literature, including trust-building for legitimacy. The totality of the new theory is to create Communities of Inclusiveness and Self Reliance.

The hypothesis that residents of informal settlements think differently than development professionals about programs to reduce extreme poverty is true for this sample of 500 residents. However, its truth is nuanced in ways not anticipated along various levels of program development and delivery. Through the efforts and conclusions of this research, a new Freirean-based theory can be used in development to reduce intercultural communication deficits that lead to continued poverty.

The *Theory of Extreme Poverty Reduction* has five conditions for success:

## 1. Cultural Dialogics or Self-Analysis

-   Use Freirean-themed questions to aid critical thinking for long-term solutions

-   Harness existing community capital in local leaders

-   Inclusiveness of women, youth, elders, and persons with disabilities

## 2. Engagement

-   Create productive community spaces for continued community dialogue and vital information to be disseminated

-   Identify a leading aid organization to analyze the needs of the community

### 3. Blended Knowledge

- Incorporate lived experience from those in poverty blended with knowledge from development professionals to create programs
- Identify pitfalls

### 4. Program Development/Community-Led

- Foster authentic human-centered programs that are community-led
- Provide micro-entrepreneurship and other necessary training for women, youth, men, and persons with disabilities

### 5. Communities of Inclusiveness and Self-Reliance (CISR)

- Begin with foundational job creation within the informal settlement to serve people who live in the informal settlement
- Maintain and develop more productive community spaces as points of contact for updates, emergencies, etc.

Communities of Inclusiveness and Self-Reliance (CISR) are self-contained and provide services to themselves. Unlike the failed Millennium Village programmed by Jeffery Sachs[112] for the UN, CISR forms organically. Residents would engage in self-analysis or dialogue led by a community-identified leader. Leaders identified by the community have different talents. Some are mobilizers. Others are innovators, connectors, or motivators. Development professionals can decolonize development by facilitating community leaders to take the lead in problem-solving. Either method (self-analysis or dialogue) should follow Freirean-themed questions as prompts that lead to deeper analysis and critical consciousness about issues surrounding poverty and how to address those issues. Residents must include men, women, youth, children, elders, and persons with disabilities. Chiefs should be present if culturally dictated. Once mobilized, communities should engage in the creation of a Productive Community Space that serves as the meeting point for knowledge sharing and dissemination of vital information.

These spaces would serve not only as a place for leaders to speak but also for future engagement with other non-profit organizations whereby the co-creation of programs can begin. In essence, the Community Productive Space would continually be used for further dialogue, monitoring and evaluation, updates, urgent information, etc. The role of development professionals would be programming to train existing community leaders, who then train the community in skills needed for self-reliance. There are residents of the informal settlement with Bachelor's and Master's degrees who can train others in micro-entrepreneurship, life skills, basic education, human rights, democracy, etc.

The shift for development professionals lies in how budgets are spent. Funding would be allocated to pay community leaders for their work and stipends for those who attend the training. Investing in community leaders creates the foundation and community capital for onboarding more comprehensive programs that fit into the political context of the state. Funding would also go toward supporting job creation, with an emphasis on financial support for business licenses and financial training for entrepreneurship. CISR should be supported for three to five years to allow enough time for self-reliant systems within the community to emerge in areas of health, education, housing, and food security.

One must consider that people living in extreme poverty, such as Mukuru, have lived in a state of stress and trauma that has become the norm. In comparison to others, some of these residents may not be looking to enter the "big-girls world," aka "modern society," where quick facts and figures are sputtered by secretaries and CEOs. The question for residents is, "What is success to you?" Development must meet their needs, not ours.

The following figure outlines a new theory that serves as crash prevention for the development of effective programs to reduce extreme poverty.

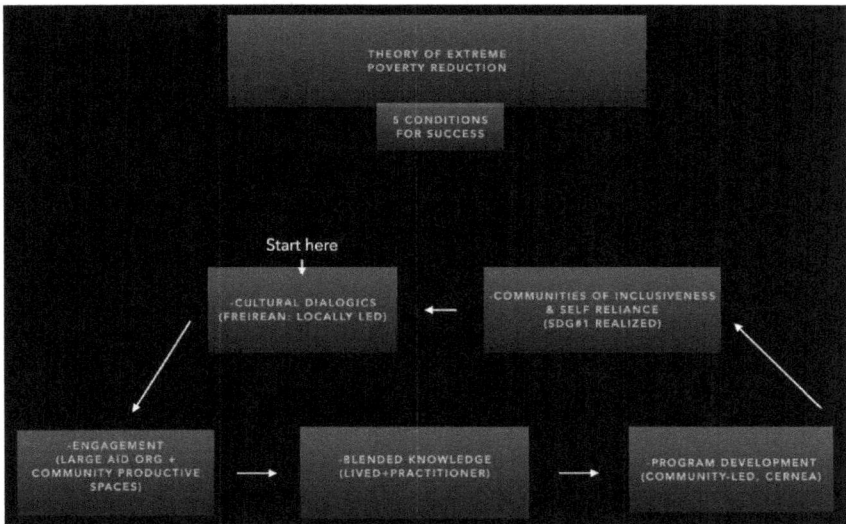

**Figure 6.1.** Theory of Extreme Poverty Reduction; CISR

### 6.2.1. CISR Economic Potential

The economy of Nairobi's Mukuru informal settlement is 7bn Kenyan Shillings or $60m dollars/year (Muungano Alliance, 2017). The Kenyan Institute for Public Policy Research and Analysis published new research confirming that 70% of Nairobi residents live in slums (KIIPRA, 2023). Approximately 71% of all Africans work informally (Bloomberg.com, 2020, Mumbai Dharavi). The economy of all informal settlements in Africa could contribute to government tax revenue if tenure issues were settled. The problem is that infrastructure would become a right for residents as well as other public services. If the $865 million dollars given annually to Kenya in development aid was used to offset the cost of infrastructure in Nairobi's informal settlements, economic poverty may still exist, but multi-dimensional poverty could be lessened by having access to WASH, safe housing, and energy. Moreover, if a portion of the $865million were used to offset education, health needs, or business set-up, residents of informal settlements could potentially be on the way to successfully making the leap out of extreme and thereby closer to reaching the #1 Sustainable Development Goal as well as goals #2-4, and #6-9. Mukuru residents in this research have made it clear that they are ready and well-trained for jobs, but there are no job opportunities. Community-driven development[113] is an approach that creates jobs within the community, for the community – an approach that I have long advocated for.

This research contributes an alternative approach to extreme poverty reduction in the informal settlement of Mukuru. The use of critical consciousness as a development tool to foster authentic dialogue requires a paradigm shift (Kuhn, 1970) in the development sector, whereby a change in foundational approaches creates a new way of addressing an old issue. Critical consciousness can serve as a bridge between those who live in extreme poverty and development professionals, both of whom seek to create effective programs for long-term resilience and the eradication of extreme poverty. If the object of development aid is to help people manage their lives independently, then help them do just that. Communities of Inclusiveness and self-reliance may produce an even greater economy for residents of informal settlements.

### 6.2.2. Support of Theory

This research stands on its own but also answers the call of William Easterly, who appealed in The White Man's Burden (2006) for academics to provide public service by evaluating development programs and approaches. Easterly believes that aid organizations follow short-sighted goals monitored and evaluated based on metrics set by the organization and not by the people they serve. Therefore, organizations never find out if the aid programs developed have satisfied their client (the poor). The critical consciousness element of this research adds novelty to Easterly's work in that it assures "effectiveness" is understood equally by the "client" and the "service provider." By allowing the community groups to work out what kinds of programs would be effective on their own, communication and definitive meaning are clear. This clarity can then be shared with development professionals. This is important because Easterly's "planners" represent large aid organizations who think about effective poverty reduction programs in different ways than their client – the poor, tested in this research. The failure of Western aid to reach the extremely poor in informal settlements like Mukuru is "The White Man's Burden." This work takes a novel approach to reducing misdirected communication between the two.

Centered on the client, this research reveals the value of knowledge collected directly from the poor. The potential for creating an internal market to create jobs is part of effective poverty reduction by providing the poor with access to markets (Prahalad, 2006). This research led to the discovery of a 7bn KES ($60m) economy already present in Mukuru (Muungano, 2017). It serves as testimony to the importance of taking a different approach to poverty reduction using existing economic dimensions, as noted by Prahalad, a scholar whose work in The Fortune at the Bottom of the Pyramid (2006) concurs with this position.

Not only are the economics of the poor essential to creating better poverty reduction programs, but the trust and legitimacy of leaders to plan alongside development professionals is irrefutably important. The notion of "habitus" must be front and center in the approach to access communities with a sense of trust and legitimacy, backed up by the work of Pierre Bourdieu (1993) and the ability to have access to informal settlements.

Additionally, this defense is backed by the work of Oteros-Rozas et al. (2015), demonstrated by their focus groups who were stimulated by "creative thinking and raising awareness" (Oteros-Rozas et al., 2015). Creative and critical thinking helps identify drivers of change that are reflected in my research. Drivers of change include removing structures of "us" and "them" (Boone et al., 2019). This research stands foundationally on the removal of structures that create a culture of silence and passive compliance, in alignment and bolstered by the work of Boone et al., 2019.

Cultures of passive compliance by aid recipients are likely a common occurrence. I situate my research with that of Barry Zimmerman, who posits that people who gather formally or informally in community groups exhibit (1) a better understanding of their life situations, (2) the development of a stronger sense of agency, and (3) a sense of mastery over their lives, (Zimmerman, 1992). Along the same philosophy about passive compliance, this work is bolstered by Franz Fanon, who stated that the "inherent unconsciousness" of impoverished people makes them likely to be excluded from the dialogue about planning, policy, and governance (Fanon, 1963). If the oppressed are educated by the oppressor to believe self-degrading thoughts (Fanon, 1963), how can thoughts of inferiority be removed in a structure that unconsciously maintains notions of "us" and "them." Herein lies a strong defense of the work in this book. Horizontal alignment of ideology is necessary for change to be sustainable (Todes et al., 2018). This research lines up with the same position through community-led ideology that aligns with the capacity of aid organizations.

Euro-centric perspectives in development that are not aligned with place-based human-centered design are not effective at reducing extreme poverty. This work, coupled with the work of Marimba Ani, explains Conscientization 101[114] as the importance of awakening the consciousness of African people to the influences of European culture (Ani, 1994). This research helps to explain the weight of colonial influences on decision-making for self-help.

Finally, this book is strengthened by the ideology of Kenyan scholar Ali Mazrui, that development needs a theory of "crash-prevention" (Mazrui, 1980). This book concludes with a new theory, the Theory of Extreme Poverty Reduction. The theory employs intercultural communication to address the deficit that leads to continual ineffective aid programs. All these scholars have conducted experimental and theoretical research to improve human agency and communication for the betterment of human development. The outcome of my research is bolstered by the work of the aforementioned key interdisciplinary scholars.

### 6.3. Recommendations

The economics of Mukuru, coupled with enhancing critical thinking, point to a viable base for job creation as a form of increasing income to reduce poverty. A market structure within the community offers equitable access for all. Communities of inclusion and self-reliance are self-sustained cities within a city, necessary because the COVID-19 pandemic taught us that governments, communities, and individuals must be self-reliant. Social security nets offer limited help and are not typically available in developing countries. Economic recovery from the pandemic is not expected for Kenya or other African states until 2023 (World Bank, 2021).

Covid-19 social distancing and work shutdowns have put the need for social safety nets front and center in public policy. Residents of informal settlements who earn less than $1.90/day have no social safety net and sometimes depend on visits from non-profits into the informal settlement to help them get by.

When the pandemic shutdowns occurred, residents had no income saved to rely on and no access to charitable services. The solution for sustainability may involve placing services within a community run by community members who will not pack up and leave at a time of great need, like during a pandemic. Health and safety measures should not be ignored, but services must remain at critical times of need. This issue comes back to the need for direct relations between the Kenyan government and a government-backed large Kenyan Aid Organization.

Communities of Inclusiveness and Self-reliance can be built through a combination of innovation, technology, and existing development/humanitarian services that are founded on entrepreneurship. This approach puts the earnest on communities to help themselves with the support from the development community in a way that builds long-term solutions.

### 6.3.1. Example #1 Fresh Water

The need for freshwater can be met by companies such as JIBU, a franchiser of water purification systems. The system comes with a small, mobile laboratory (approx.10ft x 8ft) and value-chain opportunities to deliver filtered water to households and collect empty containers. The purification process is fast and simple. Training can be completed within 2-3 weeks, providing job opportunities in the lab while fostering a new group of entrepreneurs to open another lab in a different area of the informal settlement. Alternatively, the lab on wheels is a match for movement to various locations. Multiple services such as JIBU can become the water source for several informal settlements in Nairobi. Water sold by cartels at 300% higher cost will be stopped. The role of development professionals is to foster sustainability. Such services with value chain opportunities are being ignored.

### 6.3.2. Example #2 Health

Ilara Health is an innovative, award-winning SME that offers medical entrepreneurship through a diagnostic mobile phone application. Small health stations can be opened, serving as few as three patients at a time. Opening several stations throughout the settlement and training men and women to use the app could mitigate the need for large clinics in areas where there is no open space. Training is less comprehensive than that of a Registered Nurse, and services are not invasive. Diagnostics through the application can detect pregnancy, prenatal health, and heart and lung issues. The cell phone acts as a sonogram screen. The app can also test for AIDS, HIV, TB, cancer, and influenza. Backed by the Gates Foundation and Butterfly Network, real-time feedback to remote doctors is also available. There are three centers currently in Nairobi, one located in Mukuru kwa Njenga. Costs are minimal for tests, from $10-$15 dollars. Pre-pandemic, Ilara was working on "cough analysis" through the app to determine the likelihood of serious diseases.

Similarly, residents of informal settlements could also serve in parastatal businesses managed by the state using innovative equipment such as electronic temperature readers to send data automatically to ministers of health to track indicators of illness. In the case of COVID-19, contact tracing and other health metrics could be accomplished. The role of development professionals is to provide training and expertise where needed to foster the success of systems within the informal settlements.

### 6.3.3. Example #3 Food Security

Mukuru Orange Booths is a franchise from South Africa. The booths are staffed by one person who offers access to quick loans, credit, and distributes cash from remittances. The booths also offer groceries from pre-set food packs to be delivered or picked up. Additionally, school supplies from pre-set school packs are offered. These items can be purchased through a phone app. The system supports orders placed by outside sources such as governments, NGOs, and remitters. This option addresses food insecurity and inequities in school supplies. Development professionals are not using these systems, which not only provide goods but also create jobs. Additionally, there is some evidence that micro-agriculture within Mukuru and other informal settlements is helping families remain food secure[115].

### 6.3.4. Example #4 Safe Shelter

An innovative team from the community created fire-proof housing in prefabricated slabs that can be erected in one day. The structure costs approximately $2500 for a 10ft x 8ft space. Structures can be added to and/or removed if land tenure problems arise. Some of these structures already exist in the informal settlements of Nairobi. Access to financing and advocacy for housing is what stops residents from purchasing more of these homes. Renovation of existing homes fosters entrepreneurship opportunities to sell roofing material and flooring. Other value chain opportunities arise organically as needs arise for the delivery and installation of home renovation materials. The role of development professionals should be limited to providing access to financing but include expertise in home improvement services within the informal settlement.

### 6.3.5. Example #5 Electricity

Solar home kits are readily available for individuals with small living spaces. However, residents need education and training on the installation and maintenance of the mini-solar panels. This would lower the demand for electricity, which cartels sell electricity at a 142% increase of the normal cost. Furthermore, development professionals could offer training to teach community leaders how to make solar lights to brighten dark walking paths. Community leaders who are trained can be subsidized to teach others. If development funds are invested in job creation within the community, poverty reduction might have a path forward toward effective change.

### 6.3.6. Example #6 Financial Insecurity

Savings groups in informal settlements are a popular alternative to traditional banking systems. Women have been successful at "Table Banking," where group members add weekly amounts to a collective savings pot. Members can borrow up to 50% of what they deposit. Most members make withdrawals to mitigate tough times like job loss during the COVID-19 pandemic. Others withdraw to start businesses. These groups are known in the professional development sector as Village Savings and Loans Groups (VSLGs). Kenya Post Office Bank and Hand in Hand International are two large NGOs that encourage Table Banking by offering business licensing after nine months of free additional financial training. Development professionals could play a role in funding the scale-up of businesses for graduates of the training.

### 6.3.7. Example #7 Education

Residents of Mukuru agree with development professionals about the importance of education. However, the choice between paying rent or school fees is apparent. Additionally, families must pay for uniforms and books. For families with more than one school-aged child, attendance is often staggered: one child per semester and a different child the next semester. The pattern leads to children falling behind in their studies or dropping out. Residents go hungry or get deeper into debt trying to get an education. By utilizing residents who have High School, Bachelor's, and Master's degrees as informal instructors, basic education can be provided likely at a lower cost. This would not be realized in the form of a private school but rather a community-based school operating for the common good of community empowerment.

Graduation certificates may not be valid, but general knowledge will be gained for life skills, while unemployed MA degree holders who live in the community will be employed. The role of development professionals would be to train the teachers and include democratic values, human rights, and entrepreneurship in education. Formal education remains available later for those who can afford it and wish to hold a legal credential for upward job mobility in the formal sector. The informal education system provides jobs within the community, further reducing extreme poverty while increasing empowerment and knowledge sharing.

In all matters regarding extreme poverty reduction, solutions to the everyday challenges of residents should be in the hands of community-led groups. Daycare, micro-farms, and gender-based empowerment groups could be created using leaders within the community, including beloved local chiefs and elders. If, at this point, you are still asking, What kind of residents are we dealing with here? What knowledge do they have to design programs? How are residents part of developing programs? Then you have missed the point of the research. Residents are not involved enough in developing programs – this is the problem. As development professionals, we do not have all the expertise necessary for programs to be effective. And the residents this research has focused on are typical residents of an informal settlement in Africa.

### 6.4. Future Research

Future research would include testing the Theory for Extreme Poverty Reduction as a community-led development pilot program in Mukuru. In effect, the research is looking to rectify the intercultural communication deficit that leads to continued poverty. Applying the theory and monitoring the results would provide measurable data to determine success. Research would include working with development professionals in this approach. Similar research could be conducted in other countries for comparative studies.

The need to support lives and livelihoods in informal settlements is urgent. It is time for perpetual extreme poverty to end. Obtaining perspectives directly from the most marginalized is essential. It puts locals in the lead regarding their development and allows them to take ownership of development programs. Residents of the informal settlement become "the planners," and development professionals become "the implementors" who help the residents plan for their own version of self-reliance. Communities of Inclusiveness and Self-reliance (CISR) are poised to be the future of third-world development.

### Chapter 6 - Key points

### Intercultural Communication Deficits Lead to Continued Poverty

*Six Takeaways:*

- Job creation
- Program reach

- Human-centered development

- Program effectiveness

- Human capital

- Top causes of extreme poverty in Mukuru

*Four themes:*

- Human rights

- Housing

- Social support

- Economic support

*New theory:*

- Theory of Extreme Poverty Reduction

- Communities of Inclusion and Self Reliance (CISRs)

*Inter-sectoral/interdisciplinary recommendations:*

- WASH

- Food security

- Housing

- Education

- Economic sustainability

## "Must Do" Experiential Exercise

The following pages provide instructions for a multidimensional extreme poverty exercise that can be done alone or in groups. It is simple, yet profound in impact towards gaining an understanding of the realities living in extreme poverty.

**Chapter 6 - Experiential exercise**

**Gender And Multidimensional Poverty**

Note: The experiential exercises are intended for learning purposes. It is not intended to serve as a game. With that, I encourage you to express yourselves freely (smiles of amazement are ok), but know that the scenarios are built on the real lives of residents living in Mukuru.

1)    Select the role you wish to experience from the four identities below. If working in large groups, a group leader may assign the roles. Take on any role regardless of your sex. Each role can be adopted by up to five people, i.e., five women farmers, five gay men, etc. In larger forums, break-out rooms are encouraged or sectioned areas where no more than 20 participants can engage together.

**Identities:**

- Women Farmer

- Women Table Banker

- Transgender resident

- Gay resident

2)    2.) All four identities live in the same community. Using the economic realities of the identity scenarios, your objective is to make choices to create a sustainable life while making every effort to achieve the goal noted per identity. You may move in with another community member, barter services, marry, or pool resources in any way you wish.

3)    You have 20 minutes to work out your life. Write down what you must give up and how long it will take for you to achieve your goal.

4)    If working with large teams, reconvene in a common room. Facilitate discussion to share the results of each group.

5)    After 15 minutes, everyone should write out their reflections about the role-play. Integrate theories, readings, protocols, and programs with matching elements of the experience. Note the strategies you used to achieve your outcome and the issues that held back your development.

## IDENTITY #1 – Married Women Farmer (Goal is to gain Food Security)

- number of children (3)

- nutritional food $35 or stomach fillers $15/month

- water for cooking $5/month

- charcoal for cooking $1.25/month

- wood for cooking (free)

- clean gas for cooking $1.25/month + transportation to get gas refills

- electricity $15/month

- rent $45/month

- bus transport $4/month

- school fees $8/month per child (3 children)

- school uniform $45 per student (one-time investment)

- gum boots for working on the farm $10 (one-time investment)

- farming tools $5 (one-time investment)

- pesticides $3/month

- fertilizer $3/month
  water tank for irrigation $385 (one-time investment)

- filling the water tank (rainwater or $50/water delivery every 3 months)

- unreliable spousal income $1.90/day

- medicine:

  o 2 children are infected with malaria $3/month per person

  o 1 elder has HIV $3/month

  o you need pain medicine for farming injuries $4/month

## IDENTITY #2 – Single Women (Goal is to save $100 USD)

- number of children to feed (3)

- nutritional food $35 or stomach fillers $15/month

- water for cooking $5/month
- charcoal for cooking $1.25/month
- wood for cooking (free)
- clean gas for cooking $1.25/month + transportation to get gas refills
- electricity $45/month
- rent $55/month
- bus transport $4/month
- school fees for two children @ $8/month per child
- school uniform $45 per student (one-time investment)
- income of $1.90/day
- loss of work time/menstruation $10 less/month
- medicine:
  - you have HIV $3/month
  - 1 child has malaria $3/month

**IDENTITY #3 – Single Male (Goal is sustainability)**

- nutritional food $35/month or stomach fillers $15/month
- water for cooking $5/month
- charcoal for cooking $1.25/month
- wood for cooking (free)
- clean gas for cooking $1.25/month + transportation to get gas refills
- electricity $45/month
- rent $55/month
- bus transport $4/month
- income $30/month
- support for your patents $15/month
- medicine:

- o   your youngest sister has malaria $3/month
- o   -you have Hep B $3/month
- o   Your father has HIV $3/month

## IDENTITY #4 - Gay Male with a partner (Goal is Entrepreneurship/Men's grooming salon)

- nutritional food $35/month or stomach fillers $15/month
- water for cooking $5/month
- wood for cooking (free)
- clean gas for cooking $1.25/month + transportation to get gas refills
- charcoal for cooking $1.25/month
- electricity $45/month
- rent $65/month
- bus transport $4/month
- your income $1.90/day
- additional income from your lover/partner $4/day
- medicine:
  - o   your partner has cancer $30/month toward $6000 hospital debt
  - o   you have a lower respiratory tract infection $6/month
  - o   you also have HIV $3/month
- business location rent $75/month
- business water $5/month
- business robe/uniform $8/each
- business mirror for clients $1/each
- business chairs for clients $6/each
- business hair comb for clients $.50/each
- business mustache comb for clients $.50/each
- business hair clipper/buzzer $5/each

- business hair pieces/wigs $2/each

- business hair-dressing cape for client $1/each

- business dry shampoo and lotion, free from local NGO

**Experiential Exercise Reflections:**

Below are two reflections that amplify critical factors of multidimensional poverty. The reflections are from two different students who study international development, yet both were unaware that at least 50% of the world's extreme poor make life-retracting decisions every day.

**Reflection #1**

*For this exercise, I was part of the women farmers group. I found the exercise to be eye-opening and frustrating for many reasons. While I had a general understanding of the setbacks a woman farmer might face in a poor area, I had no concept of just how many barriers there are. It was incredibly helpful to have these barriers listed together to fully understand the costs and pressures that women farmers face and how they might influence their decisions. I was shocked at how certain "barriers" that I would have prioritized outside of the exercise fell to the wayside. For instance, after calculating our monthly income based on our husband's salary, my partner and I quickly realized that we couldn't afford to put our children through school. The costs of running the farm were more pressing in order to ensure our family would survive. This is what all of our decisions came down to in the end: whether they were going to help sustain the family unit. Having to make these decisions ourselves made it so clear to me why issues like lack of education and malnutrition occur. When you're in survival mode, yor're not as worried about what your child is learning or eating as long as they are full and alive.*

*Something else that stood out to me in this exercise was how complicated figuring out our finances was. It was hard enough deciding what we could or couldn't live without and how our monthly expenses and earnings would change as our farm grew. When we took on the responsibility of feeding and housing the women's shelter group to help shore up the cost of our living expenses, it was a headache to calculate a fair monthly rate to charge and what our finances would look like in the end. I'm certainly no math whiz, but I wouldn't be surprised if I've been taught more math than the people this exercise represents. If college students with the privilege to have had years of math education struggle to come to a food-secure financial plan, how are people with significantly less education supposed to? I'm sure people living in this reality have experience with prioritizing certain expenses and such, but the thought of having to create an innovative plan meant to keep my family alive without access to certain resources or education was crushing.*

*I was also struck by how easily everything could fall apart if something went wrong. If there was a dry spell, the crops could die, and the family would be without food or a source of income. If another family member contracted malaria or fell ill, the family would have to factor in medical expenses that they may not have budgeted for. If the farmer's husband died, the family would be left without a patriarch to complete more physically demanding tasks and bring in the income, as is practiced in many places where this simulation plays out. Left to tend to the entire farm and three kids by herself, the woman farmer would likely have to bring in more help or sell her land and find work on another farm. With so few resources, there was less room for something to go wrong and a greater likelihood that something would.*

*This exercise immediately reminded me of the piece "Investigating the Gender Gap in Agricultural Productivity: Evidence from Uganda," because it broke down the expenses of running a farm and contextualized the responsibility women farmers take on when running a farm without a male presence and in the face of gendered inequalities in access to resources. It also made me think of Vygotsky's Sociocultural Theory of Cognitive Development in that children in families such as this one are exposed to the gender dynamics of farming in such an immediate and intense way. I imagine young girls learn to follow in their mother's footsteps of working the farm while young boys are raised to see themselves as the next patriarchal figure on the farm. Finally, the exercise directly pertained to Ester Boserup's argument in "An interdisciplinary visionary relevant for sustainability" that subsistence farmers respond to household consumption more than market demand to meet the pressing needs of the family first. Without the resources to address family needs, Western initiatives to connect farmers with "tech managerial assistance" in order to heighten production for retail are often fruitless and even detrimental for women farmers.*

## Reflection #2

*Throughout my academic career, I have done extensive assignments, readings, and research on poverty and poverty-related issues. However, these numbers and stories all too often lose their human face. Frequently discussing poverty in my classes sometimes makes it seem more like a statistic than the reality of life for hundreds of millions of people. Furthermore, as someone who has never lived anywhere close to poverty, it is impossible for me to truly understand what it is like to live on $1.90 a day. Obviously, this in-class exercise was nowhere close to the true experience, but it helped bring me away from the desensitized academic view of poverty and reminded me of the true lived experience.*

*Another student and I were in the women's savings group with a goal of saving $100 between us. The first thing we did was add up our total monthly incomes. We lived right at the international poverty line and made $1.90 a day. We were fortunate enough that we were both married, so our income was doubled. Our total monthly income was $114 each. Next, we went through the list to determine how much everything cost and what could be considered "optional." The first thing we noticed was that we had to subtract $10 from our monthly income due to loss of work time because of menstruation. This is something we had no control over – this was not something we could choose to opt out of, and there was nothing we could do to avoid the loss of income. We only had $104 to work with for each month. Rent was $75 a month, leaving us with $29 a month to feed ourselves, our husbands, and three children.*

*We went through the list several times, trying to see what we could cut out. It was immediately clear that sending our children to school was not an option. With the cost of rent and HIV medication, we could not even afford food. We quickly realized that our only real possibility was to try to convince the women farmers to let our families move in with them. After negotiations, they agreed to let us live on their farm for $25 a month. As a result, we not only significantly decreased our rent payment but were able to forgo the costs of things like electricity and water for cooking. However, this was not without significant tradeoffs. While we had a place to live for cheap, there were about 20 people living together in one space. While our children were out of school, they were working on the farm. We did not have a place of our own, and we had zero privacy or alone time.*

*But with careful budgeting, we were able to come up with a plan to eventually create a plan to send our children to school in four months. Luckily for us, only two of our three children were school-aged. It took two months of saving to send our first child and an additional two months to send our second child. After four months, between the two of us, we would be able to reach our $100 savings goal. But again, this involved substantial tradeoffs. Both children would be starting school late and would be significantly behind their classmates. Because the farmers' children were not in school, our children would have to teach theirs each day. Our kids had the responsibility of the babysitter and the teachers. They would likely be exhausted each day and unable to perform well in school.*

*The most difficult and eye-opening part of this exercise for me was deciding what we could consider nonessential. Before deciding to move in with the farmers, things like electricity, transportation, and water/charcoal for cooking were "nonessential." These things are part of my everyday life, and I had a very hard time imagining living without them. It is difficult to understand that these things have to be nonessential for people to survive each month. But this is a reality for hundreds of millions of people.*

*Additionally, I appreciated that these were real prices taken from a slum in Nairobi. An income of $1.90 a day means very different things in different places. Prices and the cost of living vary greatly between DC and Nairobi. When analyzing and quantifying poverty, we often assume that Western conditions apply everywhere. This is not to say that living on $1.90 a day is sufficient for anyone, but that using this number without considering the specific contexts of the places we are studying does not accurately represent the situation. However, I was still surprised at the cost of things proportional to the monthly income. Even though public schools are "free," the fees and uniform costs are substantial. It took us months to save enough to buy uniforms for our kids; one uniform cost nearly half of our monthly income.*

*The reality of multidimensional poverty became clearer as each group shared their budgets with the class. As the groups discussed giving up food and medication, we talked about how that would impact their earning, health, and well-being in general. Additionally, each group had to give up something significant and save for months to be able to afford essentials. All of these factors interact with each other and further entrap people into the poverty cycle. The social theories of gender also came to mind while performing this exercise, as I had to put myself in the position of and consider the roles and responsibilities that came with being a woman. Relevant gender norms meant that we had to consider things such as childcare and cooking meals for our children and husbands. These duties were part of the budgetary restraints and decisions we made. Even after deciding to move in with the farmers, we had to consider how we could cook, clean, and raise our children in a house with so many people.*

For in-person appearances to conduct this experiential exercise, contact apashayan@american.edu

Pollution at a bridge in Nairobi's Mathare Slum, and Rooftops of typical dwellings in Nairobi's slums (Pashayan, 2022)

Place of defecation for Mukuru residents, and the polluted Ngong River that flows through Mukuru Slum (Pashayan, 2018)

Remains from a fire in the Viwandani village of Mukuru Slum, a common occurrence due to lack of housing policy and safety standards (Pashayan, 2022)

Typical trash build-up in the kwa Ruben area of Mukuru slum, and artistic expression "Stop Corona" during the COVID-19 pandemic (Pashayan, 2020).

## Notes

[108] Gadi conducted research in Nigeria on outcomes of individuals with and without post-secondary education. She found that post-secondary education is not a guaranteed path to employment.

[109] Auerbach wrote a dissertation of the slums of India and the use of human agency to create a democratic process within and among slum residents. His research demonstrates

the possibility of leadership and cohesion in the slums regardless of formal governance. Auerbach's dissertation was commended at APSA in 2019 https://bit.ly/3LYzUK1

[110] For more resources, Africapay.org provides average pay per hour for a variety of jobs in Kenya. The wages are sourced from the Regulation of Wages in 2017 and updated to show valid wages as of April 2022. On this site, one can see that house servants earn 1.20USD/hour. Retrieved at: https://africapay.org/kenya/salary/minimum-wages/2182-cities-nairobi-mombasa-and-kisumu

[111] Fires in the slum burn wild until they burn out. The Fire Department has no feasible access because of the complexity of dirt paths leading to slum dwellings, and no taps to pump water within the slum. The work of M.K. Aiyabei and Elijah Odhiambo explain a fire disaster in Mukuru Slum (Aiyabei and Odhiambo, 2020).

[112] The Jeffrey Sachs Millennium Village program required a buy-in of IDA funds allocated to every person in the village. The information about the planning of the village can be retrieved at: https://www.un.org/esa/coordination/Alliance/Earth%20Institute%20-%20The%20Millennium%20Villages%20Project.htm

[113] Community-driven or Community-led Development is a movement that gives control of programming and the investment of resources to the community being served. More can be found at mcld.org

[114] This online site highlights cultural works of scholars and pro-Africa activists, https://conscientization101.com/video/dr-marimba-ani-the-fundamentals-of-yurugu/

[115] A report written by Owuore et.al, 2017 and published as part of the Food Studies Common in coordination with the University of Nairobi and the Urban Studies and Planning Commons of Wilfrid Laurier University, Canada, suggests that urban food systems fare improving for residents of informal settlements like Mukuru, Kibera, and Mathare. Food is grown vertically by small local co-ops despite the density of the population. https://scholars.wlu.ca/cgi/viewcontent.cgi?article=1019&context=hcp

# Appendix A.1 – Community Survey

**Community Survey Frequencies (N500)**

Q1 What is your name? - No frequencies Q2 What is your age

| Age | # Of responses | Frequencies |
|---|---|---|
| 18-24 | 143 | 29% |
| 25-34 | 221 | 44% |
| 35-44 | 94 | 19% |
| 45-54 | 28 | 6% |
| 55-64 | 11 | 2% |
| 65 | 1 | 0% |

Q3 Are you married?

| Marital Status | # Of responses | Frequencies |
|---|---|---|
| Yes | 272 | 54.4% |
| No | 58 | 11.6% |
| Divorced | 50 | 10% |
| Separated | 59 | 11.8% |
| Partner comes and goes | 55 | 11% |

Q4 What is your contact/cell - No frequencies

| # Of children | # Of responses | Frequencies |
|---|---|---|
| 1 | 68 | 13.6% |
| 2 | 126 | 25.2% |
| 3 | 115 | 23% |
| 4 | 81 | 16.2% |
| 5 | 31 | 6.2% |

| 6 | 11 | 2.2% |
|---|----|------|
| 7 | 9 | 1.8% |
| No children | 59 | 11.8 |

Q6 Were your children born at home or in hospital?

| Location born | Frequency of responses | Percentage |
|---------------|------------------------|------------|
| Home | 120 | 24% |
| Hospital | 336 | 67.2% |

Q7 Do you live in Mukuru?

| Mukuru resident | # Of responses | Frequencies |
|-----------------|----------------|-------------|
| Yes | 500 | 100% |
| No | 0 | 0% |

Q8 Do you consider yourself living in poverty?

| Living in Poverty | # Of responses | Frequencies |
|-------------------|----------------|-------------|
| Yes | 459 | 91.8% |
| No | 34 | 6.8% |

Q9 How long have you lived in Mukuru?

| # Of years | # Of responses | Frequencies |
|------------|----------------|-------------|
| 1-2yrs | 57 | 11.4% |
| 3-5yrs | 99 | 19.8% |
| 6-10yrs | 100 | 20% |
| 11-15yrs | 88 | 17.6% |
| 16-20yrs | 65 | 13% |
| 20yrs+ | 85 | 17% |

Q10 How did you come to live in Mukuru?

| Mukuru arrival how | # Of responses | Frequencies |
|---|---|---|
| Ancestors moved here from rural area | 209 | 41.8% |
| Ancestors moved here from another country | 4 | 0.8% |
| Moved here due to early marriage | 53 | 10.6% |
| Moved here because parents died | 28 | 5.6% |
| My parents left me here | 30 | 6% |
| Moved here to start a life on my own | 128 | 25.6% |
| Other | 29 | 5.8% |

Q11 What are your daily challenges?

| Daily challenge | Frequency of responses | Percentage |
|---|---|---|
| Rent | 473 | 94.6% |
| School fees | 456 | 91.2% |
| Food | 436 | 87.2% |
| Hygiene | 395 | 79% |
| Water | 362 | 72.4% |
| Health issues | 392 | 78.4% |
| Bribes | 339 | 67.8% |
| Shelter | 339 | 67.8% |
| Childcare | 323 | 64.6% |
| Safety | 282 | 56.4% |
| Transportation | 222 | 44.4% |
| Eldercare | 202 | 40.4% |
| No spouse | 140 | 28% |
| Police Brutality | 117 | 23.4% |
| Other | 17 | 3.4% |

Q12 Has COVID-19 increased your poverty?

| Increased poverty how | Frequency of responses | Percentage |
|---|---|---|
| Less/no income | 434 | 86.8% |
| Hunger | 436 | 87.2% |
| Less services available | 388 | 77.6% |
| Domestic violence | 378 | 75.6% |
| Increased anxiety | 273 | 54.6% |
| Bribes in general | 331 | 6.2% |
| Child abuse | 290 | 58% |
| No mask/PPE | 294 | 58.8% |
| Lost my shelter | 281 | 56.2% |
| Divorce or separation | 243 | 48.6% |
| Small space to quarantine | 222 | 44.4% |
| Curfew/Police brutality | 205 | 41% |
| Bribes to get out of hospital | 81 | 16.2% |
| Other | 4 | 0.8% |

Q13 Pre-COVID-19, did you have any children home because you could not afford school fees?

| Children home due to school fees | # Of responses | Frequencies |
|---|---|---|
| Yes | 289 | 57.8% |
| No | 175 | 35% |
| I do not have children | 8 | 1.6% |

Q14 How do you earn money each day?

| How money is earned | Frequency of responses | Percentage |
|---|---|---|
| Construction work | 197 | 39.4% |
| Recycling | 191 | 38.2% |
| Washing Clothes | 178 | 35.6% |

| Cash transfers | 142 | 28.4% |
| I own my own business | 87 | 17.4% |
| Selling food | 71 | 14.2% |
| Spouse/partner contributes | 73 | 14.6% |
| Government disbursements | 44 | 8.8% |
| Steady job | 24 | 4.8% |
| Remittances | 2 | 0.4% |
| Other | 0 | 0% |

Q15 If a family is short of money, or has a family member that is sick or dies, will people in the informal settlement help that family?

| Community help when someone is sick | # Of responses | Frequencies |
|---|---|---|
| Yes | 443 | 88.6% |
| No | 44 | 8.8% |
| Maybe | 9 | 1.8% |
| Don't know | 0 | 0% |
| Other | 0 | 0% |

Q16 Is there someone in your community that you consider a leader?

| Community Leader | # Of responses | Frequencies |
|---|---|---|
| Yes | 373 | 74.6% |
| No | 90 | 18% |
| Don't know | 3 | 0.6% |
| Yourself | 0 | 0% |
| Other | 0 | 0% |

Q17 What do you think causes poverty? (Psychologism)

*Qualitative answers are within the findings, analysis, and conclusions – see the word cloud of frequencies with a chart of mentions.

Poor leadership ........, Joblessness corona tribalism income
Unemployment poor Corruption money Lack
alcoholism Lack job capital education drugs
Lack employment Laziness

| Words expressed | Frequency of mentions |
|---|---|
| Lack | 54% |
| Corruption | 52% |
| Lack job | 24% |
| Unemployment | 16% |
| Education | 16% |
| Tribalism | 16% |
| Lack of employment | 14% |
| Joblessness | 14% |
| Laziness | 12% |
| Poor leadership | 10% |
| Money | 10% |
| Poor | 10% |
| Alcoholism | 8% |
| Income | 8% |
| Capital (cash) | 8% |
| Corona | 8% |
| Drugs | 6% |
| Insecurity | 6% |

| Groupings-what causes poverty | Percentages |
|---|---|
| Bad governance | 30% |
| Illness | 20% |
| Lack of education | 20% |
| Alcoholism and drug abuse | 18% |
| Tribalism | 9% |
| High population | 1% |
| Other | <1% |

Q18 Do you think there is a way out of poverty? (Psychologism)

| A way out? | # Of responses | Frequencies |
|---|---|---|
| Yes | 476 | 95.2% |
| No | 13 | 2.6% |
| Maybe | 6 | 1.2% |
| Don't know | 1 | 0.2% |
| Other | 0 | 0% |

Q19 What do you think is the best solution to reduce extreme poverty?

| Solutions to poverty | Percentage |
|---|---|
| Better governance | 26% |
| Free public education | 26% |
| Better clinics | 22% |
| Reduced corruption | 14% |
| Job training | 12% |
| Other | <1% |

Q20 Do you think poverty is an issue for you alone? (Subjectivism)

| Issue only for you | # Of responses | Frequencies |
|---|---|---|
| No | 500 | 100% |
| Yes | 0 | 0% |

| Maybe, Don't Know, Other | 0 | 0% |
|---|---|---|
|  |  |  |

Q21 What do you need to reduce poverty short-term? Long-term?

*Qualitative answers are within the findings, analysis, and conclusions – see the word cloud of frequencies with chart of mentions.

start business creation good leadership government jobs money
education Self Help Groups business training
capital soft loans Employment opportunities
job creation funds job opportunities good
fight corruption Job availability

| Words expressed | Frequency of mentions |
|---|---|
| Capital (cash) | 40% |
| A business | 38% |
| Employment | 32% |
| Education | 24% |
| Job creation | 18% |
| Jobs | 16% |
| Job opportunities | 12% |
| Good leadership | 8% |
| Fight corruption | 8% |
| Business | 8% |
| Training | 8% |
| Self-help groups | 6% |
| Soft loans | 6% |
| Money | 6% |
| Opportunities | 6% |
| Government | 6% |
| Funds | 6% |

| Creation | 6% |
|---|---|
| Good | 6% |

Q22 Do you think your government has the funds to help you?

| Gov't funds meant to help? | # Of responses | Frequencies |
|---|---|---|
| Yes | 492 | 98.4% |
| No | 0 | 0% |
| Maybe | 0 | 0% |
| Don't know | 0 | 0% |
| Refused | 8 | 1.6% |

Q23 If so, how does. Your government help you?

| How does your gov't help? | Frequency of responses | Percentage |
|---|---|---|
| Fresh water | 289 | 57.8% |
| Protection from harm | 268 | 53.6% |
| Health program | 222 | 44.4% |
| Food program | 166 | 33.2% |
| Jobs | 163 | 32.6% |
| Childcare program | 114 | 22.8% |
| Elder & disabled care | 121 | 24.2% |
| Free education | 102 | 20.4% |
| Shelter program | 89 | 17.8% |
| Cash disbursements | 76 | 15.2% |
| Easy business license | 43 | 8.6% |
| Loans | 30 | 6% |

Q24 If not, why doesn't your government help you?

| Why do they not help? | Frequency of responses | Percentage |
|---|---|---|
| Corruption | 295 | 59% |

| They don't care | 143 | 28.6% |
|---|---|---|
| They are busy | 24 | 4.8% |
| I don't know | 11 | 2.2% |
| Other | 1 | 0.2% |
| They are still making plans | 5 | 1% |
| Not enough money | 1 | 0.2% |

Q25 Did you vote in the last election?

| Vote? | # Of responses | Frequencies |
|---|---|---|
| Yes | 466 | 93% |
| No | 35 | 7% |

Q26 If not, why didn't you vote? (N35 did not vote)

| Why not? | Frequency of responses | Percentage |
|---|---|---|
| Not registered | 24 | 4.8% |
| Because nothing changes | 5 | 1% |
| Afraid of violence at polls | 3 | 0.6% |
| No time | 2 | 0.4% |
| Poll was too far | 1 | 0.2% |
| I didn't want to be bribed | 0 | 0% |
| I was not in town | 0 | 0% |
| Other | 3 | 0.6% |

Q27 If so, why did you vote?

| Why did you vote? | Frequency of responses | Percentage |
|---|---|---|
| I want things to change | 433 | 86.6% |
| Everyone votes | 49 | 9.8% |
| I want my tribe to stay in power | 28 | 5.6% |
| Opponents can make things worse | 18 | 3.6% |

| I was bribed to vote | 7 | 1.4% |
|---|---|---|
| Don't know | 1 | 0.2% |
| Other | 10 | 2% |

Q28 Do you think you have what it takes to be successful? (Subjectivism)

| Have what it takes? | # Of responses | Frequencies |
|---|---|---|
| Yes | 387 | 77.4% |
| No | 103 | 20.6% |
| Maybe | 7 | 1.4% |

Q29 What kinds of programs do you think will reduce poverty? (Psychologism)

*Qualitative answers are within the findings, analysis, and conclusions – see the frequency of mentions in this chart:

| Words expressed | Frequency of mentions |
|---|---|
| Advocacy | 813 |
| Job training | 485 |
| Entrepreneurship | 454 |
| Cash | 426 |
| Education | 444 |
| Hygiene | 453 |
| Housing | 438 |
| Gender equality | 423 |
| Health | 420 |
| Childcare | 408 |
| Elder/disabled care | 384 |
| Savings groups | 382 |
| Drug/Alcohol abuse | 284 |
| Urban agriculture | 348 |
| Climate/environment | 272 |
| Other | 10 |

Q30 What do you think of job training? How likely is it to help reduce poverty?

| Job training helpful | Frequency of mentions | Percentage |
|---|---|---|
| Very likely | 440 | 88% |
| Likely | 60 | 12% |
| Neither likely nor unlikely | 0 | 0% |
| Unlikely | 0 | 0% |
| Very unlikely | 0 | 0% |

Q31 Have any of these programs helped you?

| Programs by name | Frequency of mentions | Percentage |
|---|---|---|
| The Ruben Center | 474 | 61% |
| The Red Cross | 309 | 61% |
| Pay showers & toilets | 277 | 55% |
| USAID | 251 | 50% |
| Community Organizations | 176 | 35% |
| Save the Children | 70 | 14% |
| Muungano Alliance | 39 | 7.8% |
| World Bank KYEOP | 33 | 6.6% |
| Sanergy waste removal | 30 | 6% |
| UN housing KENSUP | 25 | 5% |
| Pamoja Trust | 3 | 0.6% |

Q32 If you could develop a poverty reduction program for informal settlements with an unlimited budget, what would it include? (Psychologism)

| Program feature | Frequency of mentions |
|---|---|
| More health clinics-24hrs | 468 (93%) |
| Free public school | 465 (93%) |
| More pay-toilets/showers | 439 (88%) |
| Electricity | 418 (84%) |

| | |
|---|---|
| New housing in the community | 402 (80%) |
| Concrete paths for walking | 398 (80%) |
| Plumbing | 394 (79%) |
| Home improvements | 397 (79%) |
| Paths for fire safety | 374 (75%) |
| Childcare | 372 (75%) |
| Community social groups | 370 (74%) |
| Easy business licensing | 355 (71%) |
| Safe cook stoves | 351 (70%) |
| Community vegetable gardens | 351 (70%) |
| Savings groups | 326 (65%) |
| Solar electricity | 307 (61%) |
| Elder & disabled care | 306 (61%) |
| Advocacy groups | 278 (56%) |
| Community watch-safety | 278 (56%) |
| New housing away from the community | 179 (36%) |

Q33 Is there anything else you would like to add?

*Qualitative answers are within the findings, analysis, and conclusions – see the word cloud of frequencies with chart of mentions.

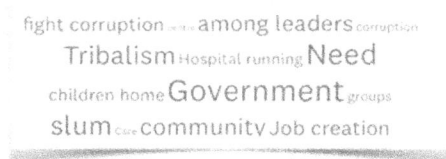

| Words expressed | Frequency of mentions |
|---|---|
| Government | 19% |
| Need | 9% |
| Slum | 9% |

| Tribalism | 9% |
|---|---|
| Community | 9% |
| Leaders, Job creation, | 7% |
| Fighting corruption | 7% |
| Fight corruption | 7% |
| Children at home | 7% |
| Hospital running | 7% |
| Groups | 7% |
| Corruption | 7% |
| Care | 7% |

# Appendix A.2 – Interview Questions

**Interview Frequencies (N100)**

Q1 What is your age?

| Age | # Of responses | Frequency |
|---|---|---|
| 18-24 | 19 | 19% |
| 25-34 | 18 | 18% |
| 35-44 | 40 | 40% |
| 45-54 | 16 | 16% |
| 55-64 | 6 | 6% |
| 65 | 1 | 1% |

Q2 What is your gender?

| Sex | Frequency |
|---|---|
| Female | 41% |
| Male | 37% |

Q3 How many years of experience do you have in this line of work?

| Years of experience | Frequency |
|---|---|
| 1-5 | 45% |
| 6-10 | 26% |
| 11-15 | 17% |
| 16 | 15% |

Q4 What is the name of the organization where you work?

| CATEGORY: GOVERNMENT (N10) | YEARS OF EXPERIENCE |
|---|---|
| Kenyan Ministry of Health | 24yrs |
| Kenyan Ministry of Education | 4yrs |
| Kenyan Refugee Secretariat | 5yrs |
| Danish Refugee Council | 19yrs |
| Kenyan Ministry of Interior | 8yrs |
| Nairobi City Council | 6yrs |
| Judiciary Kibera Law Courts | 5yrs |
| Kenyan Population Council | 15yrs |
| Kenyan Ministry of Gender & Social Services | 15yrs |
| EU Delegation to Kenya | 1yr |

| CATEGORY: PROMINENT AID ORGANIZATION (N23) | YEARS OF EXPERIENCE |
|---|---|
| Kenyan Red Cross (2) | 11yrs, 5yrs |
| World Vision | 14yrs |
| The Rotary Club Kenya | 7yrs |
| The Homeless Org. Kenya | 8yrs |
| KYEOP-World Bank | 3yrs |
| Kwetu Home of Peace | 18yrs |
| RTI International | 8yrs |
| Pamoja Trust | 2yrs |
| Street Families Rehabilitation Trust Fund | 14yrs |
| UN Habitat | 25yrs |
| UNHCR | 20yrs |
| Plan International (2) | 6yrs, 6yrs |
| Mukuru Slum Development Project | 9yrs |
| Hope Worldwide | 5yrs |

| Compassion International | 6yrs |
| HROC Friends Peace Teams | 2yrs |
| USAID (2) | 30yrs, 21yrs |
| Global Alliance Africa | 19yrs |
| UNaids.org | 12yrs |
| Center for Global Development | 5yrs |

| CATEGORY: ACADEMICS (N19) | YEARS OF EXPERIENCE |
| --- | --- |
| Pwani University (2) | 19yrs, 3yrs |
| Nairobi University (2) | 2yrs,3yrs |
| Cooperative University | 2yrs |
| Mt.Kenya University (2) | 2yrs,2yrs |
| Joe University of Nairobi | 3yrs |
| Kisii University | 4yrs |
| Kenyatta Ag & Tech University (2) | 4yrs, 3yrs |
| Wayland Baptist University | 4yrs |
| Daystar University | 2yrs |
| Strathmore University Kenya (2) | 2yrs, 2yrs |
| Masinde Muliro University | 4yrs |
| Kibera Salem Academy | 7yrs |
| University of Maryland Kenya | 8yrs |
| Jua Kali Artisan University | 1yr |

| CATEGORY: HEALTH (N9) | YEARS OF EXPERIENCE |
| --- | --- |
| AMREF Health Kenya (2) | 4yrs, 12yrs |
| Mater Hospital (2) | 10yrs,15yrs |
| Kitengela Medical Center | 10yrs |
| Mbagathi Hospital | 10yrs |
| Ilara Health | 10yrs |

| Pipeline Health Center | 14yrs |
|---|---|
| Safari Doctors | 4yrs |

| CATEGORY: CSO/NON-PROFITS (N30) | YEARS OF EXPERIENCE |
|---|---|
| Mukuru Promotion Centre | 2yrs |
| Mwalimu Kingi Madzo Investment | 16yrs |
| Kenya Institute of Management | 5yrs |
| Mothers2Mothers | 20yrs |
| Kounkuey Design Initiative (KDI) | 13yrs |
| The Lutheran Church | 15yrs |
| Good Hope Community Center | 12yrs |
| Mennonite Center | 8yrs |
| Good Neighbors Int'l | 5yrs |
| St. John's Community | 12yrs |
| PCEA Eastleigh | 8yrs |
| Action Aid Kenya | 7yrs |
| Life Song Kenya | 5yrs |
| Kwangu Kwako | 8yrs |
| Mathare Community Initiative | 4yrs |
| Group for Transcultural Relations | 3yrs |
| Caritas Nairobi | 13yrs |
| Call Africa | 4yrs |
| Napenda Kuishi Trust | 10yrs |
| Homeless of Nairobi | 9yrs |
| New Life Mwangaza Rehabilitation Center | 4yrs |
| Tugutuke Youth | 4yrs |
| AVP Trust | 7yrs |
| Inua Jamii | 3yrs |

| | |
|---|---|
| KISPED | 3yrs |
| Agape Model Solutions | 4yrs |
| Jitegemee Kenya Pamoja | 5yrs |
| Mukuru Land Mawe Resource Centre | 6yrs |
| Mukuru Promotion Center | 1yr |
| Volunteers Oversees | 20yrs |

| CATEGORY: Requested generalized name be used instead of actual organization (N9) | YEARS OF EXPERIENCE |
|---|---|
| Kenyan Government | 17yrs |
| US Bilateral Organization (2) | 4yrs,15yrs |
| US Private Sector Aid Organization | 10yrs |
| US Investment Assurance Organization | 10yrs |
| US Multilateral Financial Organization (2) | 3yrs, 17yrs |
| US Development Organization | 14yrs |
| US Government | 20yrs |

Q5 Where is the organization headquartered?

| HQ location | Frequency |
|---|---|
| Kenya | 72.73% |
| USA | 12.12% |
| Other | 15.15% |

Q6 What kind of organization is it?

| Organization Type | Frequency |
|---|---|
| Governmental | 18% |
| Non-governmental | 54% |
| Community Organization | 11% |
| Educational Institution | 17% |

Q7 Based on the number of staff, how large is the organization?

| Organization Size | Frequency |
|---|---|
| 1-10 workers | 17.2% |
| 11-50 workers | 23.2% |
| 51-200 workers | 21.2% |
| 201-500 workers | 13% |
| Up to 1000 workers | 1.1% |
| Up to 3000 workers | 5.1% |
| Up to 5000 workers | 19.2% |

Q8 What is the focus of the organization?

| Organization focus | Frequency (multi-focus included) |
|---|---|
| Loans/Cash/Finance | 13% |
| Training | 27% |
| Education | 24% |
| Agriculture | 3% |
| Health | 17% |
| Entrepreneurship | 34% |
| Environment | 0% |
| Housing | 5% |
| Women/Gender | 6% |
| Advocacy | 1% |

Q9 How long have you worked at the organization?

| Years at the organization | Frequency |
|---|---|
| Under 5 years | 51% |
| 6-10 years | 32% |
| 11-15 years | 9% |
| 16-20 years | 5% |
| 21+ years | 3% |

Q9a What is your job title at the organization?

*See the word cloud of frequencies and chart of job categories.
** The word" Bachelor" in the word cloud represents a degree in development studies.

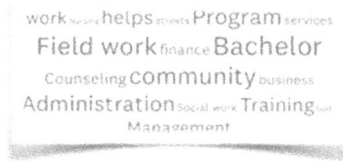

| Job title | Frequency |
|---|---|
| Monitoring and Evaluation | 5% |
| Community Services Administrator | 5% |
| Nurse Clinician | 7% |
| Social Worker | 3% |
| Accountant | 4% |
| Program Development Manager | 11% |
| Hydrospacial Engineering | 1% |
| University Studies in Development | 14% |
| Legal Advocat | 1% |
| Nutrition Training Associate | 2% |
| Livelihood Assessment | 2% |
| Field Officer | 15% |
| Program Coordinator | 3% |
| Training Manager | 7% |
| Micro-Finance Associate | 4% |
| Entrepreneurship Coordinator | 2% |
| Micro home building for informal settlements | 2% |
| Gender Specialist | 1% |
| Food Security | 1% |
| Family Planning | 1% |
| Child Counselor & Protection | 2% |
| Adult Counselor | 2% |

| Research | 1% |
|---|---|
| Chairman/Founder/CEO | 3% |
| ICT Specialist | 1% |

Q10 How much time do you spend in the field vs the office at your organization?

| Time allocation at work | Frequency |
|---|---|
| Mostly in the office | 46% |
| Mostly in the field | 24% |
| Equal split | 30% |

Q11 Does the organization run programs in informal settlements?

| Programs in informal settlements | Frequency |
|---|---|
| Yes | 78% |
| No | 22% |

Q12 What is your understanding of informal settlements?

*See the word cloud of frequencies and the corresponding chart of frequencies

mostly lack proper water little income good high areas without
lack basic social overcrowded lack basic grid
proper social amenities low income electricity
basic social amenities land poor
Residential areas crowded

Unplanned structures temporary people
people low income slums Informal settlement
housing Dwelling infrastructure poverty areas
buildings settlement understanding informal settlement
Unplanned structures lack basic amenities living acces

temporary structures characterized Places toilets
people living urban overcrowded

| Definitions to describe informal settlements | Frequency |
|---|---|
| No legal occupancy | 17% |
| Unplanned urban area | 8% |
| Overcrowded area | 12% |
| Geographical area below poverty line | 7% |
| For the less civilized | 1% |
| Unpleasant and full of struggle | 7% |
| No amenities (water, electricity, plumbing) | 21% |
| Temporary disorganized structures | 6% |
| Socio-economically deprived area | 14% |
| Off-grid | 7% |

Q13 Does the organization have restraints on where to run programs?

| Program restraints? | Frequency |
|---|---|
| Yes | 34% |
| No | 66% |

Q13a If so, what are the restraints?

*See the word cloud of frequencies from 43 organizations that mentioned some type of restraint and chart of corresponding frequencies.

Financial capacity institution Funding Program
Location government None work
Geographical coverage

| Types of restraints | Frequency |
|---|---|
| No restraint | 21% |
| Location | 12% |
| Geographical | 12% |
| Funding | 10% |

| Coverage | 10% |
|---|---|
| Financial capacity | 7% |
| Government | 7% |
| Program | 7% |
| Work | 7% |
| Institutional | 7% |

SCRIPT: Now, I want to talk about what types of programs help people who live in informal settlements. Extreme poverty is defined by The World Bank as those earning less than $1.90/day. In your opinion:

Q14 Have traditional poverty reduction programs (like job training, health/hygiene, and education) helped people who live in informal settlements?

| Are traditional programs helpful? | Frequency |
|---|---|
| Yes | 63% |
| No | 12% |
| Maybe | 24% |
| Don't know | 1% |

Q15 Do you think traditional development programs reach people living in informal settlements?

| Do traditional programs reach informal sesttlement | Frequency |
|---|---|
| Yes | 51% |
| No | 11% |
| Maybe | 38% |
| Don't know | 0% |

Q16 How has COVID-19 affected your program and its recipients?

*See the word cloud and chart of corresponding frequencies.

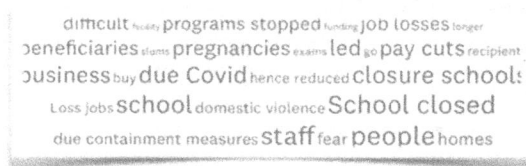

difficult programs stopped funding job losses longer beneficiaries slums pregnancies exams led go pay cuts recipient business buy due Covid hence reduced closure schools Loss jobs school domestic violence School closed due containment measures staff fear people homes

| Ways programs were affected | Frequencies |
|---|---|
| Staff infected | 3% |
| Shift to virtual | 2% |
| No face-to face visits | 19% |
| Staff cuts | 12% |
| Insufficient funds for PPE | 2% |
| Program stopped | 19% |
| Program scaled down | 10% |
| No problem – fully digital program | 3% |
| Recipient loss income | 12% |
| Recipient hunger | 5% |
| Recipient pregnancies & domestic violence | 2% |
| Recipient default on loans, loose homes | 4% |
| Recipient digital divide when schools closed | 5% |
| Recipient drug abuse increased | 2% |

Q17 How likely does Aid help reduce poverty in informal settlements? And why?

| Aid reduces poverty? | Frequencies |
|---|---|
| Very likely | 20% |
| Likely | 44% |
| Neither likely nor unlikely | 24% |
| Unlikely | 8% |
| Very unlikely | 4% |

Q18 Which of these programs are you familiar with?

| Programs that are familiar | Frequencies (includes multiple mentions) |
|---|---|
| UN KENSUP | 29% |
| World Bank KISIP | 5% |

| World Bank KYEOP | 28% |
| --- | --- |
| Sanergy Waste Removal | 0% |
| Muungano Alliance | 1% |
| Mercy Corps. | 1% |
| Save the Children | 67% |
| The Ruben Center | 18% |
| Mukuru Art Center | 0% |
| SHOFCO | 3% |
| Community Coops | 0% |
| Micro-loans | 8% |

Q19 How likely do these programs help reduce poverty in informal settlements?

| Programs that are familiar | Very likely | Likely | Neither/Nor | Unlikely | Very Unlikely | Not Sure |
| --- | --- | --- | --- | --- | --- | --- |
| UN KENSUP | 16% | 11% | 40% | 4% | 9% | 20% |
| World Bank KISIP | 28% | 39% | 17% | 6% | 6% | |
| World Bank KYEOP | 26% | 60% | 6% | 6% | 0% | 3% |
| Sanergy Waste Removal | 47% | 26% | 5% | 11% | 5% | 5% |
| Muungano Alliance | 20% | 40% | 20% | 20% | 0% | 0% |
| Mercy Corps. | 33% | 17% | 33% | 0% | 17% | 0% |
| Save the Children | 10% | 43% | 10% | 33% | 0% | 5% |
| The Ruben Center | 81% | 11% | 4% | 4% | 0% | 0% |
| Mukuru Art Center | 50% | 25% | 25% | 0% | 0% | 0% |
| SHOFCO | 20% | 40% | 40% | 0% | 0% | 0% |
| Community Coops | 40% | 40% | 20% | 0% | 0% | 0% |
| Micro-loans | 47% | 41% | 0% | 0% | 6% | 6% |

Q20 What types of programs or strategies are the most effective at reducing poverty in informal settlements?

*See the word cloud with corresponding frequencies, including program types.

| Word use | Frequencies |
|---|---|
| Education | 34% |
| Empowerment programs | 21% |
| Housing programs | 18% |
| Education(al) training | 16% |
| Entrepreneurship | 13% |
| Skills training | 11% |
| Health education | 9% |
| Health programs | 9% |
| Skills | 9% |
| Training | 9% |

| Types of programs | Frequencies |
|---|---|
| Income generating opportunities | 4% |
| Capacity building | 4% |
| Entrepreneurship | 28% |
| Education | 11% |
| Loan oversight and education | 7% |
| Skills training | 8% |
| Drug Abuse programs | 3% |
| Health/WASH | 9% |

| | |
|---|---|
| Slum clearance | 1% |
| Housing | 3% |
| Programs that are not "free" aid | 1% |
| Programs that are locally conceived | 4% |
| Gender and youth programs | 10% |
| Advocacy | 2% |
| Food security | 2% |
| Fire reduction | 2% |
| Not sure | 1% |

Q21 How likely or unlikely are these types of programs able to help reduce poverty in informal settlements?

| Helpful programs | Very likely | Likely | Neither/Nor | Unlikely | Very Unlikely | Not Sure |
|---|---|---|---|---|---|---|
| Health programs | 64% | 36% | 0% | 0% | 0% | 0% |
| Training | 43% | 29% | 19% | 5% | 5% | 0% |
| Education | 55% | 45% | 0% | 0% | 0% | 0% |
| Entrepreneurship programs | 67% | 33% | 0% | 0% | 0% | 0% |
| Agriculture programs | 10% | 10% | 40% | 20% | 20% | 0% |
| Loans/Cash | 23% | 29% | 71% | 7% | 21% | 14% |
| Gender equality | 25% | 33% | 17% | 8% | 0% | 17% |
| Advocacy | 25% | 50% | 0% | 0% | 25% | |
| Climate/environment | 0% | 0% | 11% | 33% | 11% | 44% |
| Housing programs | 29% | 29% | 29% | 0% | 0% | 14% |

Q22 Programs that use Human-centered design take input from communities before formulating the poverty reduction program. Does your organization use human-centered design?

| Using human-centered design? | Frequency |
|---|---|
| Yes | 99% |

| | |
|---|---|
| No | 0% |
| Don't know | 1% |

Q23 If you had an unlimited budget to create a poverty reduction program for the informal settlements, what type of program would you create?

*The word cloud reflects elements that should be included in new programs.

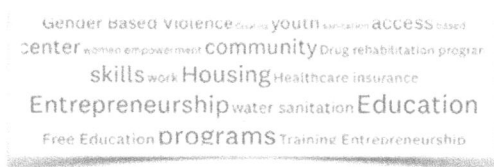

| Word use | Frequencies |
|---|---|
| Programs (maintain some) | 32% |
| **Include more programs with an emphasis on:** | |
| Education | 30% |
| Health | 23% |
| Entrepreneurship/Finance | 23% |
| Practical skills training | 14% |
| Housing | 11% |
| Community (WASH, gender, food security) | 8% |

| Dream program | Frequencies |
|---|---|
| Income-generating savings groups | 2% |
| Business start-up programs | 24% |
| Vocational skills | 11% |
| Creating job opportunities | 1% |
| Education | 7% |
| Loans and cash | 3% |
| Empowerment | 2% |

| | |
|---|---|
| Strategy with the community | 4% |
| Health | 11% |
| Improved housing | 10% |
| Waste management | 2% |
| Drug and substance abuse | 6% |
| Teen pregnancy | 1% |
| Urban farming | 1% |
| Gender empowerment | 5% |
| Comprehensive Millennium Village | 6% |
| UN refugee camp | 1% |
| Nutrition/Food Security | 3% |

# Appendix A.3 – Terminology

### Industry Terminology:

*Development professional*

Those who work in organizations that create and/or implement programs to help the poor develop socially and economically.

*Development program*

Programs created to empower the poor socially and/or economically.

*Inclusive development*

The concept is that every person, regardless of identity, is instrumental in the transformation of their own societies (USAID Operational Policy Manual).

*Informal sector*

An informal economy that is not taxed or regulated by the government and is typically sustained by the inner systems of those who live in poverty, mainly in the informal settlements.

*Informal settlement*

Areas where groups of housing units have been constructed on land that the occupants have no legal claim to or occupy illegally; unplanned settlements in areas where housing is not in compliance with current planning and building regulations (OECD).

*Non-governmental organization*

A nonprofit organization that operates independently of any government, addressing social, humanitarian, political, or advocacy issues.

*Non-profit organization*

Organizations that intentionally do not take profit and instead reinvest any surplus funds to achieve their charitable purpose.

### Foreign Direct Investment

An investment made by a company or individual from one country into another country.

### Public-Private Partnership

A collaboration between a government agency and a private-sector company is typically used to finance programs for the benefit of a country's citizens.

### Civil society organization

Organizations not associated with government and operate as grass-roots advocacy groups for communities, including community organizations and faith-based organizations.

### Foreign Aid

A voluntary transfer of public resources from a government to another independent government, to an NGO, or an international organization (such as the World Bank or the UN Development Program) with at least a 25% grant element, one goal of which is to better the human condition in the country receiving the aid (Lancaster, 2006).

### Millennium Village Project

2005 Jeffrey Sachs project supported by the United Nations, aimed at rural Africa inclusive of training manuals and funding to create sustainable, self-governing villages for those living in extreme poverty. Funding was provided by the World Bank, governments, and private contributions, including funds from George Soros.

### Multi-dimensional poverty

Poverty is measured by income, nutrition, education, cultural stigmas, gender issues, access to water, electricity, health services, and legal advocacy in terms of public safety, immigration, and land tenure rights.

### Social entrepreneurship

A person who pursues a for-profit business idea with the potential to solve a community problem.

### *Third World Poverty Index*

An index devised by World Bank economists as a marker for people living in low-middle income countries. Earning $1.90/day is considered living in extreme poverty, $3.20/day for nutritionally sustainable poverty, and $5.50/day is the highest marker to be considered living in poverty.

### *Power Africa*

Program developed by USAID to bring electricity to the African continent in rural and dark areas.

### *Prosper Africa 2019*

Government initiative under the Trump Administration that offered incentives for U.S. businesses to engage in emerging markets in Africa.

### Local (Nairobi) Terminology:

### *Mabati*

The literal translation is "iron sheets," the term is used to describe a type of dwelling in informal settlements made of corrugated iron sheets fastened together by gravity or nails if available.

### *Mukuru*

The informal settlement that stretches across three counties in Nairobi, Kenya.

### *Mzungu*

The literal translation is "wanderer," used first to describe European explorers in the eighteenth century, now used as a name for white people.

### *Slum Dweller*

A resident of an informal settlement.

### Freirean Theory Terminology:

### *Banked knowledge*

Model of teaching/learning whereby students are considered empty containers that must be filled with knowledge not based on their own experiences or understandings.

### Co-creation of knowledge

Model of teaching/learning whereby students and teachers are encouraged to express and expound on their life experiences as relative to a subject matter they are teaching/learning.

### Critical consciousness

Freire refers to critical consciousness as "conscientizacao," the process of people understanding the fullness of their situation in terms of factors that relate to keeping them in poverty.

### Dialogics

Dialogue that consists of implied meanings of words and expressions that foster shared understandings.

### Praxis

Method or "practice" of teaching/learning that embodies firsthand experiences: a combination of theory and practice into action.

### Psychologism

Self-reflection to change one's reality.

### Radicalization

Active truth that cannot remain passive in the face of oppression

### Sectarianism

False truths about a group or "sect" you are a part of.

### Subjectivism

A self-created oppressive reality.

### New Theory Terminology:

### CISR

Communities of Inclusiveness and Self-reliance: informal settlements that use their informal economy to create an integrative economic and social system that supports sustainability above the poverty level with little to no local government support.

# Bibliography

**Primary sources**

**Aiyabei, M. K., & Odhiambo, E**. (n.d.). Fires in Mukuru informal settlements in Nairobi, Kenya. Retrieved June 26, 2020, from Researchgate: https://www. researchgate.net/profile/Elijah-Odhiambo-2/publication/341900872_FIRES _IN_MUKURU_INFORMAL_SETTLEMENTS_IN_NAIROBI_KENYA_UNINF ORMED_OR_UN-ENFORCED/links/5f38389f458515b729245d63/FIRES-IN-MUKURU-INFORMAL-SETTLEMENTS-IN-NAIROBI-KENYA-UNINFORME D-OR-UN-ENFORCED.pdf

**Afolabi, O. S**. (2020). Conducting Focus Group Discussion in Africa: Researching the Nexus Between the State and Election Administration. *SAGE Research Methods Cases*. https://dx.doi.org/10.4135/9781526499141

**AUDA-NEPAD**. (n.d.). African Union Development Agency - The New Partnership for Africa's Development. Ethiopia, African Union. Retrieved from https://www.nepad.org

**Auerbach, A. M**. (2018). Demanding development: democracy, community governance, and public goods provision in India's urban slums. *UW-Madison Libraries Catalog*. Retrieved January 16, 2020, from https://search. library.wisc.edu/catalog/9911183229602121

**Australian Government**. (n.d.). Family and Children outcomes measurement matrix; explanatory notes.

**Australian Institute of Family Studies**. Retrieved from https://aifs.gov.au /cfca/expert-panel-project/families-and-children-outcomes-measurement-matrix-explanatory-notes

**Bates, R. H**. (1981). Markets and States in Tropical Africa: The Political Basis of Agricultural Policies. Los Angeles: University of California Press. ISBN: 978052028256.

**Beegle, K., & Christiaensen**. (2019). Accelerating poverty reduction in Africa. Washington, DC: World Bank Publication.

**Beegle, K., Honorati, M., & Monsalve, E**. (2018). Reaching the poor and vulnerable in Africa through social safety nets. In *Realizing the Full Potential of Social Safety Nets in Africa* (pp. 49–86). https://doi.org/10.1596/978-1-4648-1164-7_ch1

**Boone, K., Roets, G., & Rudi**. (2019). Raising critical consciousness in the struggle against poverty: Breaking a culture of silence. *Sage Publications*. Retrieved May 6, 2020, from https://journals.sagepub.com/doi/full/10.117 7/0261018318820233

**Brown, P. M**. (2013). An examination of Freire's notion of problem-posing pedagogy: The experiences of three middle school teachers implementing theory into practice (Doctoral dissertation).

**Candiracci, S., & Syrjanen, R**. (2007). UN-Habitat and the Kenya Slums Upgrading Programme. UN Publishing. Retrieved from https://unhabitat. org/un-habitat-and-kenya-slum-upgrading-programme-kensup

**Centers for Disease Control and Prevention.** (2018, November 15). Bushmeat importation policies. Retrieved April 7, 2022, from https://www.cdc.gov/imp ortation/bushmeat.html

**Cernea, M.** (1991). *Putting People First: Sociological variables in rural development* (revised edition). New York: Oxford University Press.

**Cheruiyot, K.** (2020, April 18). Kenyans bribing to get out of quarantine. *The Star.* https://www.the-star.co.ke/covid-19/2020-04-18-kenyans-bribing-to-get-out-of-quarantine/

**Dahir, A. L.** (2020, May 8). Kenyans held for weeks in Quarantine were told to pay to get out. The *New York Times.* https://www.nytimes.com/2020/05/08/world/africa/kenya-coronavirus-quarantine.html

**Decampo, P., & Langat, A.** (2019, February 15). What went wrong? Citizen reports of foreign aid in Kenya. *Pulitzer Center.* Retrieved February 10, 2020, from https://pulitzercenter.org/projects/what-went-wrong-citizen-reports-foreign-aid-kenya

**Diemer, M., & Li, C.** (2011). Critical consciousness development and political participation among marginalized youth. *JSTOR.* Retrieved April 10, 2020, from https://www.jstor.org/stable/41289885

**Ezeanya, C.** (2014). Indigenous Knowledge, Economic Empowerment and Entrepreneurship in Rwanda: The Girinka Approach. *The Journal of Pan African Studies,* 6(10), 241-263. http://www.jpanafrican.org/docs/vol6no10/6.10-19-Ezeanya.pdf

**Fox, S.** (2014). The political economy of slums: Theory and evidence from Sub-Saharan Africa. *World Development,* 54, 191–203. https://doi.org/10.10 16/j. worlddev.2013.08.005

**Gadi, K.** (2020, March 14). Beyond Learning Outcomes: Implications of Postsecondary Education on Market and Non-Market-Related Outcomes for Individuals in Nigeria. Paper presented at the National Conference of Black Political Scientists, Georgia State University, Atlanta, GA.

**Galistcheva, N. V.** (2020, July). The Role of Small-Scale Industries in Achieving Sustainable Development: The Experience of India. *Mgimo University Journal.*

**GINN-*Global Impact Investing Network.*** (2019). About Impact Investing. Annual Report. Retrieved from https://thegiin.org/impact-investing/

**Godfrey, E. B., & Wolf, S.** (2016). Developing critical consciousness or justifying the system? A qualitative analysis of attributes of poverty and wealth among low-income radical/ethnic minority and immigrant women. *Cultural Diversity & Ethnic Minority Psychology, 22*(1), 93-103. doi:10.1037/cdp0000048

**Haushofer, J., & Shapiro, J.** (2016). The Short-Term Impact of Unconditional Cash Transfers to the Poor: Experimental Evidence from Kenya. *The Quarterly Journal of Economics, 131*(4), 1973-2042. doi: 10.1093/qje/qjw025. Retrieved from https://pubmed.ncbi.nlm.nih.gov/33087990/

**Higgins, A.** (2013, April 18). Why residents of Kibera slum are rejecting new housing plans. *ONE.* Retrieved March 15, 2020, from https://www.one.org/international/blog/why-residents-of-kibera-slum-are-rejecting-new-housin g-plans/

**IDA News**. (2019, May 30). World Bank/IDA Publication. Retrieved from https://worldbank.org/en/news/immersivestory/2019/05/30fromcountries cid=ECR_E_NewsletterWeekly_EN_EXT&deliveryName=DM13731

**IMF.** (2020, April). COVID-19: An Unprecedented Threat to Development. *Regional Economic Outlook Sub-Saharan Africa, IMF Publication.* ISBN 9781513538495.

**Kenya Government**. (2019, July 23). Government invests Sh 126 billion in orphans, the elderly and people living with disabilities. *Ministry of Information, Communications and Technology.* https://ict.go.ke/government-invests-sh-126-billion-in-orphans-the-elderly-and-people-living-with-disabilities/#:~:t ext=Communications%20and%20Technology-,Government%20invests%20S h%20126%20billion%20in%20orphans%2C%20the%20elderly%20and,prote ction%20program%20called%20Inua%20Jamii.

**Kenya-Nairobi Government Census Statistics**. (2019). *Kenya: Kenya National Bureau of Statistics (KNBS).* Retrieved from https://nairobi.go.ke/growing-nairobi-population-indicator-opportunities-sonko/

**Kenya National Bureau of Statistics (KNBS).** (2019). Retrieved from https://www.knbs.or.ke

**Kinchin, I., Jacups, S., Tsey, K., & Lines, K.** (2015, August 21). An empowerment intervention for indigenous communities: An outcome assessment. *BMC Psychology.* Retrieved February 26, 2020, from https://www.ncbi.nlm.nih.gov/pubmed/26293685

**Lines, K., & Makau, J.** (2018). Taking the long view: 20 years of Muungano WA Wanavijiji, the Kenyan Federation of Slum Dwellers. *Environment and Urbanization, 30* (2), 407–424. https://doi.org/10.1177/0956247818785327

**Moore, G. W.** (2020, April 11). Curfews are a safer plan than total lockdowns to slow COVID-19's spread in informal economies. *Quartz.* Retrieved April 26, 2020, from https://qz.com/africa/1836458/curfews-not-lockdowns-will-slo w-covid-19-spread-in-africa/

**Muungano wa Wanavijiji**. (n.d.). Retrieved from https://www.muungano.net/

**Mwenga, F. M**. (2009, January). A case study of Aid Effectiveness in Kenya. Retrieved March 10, 2020, from https://ciaotest.cc.columbia.edu/wps/bi/00 16268/f_0016268_14066.pdf

**Ngunjiri, W.** (2019, June 25). List of Nairobi County wards. Tuko.co.ke - Kenya *news.* Retrieved April 6, 2022, from https://www.tuko.co.ke/285791-list-nairobi-county-wards.html

**Obama White House Archives**. (2014, August 5). FACT SHEET: the Doing Business in Africa Campaign. DC: White House Press Release. Retrieved from https://obamawhitehouse.archives.gov/the-press-office/2014/08/05/f act-sheet-doing-business-africa-campaign

**Oteros-Rozas, E., et al.** (2015). Participatory Scenario Planning in Place-Based Social-Ecological Research: Insights and Experiences from 23 Case Studies. *Ecology and Society, 20* (4). JSTOR. Accessed December 20, 2020, from www.jstor.org/stable/26270296.

**Owuor, S., Brown, A., Crush, J., Frayne, B., & Wagner, J.** (2017). The Urban Food System of Nairobi, Kenya: Hungry Cities Report No.6. Retrieved June 13, 2020, from https://scholars.wlu.ca/

**Perry, N.** (2019, October 11). In Nairobi, recycling poo is cleaning up the slums. *Phys-org Home/Earth/Environment.* Retrieved from https://phys.org/news/2019-10-nairobi-recycling-poo-slums.html

**Public Opinion Research Group (The World Bank Group).** (2019). Kenya-World Bank Group Country Survey (WBCS) 2019, Ref. KEN_2019_WBCS_v01_M. Dataset downloaded from https://microdata.worldbank.org/index.php/catalog/3516/study-description on January 10, 2021.

**Pumza, F.** (2015, February 23). Kenya's Kibera slum gets a revamp. *BBC News, Nairobi.* Retrieved from https://www.bbc.com/news/world-africa-31540911

**Reuters, T.** (2020, April 6). Kenya rolls out testing in Nairobi slums, but some fear stigma.

**Salaries and Remuneration Commission.** (2020, July). Phase IV Salary Review for County Government Employees at the Executive. *Government of Kenya.* Retrieved from: https://src.go.ke/wp-content/uploads/2020/07/Phase-IV-Salary-Review-for-County-Government-Employees-at-the-Executive.pdf

**Sanyal, S.** (2018, July 27). Kenyans are developing solutions for their own country. Interview with Edward Mungai. Retrieved February 26, 2020, from https://medium.com/thebeammagazine/kenyans-are-developing-solutions-for-their-own-country-f2584aea0982

**Scott, J. C.** (1985). *Weapons of the Weak: Everyday Forms of Peasant Resistance.* New Haven, CT: Yale University Press.

**Selbin, E.** (2010). *Revolution, Rebellion, Resistance: The Power of Story.* London: Zed Books. ISBN: 9781848130173.

**Un-authored.** (2020, March 28). Kenya police under fire over 'excessive force' as curfew begins. *Coronavirus pandemic News | Al Jazeera.* Retrieved April 10, 2020, from https://www.aljazeera.com/news/2020/03/kenya-police-fire-excessive-force-curfew-begins-200328101357933.html

**Un-authored.** (2020, June 10). Nairobi evicts 8,000 people amidst a pandemic and curfew. *African Arguments.* Retrieved February 1, 2021, from https://africanarguments.org/2020/06/10/nairobi-evicts-8000-people-amidst-a-pandemic-and-curfew/

**Un-authored.** (2013, March 19). Kensup: Inside the ministry-on site in Kibera. Retrieved March 16, 2020, from https://www.muungano.net/browseblogs/2013/03/19/kensup-inside-the-ministry-on-site-in-kibera

**US Int'l Development Finance Corp.** (2020, March 12). DFC approves nearly $900 million for global development projects. *DFC Speeches and Testimony.* Retrieved April 8, 2022, from https://www.dfc.gov/media/press-releases/dfc-approves-nearly-900-million-global-development-projects

**USAID Operational Policy.** (2017, April 27). *The Automated Directives System (ADS), Chapter 205.*

**USAID Global Infrastructure Hub.** (2019). *Africa Infrastructure Program.* Retrieved from https://www.gihub.org/resources/financial-facilities/usaid-african-infrastructure-program/

**USAID Press Office.** (2017, Aug.3). US Announces $169 million in New Humanitarian Assistance for Ethiopian and Kenya. *USAID.* Retrieved from https://www.usaid.gov/news-information/press-releases/aug-3-2017-us-announces-169-million-new-humanitarian-assistance-ethiopia-kenya

**USAID.** Foreign Assistance Aid Data. (2015). *USAID.* Retrieved from https://explorer.usaid.gov/cd/KEN?measure=Obligations&fiscal_year=2015&implementing_agency_id=1

**USAID.** Staffing Report to Congress. (2016, June). *House Report 114-154, H.R. 2772.* Retrieved from https://www.usaid.gov/sites/default/files/documents/1868/2016_USAID_Staffing_Report_to_Congress.pdf

**U.S. Department of State.** (2016, May 11). *Foreign Affairs Manual and Handbook. Requirement for Sustainability Assessments, 14FAM 243.3-1.* Retrieved April 8, 2022, from https://fam.state.gov/FAM/14FAM/14FAM0240.html#M243_3_1

**Van Trottenburg, Axel.** (2020, October 17). World Bank Managing Director of Operations, Presentation delivered on End Poverty Day. *World Bank Annual Meetings.*

**V. O. A. News.** (2020, May 8). Kenyans riot in Nairobi after demolition of homes. *VOA.* Retrieved November 14, 2021, from https://www.voanews.com/africa/kenyans-riot-nairobi-after-demolition-homes

**World Health Organization.** (2021, March). *Virus Origin / Origins of the SARS-COV-2 Virus.* Retrieved from https://www.who.int/emergencies/diseases/novel-coronavirus-2019/origins-of-the-virus

**World Health Organization.** (1990, Jan. 1). *Ebola Virus: Ebola Virus in Monkeys Shipped from the Philippines to the United States of America.* Retrieved from https://apps.who.int/iris/handle/10665/227498

**Secondary Sources:**

**Akala, W. J., & Changilwa, P.** (2018). Status of Technical and Vocational Education and Training (TVET) in Post-secondary Education in Kenya. *Journal of Popular Education in Africa, 2* (7), 15-25.

**Akwei, I.** (2017, July 10). Rwanda tops UN list of countries with most women in Parliament. *Africanews.* Retrieved September 20, 2020, from https://www.africanews.com/2017/07/10/rwanda-tops-un-list-of-countries-with-most-women-in-parliament//

**Albrecht, K.** (2006). *Social Intelligence: The New Science of Success.* Wiley Press.

**American Psychological Association (APA).** (2020). Conducting research during the COVID-19 pandemic: Advice from psychological researchers on protecting participants, animals, and research plans.

**American Psychological Association.** https://www.apa.org/news/apa/2020/03/conducting-research-covid-19

**Ani, M.** (1994). *Yurugu: An African-centered Critique of European Cultural Thought and Behavior, 511-552.* African World Press.

**Ani, M. (n.d.).** *Conscientization 101.* Video lecture retrieved from https://conscientization101.com/video/dr-marimba-ani-the-fundamentals-of-yurugu/

**Asante, M. K.** (1998). *The Afrocentric Idea.* Temple University Press.

**Bateson, P., & Gluckman, P.** (2011). *Plasticity, Robustness, Development and Evolution.* Cambridge University Press.

**Bemma, A**. (2014, July 22). Creating a Slum Within a Slum. *Inter Press Service.* Retrieved from http://www.ipsnews.net/2014/07/creating-a-slum-within-a-slum/

**Bhalla, N**. (2020, July 6). Kenya orders probe into rise in violence against women and girls during pandemic. *Reuters.* Retrieved September 22, 2020, from https://www.reuters.com/article/us-health-coronavirus-kenya-women-in-violence-against-women-and-girls-during-pandemic-idUSKBN2472ER

**Bjornlund, V., Bjornlund, H., & Van Rooyen, A. F.** (2020). Why agricultural production in sub-Saharan Africa remains low compared to the rest of the world – a historical perspective. *International Journal of Water Resources Development, 36* (sup1). https://doi.org/10.1080/07900627.2020.1739512

**Bogonko, S. A.** (1992). *History of Modern Education in Kenya, 1895-1992.* Evans Brothers.

**Bourdieu, P.** (1993). *The Field of Cultural Production.* Columbia University Press.

**Carothers, T.** (2004). *Critical mission essays on democracy promotion.* Carnegie Endowment for International Peace.

**Chang, A. M.** (2019). *Lean Impact.* John Wiley & Sons.

**Collier, P.** (2008). *The Bottom Billion: Why the poorest countries are failing and what can be done about it.* Oxford University Press.

**Creswell, J. W.** (1998). *Qualitative Inquiry and Research Design: Choosing among five traditions.* Sage Publications.

**Deakin, H., & Wakefield, K.** (2013). Skype interviewing: reflections of two PhD researchers. *Qualitative Research, 14*(5), 603-616.

**DeCarlo, M.** (2018). Ch.13.1, Interview Research. In *Scientific inquiry in social work.*

**Diouf, M.** (2016). Africa in the world. *Africa Today, 63*(2), 58. https://doi.org/10.2979/africatoday.63.2.05

**Dodds, S., & Hess, A. C.** (2020). Adapting research methodology during COVID-19: lessons for transformative service research. *Journal of Service Management.*

**Easterly, W.** (2006). *The White Man's Burden.* Penguin Group. ISBN 978-0-14-303882-5

**Fanon, F.** (1963). *The wretched of the earth.* Grove Press.

**Farooq, M. B., & De Villiers, C.** (2017). Telephonic qualitative research interviews: When to consider them and how to do them. *Meditari Accountancy Research.*

**Faux, Z.** (2020, February 17). From Micro-credit to major debt. *Bloomberg Businessweek.*

**Foucault, M.** (1977). *Discipline and Punish.* Doubleday Publishing Group.

**Freire, P.** (1972). *Pedagogy of the oppressed.* Penguin Education.

**Gajaweera, N., & Johnson, A.** (2015, October 21). Why should I use interviews in my research? *USC Dornsife Center.* Retrieved from https://crcc.usc.edu/report/studying-faith-qualitative-methodologies-for-studying-religious-communities/why-should-i-use-interviews-in-my-research/

**Gardner, H**. (2011). *Frames of mind: The theory of multiple intelligences.* BasicBooks. Garvey, Marcus. *Emancipated from mental slavery: selected sayings of Marcus Garvey.* The Mhotep Corporation.

**Geda, A**. (2006). The political economy of growth in Ethiopia (Ch.4, Vol.2). Cambridge University Press. Retrieved April 4, 2022, from http://www.ww. alemayehu.com/AA%20Recent%20Publication/Growth_CambChap_Sept20 06.pdf

**Gendzier, I. L**. (2017). *Development against democracy: Manipulating political change in the Third World.* Pluto Press.

**Georgieva, K**. (2020, October). World Bank Annual Meeting. Presentation on the state of Africa.

**Gokah, T**. (2007). The Naïve Researcher: Doing Social Research in Africa. *International Journal of Social Research Methodology*, 9(1), 61-73. DOI: 10.1080/13645570500436163. Retrieved from https://www.tandfonline.com/doi/citedby/10.1080/13645570500436163?scroll=top&needAccess=true

**Goldsmith, A. A**. (2001). Foreign aid and statehood in Africa. *International Organization, 55(1)*, 123-148. Retrieved from https://www.jstor.org/stable/3078599

**Hafsaas-Tsakos, H**. (2019, June 23). The Kingdom of Kush: An African centre on the periphery of the Bronze Age World System. *Taylor & Francis Online*, 42(1), 50-70. DOI:10.1080/00293650902978590. Retrieved April 5, 2022, from https://www.tandfonline.com/doi/abs/10.1080/00293650902978590

**Haq, M., Sen, A. K., & Anand, S**. (1994). *Human Development Index: Methodology and Measurement.* Human Development Report Office, Occasional Papers. Retrieved from https///ora.ox.ac.uk/objects/uuid/98d15918-dca9-4df1-86 5360df6d0289dd/download_file?file_format=application/pdf&safe_filename =HDI_methodology.pdf&type_of_work=Report.pdf

**Herbling, D**. (2020, March 24). Kenya Seeks $1.2 Billion From IMF, World Bank amid Virus. *Bloomberg.com*. Retrieved March 26, 2020, from https://www.bloomberg.com/news/articles/2020-03-24/kenya-seeks-more-than-1-billio n-from-imf-world-bank-amid-virus

**Hickel, J., & Kenny, C**. (2018, August 27). 12 things we can agree on about global poverty. *Center For Global Development.* Retrieved February 12, 2020, from https://www.cgdev.org/blog/12-things-we-can-agree-about-global-poverty

**Howlett, M**. (2021, January). Looking at the 'field' through a Zoom lens: Methodological reflections on conducting online research during a global pandemic. *Qualitative Research.* doi:10.1177/1468794120985691

**Horn, P., et al**. (2020, June). Scaling participation in informal settlement upgrading. *University of Manchester Global Development Institute Press.*

**Huggins, R., & Thompson, P**. (2015). Culture and place-based development: A Socio-economic analysis. *Regional Studies, 49(1)*, 130–159. https://doi.org/10.1080/00343404.2014.889817

**Illich, I**. (1973). *Tools for Conviviality.* Marion Boyars Publishers Ltd. ISBN: 978-1-8423-0011-4

**IMF**. (2020, April 23). Epidemiologists Help Steer Economy Through COVID-19. Retrieved at https://www.imf.org/en/News/Podcasts/All-Podcasts/2020/04/23/MD-Epidemiologists

**IMF. (n.d.).** *Regional Economic Outlook, April 2020, Sub-Saharan Africa.* Retrieved February 14, 2021, from https://www.google.com/books/edition/ Regional_Economic_Outlook_April_2020_Sub/Jq8YEAAAQBAJ?hl=en&gbpv =1&printsec=frontcover

**Jean, C.** (1991). *Behind the Eurocentric veils: The search for African realities.* The University of Massachusetts Press. ISBN-13: 978-0870237577.

**Kelleher, A.** (1993). The need for human centered development. *The American Journal of Economics and Sociology, 52(1),* 49-50 and 100. Retrieved from https://Query=+human+centered+development.

**Kharas, H., Hamel, K., & Hofer, M.** (2018, December 13). Rethinking global poverty reduction in 2019. *Brookings.* Retrieved February 26, 2020, from https://www.brookings.edu/blog/future-development/2018/12/13/rethinki ng-global-poverty-reduction-in-2019/

**Kibera UK.** Kibera Facts & Information. Retrieved from https://www.kibera. org.uk/facts-info/

**Koltai, S.** (2018, October). Entrepreneurial Eco-system, Uganda. *Center for Development Alternatives and Aspen Network of Development Entrepreneurs.* DC: CGD Publication.

**Koltai, S.** (2016, August 15). Entrepreneurship needs to be a bigger part of U.S. Foreign Aid. *Harvard Business Review.*

**Kuhn, T.** (1970). *The structure of scientific revolutions.* University of Chicago Press.

**Lall, R.** (2017). *Making International Organizations Work the Politics of Institutional Performance.* Harvard University. Retrieved from http://nrs. harvard.edu/urn-3:HUL.InstRepos:39945354

**Lancaster, C.** (2006). *Foreign aid; Diplomacy, development, domestic politics.* Chicago University Press.

**Mazrui, A. A.** (1977). *Africa's International Relations: The Diplomacy of Dependency and Change.* Routledge Press.

**Mazrui, A. A.** (1980). *The African Condition: A Political Diagnosis by Ali A. Mazrui.* Cambridge University Press.

**Mazrui, A.** (2011, October 7). Video. Retrieved from the Library of Congress, https://www.loc.gov/item/webcast-5324/.

**Mildenstein, T., Tanshi, I., & Racey, P. A.** (1970, January 1). Exploitation of Bats for Bushmeat and Medicine. *SpringerLink.* Springer International Publishing. https://link.springer.com/chapter/10.1007/978-3-319-25220-9_12

**Morris, L., & Gomez de la Torre, A.** (2020, December 18). How to decolonize International Development: some practical suggestions. *From Poverty to Power. Oxfam Blog.* Retrieved from https://oxfamblogs.org/fp2p/how-to-decolonise-international-development-some-practical-suggestions/utm_so urce=feedburner&utm_medium=feed&utm_campaign=Feed%3A+FromPov ertyToPower+%28From+Poverty+to+Power+%3A+Duncan+Green%29

**Moyo, D.** (2010). *Dead aid: Why aid makes things worse and how there is another way for Africa.* Penguin Books.

**Muli, J. M.** (2019). Social Entrepreneurship: Sustainability and social impact by not-for-profits: Theory and evidence. *Semantic Scholar.* Retrieved February 16, 2020, from https://www.semanticscholar.org/paper/SOCIAL-

ENTREPRENEURSHIP%3A-SUSTAINABILITY-AND-SOCIAL-Muli/f5646355 0d2fcd9f6d5bf589342f556119f3d77c

**Muyembe-Tamfum, J. J., Mulangu, S., Masumu, J., Kayembe, J. M., Kemp, A., & Paweska, J. T.** (2012, January). Ebola virus outbreaks in Africa: Past and present. *Onderstepoort Journal of Veterinary Research.* Retrieved April 7, 2022, from http://www.scielo.org.za/scielo.php?pid=S0030-24652012000200003&script=sci_arttext&tlng=es

**Ndaba, B., Owen, T., & Panyane, M.** (2021). *The Black Consciousness Reader: Steve Biko and the Rise of Black Consciousness.* Jacana.

**North, D.** (2005). Consciousness and Human Intentionality. In *Understanding the Process of Economic Change* (pp. 38-47). Princeton University Press. Retrieved from http://www.jstor.org/stable/j.ctt7zvbxt.8

**Nyabola, N.** (2020, May 18). Africa is not waiting to be saved from the coronavirus. *The Nation.* Retrieved July 19, 2020, from https://www.thenation.com/article/world/coronavirus-colonialism-africa/

**Okaka, P. O.** (2001). Technical and Vocational Education and Training in Kenya. Paper presented at the sub-regional workshop on the theme Promotion and Reform of Technical and Vocational Education and Training in Africa, Kampala.

**Otiende, J. E., Wamahiu, S. P., & Karagan, A. M.** (1992). *Education and Development in Kenya: A Historical Perspective.* Nairobi: Oxford University Press.

**Polak, P.** (2008). *Out of Poverty; What Works When Traditional Approaches Fail.* Berrett-Koehler Publishers. ISBN 978-1-60509-276-8.

**Prahalad, C. K.** (2014). *The fortune at the bottom of the pyramid: Eradicating poverty through profits.* Prentice Hall.

**Rodney, W.** (1972). *How Europe underdeveloped Africa.* Tanzania Publishing.

**Rostow, W. W.** (1960). *The Stages of Economic Growth; A Non-Communist Manifesto.* Cambridge University Press. ISBN: 0-521-40928-4.

**Sachs, J. D.** (2005). *The End of Poverty; Economic Possibilities for Our Time.* Penguin Books. ISBN 978-0-14-303658-6.

**Sawyer, M.** (2005). *Racial Politics in Post-Revolutionary Cuba.* Cambridge University Press. ISBN: 9780511791031.

**Schumpeter, J. A.** (1934). *The Theory of Economic Development.* Routledge Publishers. ISBN: 978-0-87855-698-4.

**Tafira, C. K.** (2015, October 22). Mugabe's Land Reform and the Provocation of Global White Anti-Black Racism. In: Ndlovu-Gatsheni, S. J., Ed., *Mugabeism? History, Politics and Power in Zimbabwe. Open Journal of Sciences,* 7(10), 1-31. Palgrave Macmillan, New York.

**Taylor, C.** (1985). *Philosophy and the human sciences: Philosophical papers 2.* Cambridge University Press.

**Taylor, C.** (1985). *Human agency and language.* Cambridge University Press.

**Todes, A., & Turok, I.** (2018, July). Spatial inequalities and policies in South Africa: Place-based or people-centered? *Progress in Planning,* 123, 1-31. https://doi.org/10.1016/j.progress.2017.03.001

**Tong, B. (2020, November 19).** *Webinars.* OECD.org. Retrieved from https:// qpp.cms.gov/resources/webinars

**Transparency International.** (2020, September 23). Police corruption is becoming a pandemic too. *Transparency.org.* https://www.transparency. org/en/news/police-corruption-is-becoming-a-pandemic-too

**Un-authored.** (2010). *People-centered development; empowered lives, resilient nations - UNDP.* United Nations. Retrieved from https://www.undp.org/ content/dam/undp/library/corporate/UNDP-in-action/2011/English/UND P-in-Action-2011-en.pdf

**Un-authored UNEP.** (2016). *Emerging issues of environmental concern: Blurred lines of emergent disease and ecosystem health.* United Nations. Retrieved from https://wedocs.unep.org/bitstream/handle/20.500.11822/7 664/Frontiers_2016.pdf?sequence=1

**Un-authored UN.** (2003). *The challenge of Slums - UN-Habitat.* United Nations. Retrieved from https://unhabitat.org/sites/default/files/downloa d-manager-files/The%20Challenge%20of%20Slums%20-%20Global%20Rep ort%20on%20Human%20Settlements%202003.pdf

**Van Noppen, A.** (2013). *The ABCs of Affordable Housing in Kenya.* Acumen Publication. Retrieved from https///acumen.org/wp-content/uploads/201 3/03/ABCs-of-Affordable-Housing-in-Kenya.pdf

**Venkatesh, S. A.** (2008). *Off the books: The underground economy of the urban poor.* Harvard University Press.

**Vindrola-Padros, C., et al.** (2020, December 30). Carrying Out Rapid Qualitative Research During a Pandemic: Emerging Lessons From COVID-19. *Qualitative Health Research,* 14, 2192-2204. doi: 10.1177/104973232095 1526. PMID: 32865149; PMCID: PMC7649912.

**Vo, L.** (2020, March 28). Kibera Slum: When Kindness Kills Development. *Rotary Peace Center.* Retrieved from https://rotarypeacecenternc.org/2019/ 07/kibera-slum/

**Weston, M.** (2020, March 27). How to tackle coronavirus in slums. *Global Dashboard Blog covering international affairs and global risks.* Retrieved April 30, 2020, from https://www.globaldashboard.org/2020/03/27/how-to-tackle-coronavirus-in-slums/

**Weber, M., & Michael, S.** (2015). *Max Weber's theory of modernity: The endless pursuit of meaning.* Routledge.

**World Bank Group.** (2018). *Poverty and Shared Prosperity: Piecing together the poverty puzzle.* Washington, DC: World Bank Publication.

**World Bank Group.** (2016, March). While poverty in Africa has declined, the number of poor has increased. Washington, DC: World Bank Publication. Retrieved from https://www.worldbank.org/en/region/afr/publication/po verty-rising-africa-poverty-report.

**World Bank.** (1980). *Announcement of Kenyan Economy to Receive Structural Adjustment Credits on April 14, 1980.* World Bank Publication. https://docu ments.worldbank.org/en/publication/documents-reports/documentdetail/ 369891618565946396/announcement-of-kenyan-economy-to-receive-struc tural-adjustment-credits-on-april-14-1980.

**World Poverty Map**. (n.d.). Germany Federal Ministry for Economic Cooperation and Development. Live, real-time data. Retrieved from https://worldpoverty.io/map

**Yusuf, M.** (2020, May 19). Kenya evicts 7,000 from slums despite coronavirus pandemic. *VOA*. Retrieved August 12, 2021, from https://www.voanews.com/africa/kenya-evicts-7000-slums-despite-coronavirus-pandemic

**Zimmerman, M. A., Israel, B. A., Schulz, A., et al.** (1992). Further explorations in empowerment theory: An empirical analysis of psychological empowerment. *American Journal of Community Psychology*, 20(6), 707-727.

**Further reading**

**Abd Halim, M., Foozy, C. F. M., Rahmi, I., & Mustapha, A.** (2018). A review of the live survey application: SurveyMonkey and SurveyGizmo. *JOIV: International Journal on Informatics Visualization*, 2(4-2), 309-312.

**Aguirre, A. A., Catherina, R., Frye, H., & Shelley, L.** (2020, June 24). Illicit Wildlife Trade, Wet Markets, and COVID-19: Preventing Future Pandemics. *World Medical Health Policy Journal*, 12(3), 256-265. Retrieved April 9, 2022, from https://onlinelibrary.wiley.com/doi/full/10.1002/wmh3.348

**Butzer, K.** (1981). Rise and Fall of Axum, Ethiopia: A Geo-Archaeological Interpretation. *American Antiquity*, 46(3), 471-495. doi:10.2307/280596.

**Carbone, M.** (2010). The EU in Africa: Increasing coherence, decreasing partnership. In *The Foreign Policy of the European Union* (pp. xx-xx). DC: Brookings Institution Press. Retrieved from https://www.jstor.org/stable/10.7864/j.ctt6wpgwz.22

**Cusolito, A. P., & Maloney, W. F.** (2018). *IBRD/World Bank Group Productivity Revisited*. World Bank Publication. ISBN (electronic): 978-1-4648-1362-7, DOI:10.1596/978-1-4648-1334-4.

**Gawaya, R., & Mukasa, R. S.** (2005). The African Women's protocol: A new dimension for women's rights in Africa. *JSTOR*. Retrieved April 12, 2020, from https://www.jstor.org/stable/20053162

**Green, D.** (2013). *From poverty to power: How active citizens and effective states can change the world*. Practical Action Publishing.

**Hui, C., & Triandis, H.** (1985). The Instability of Response Sets. *The Public Opinion Quarterly*, 49(2), 253-260. Retrieved September 7, 2021, from http://www.jstor.org/stable/2748831

**ICT. Staff Writer.** (2015). *First Nation Relationship to the Land*. Indigenous Corporate Training Inc. British Columbia. Retrieved from https://www.ictinc.ca/blog/first-nation-relationship-to-the-land

*KFGO*. Retrieved September 10, 2020, from https://kfgo.com/2020/05/27/kenya-rolls-out-testing-in-nairobi-slums-but-some-fear-stigma/

**Lemmen, C. H. J., Bennett, R. M., McLaren, R., & Enemark, S.** (2015). A new era in land administration emerges: Securing land rights for the world is feasible: Book review. *Journal of Land Administration in Eastern Africa*, 3(2), 353. http://journals.aru.ac.tz/index.php/JLAEA/article/view/88

**Lijadu, K.** (2018, August 24). A Kenyan Nonprofit's Innovative Aerial Water System Just Won it the World's Largest Humanitarian Prize. *Quartz Africa*.

Retrieved from https://qz.com/africa/1368422/the-2018-hilton-prize-went-to-a-kenyan-nonprofit-that-builds-aerial-water-systems-for-slums/

**Lu, J.** (2018, November 13). China's Building Spree in poor nations: Does it really help the local economy? *NPR.* Retrieved March 16, 2020, from http://www.npr.org/sections/goatsandsoda/2018/11/13/651834661/china-s-building-spree-in-poor-nations-does-it-really-help-the-local-economy?utm_&

**Madavo, C., Basu, A., et al.** (2000, July 12). Assessment of the Interim Poverty Reduction Strategy Paper (PRSP) for the Republic of Kenya. DC: IDA/IMF Publication.

**Marx, K., & Engels, F.** (1848). *The Communist Manifesto.*

**Media Team.** (2021, July 26). 2021/2022 New reduced school fees structure and guidelines for all secondary schools in Kenya; Education Ministry releases guidelines. *Education News Hub.* https://educationnewshub.co.ke/2021-2022-new-reduced-school-fees-structure-and-guidelines-for-all-secondary-schools-in-kenya-education-ministry-releases-guidelines/.

**McLagan, M.** (2014, May 13). The Mukuru slum; a lesson in inequality. *Oxfam GB.* Retrieved from https://oxfamapps.org/blog/2014-05-mukuru-slum-a-lesson-in-inequality/

**Population Matters News Team.** (2020, March 13). Population growth and environmental destruction fuel deadly diseases. *Populationmatters.org.* Retrieved from: https://populationmatters.org/news/2020/03/13/population-growth-and-environmental-destruction-fuel-deadly-diseases

**Ratner, C.** (2002). Subjectivity and Objectivity in Qualitative Methodology [29 paragraphs]. *Forum Qualitative Sozialforschung / Forum: Qualitative Social Research*, 3(3), Art. 16. Retrieved from http://nbn-resolving.de/urn:nbn:de:0114-fqs0203160.

**Reid, R.** (2011). The 'Precolonial' and the Foreshortening of African History. *JSTOR.* Retrieved March 19, 2020, from https://www.jstor.org/stable/i23016264

**Republic of Kenya.** (1964). *Kenya Education Commission.* Nairobi: Government Printer.

**Runde, D. F.** (2020, March 31). Will many developing countries get old before they get rich? *Center for Strategic and International Studies.* Retrieved April 8, 2020, from https://www.csis.org/analysis/will-many-developing-countries-get-rich

**Runde, D. F.** (2020, March 27). Competition or coordination: Coronavirus in the developing world. *Center for Strategic and International Studies.* Retrieved April 17, 2020, from https://www.csis.org/analysis/competition-or-coordination-coronavirus-developing-world

**Scruggs, G.** (2015, August 10). Turning Mud Huts into Apartment Towers in Nairobi's Biggest Slum. *Bloomberg Anywhere.* Retrieved from https://www.citylab.com/equity/2015/08/turning-kiberas-mud-huts-into-apartment-towers/400787/

**Sharma, D., & Friedman, J., et al.** (2018, November 7). World Bank Data Blog. *World Bank Publications.* Retrieved from https://blogs.worldbank.org/opendata/more-money-counting-poverty-multiple-forms

**Smith, M.** (2013). European policies, African impact and international order: (Re)evaluating the EU-Africa relationship. In *The European Union in Africa* (pp. xx-xx). Manchester University Press. Retrieved from https://www.jstor.org/stable/j.ctt16mvm0n.21

**Sun, Y.** (2014). *Africa in China's Foreign Policy*. East Asia Program, Henry L. Stimson Center. Retrieved from: https://www.brookings.edu/wp-content/uploads/2016/06/Africa-in-China-web_CMG7.pdf

**Sy, M., O'Leary, N., Nagraj, S., El-Awaisi, A., O'Carroll, V., & Xyrichis, A.** (2020). Doing international professional research in the COVID-19 era: A discussion paper. *Journal of International Professional Care*, 1-7.

**Torrentira, M.** (2020). Online data collection as adaptation in conducting quantitative and qualitative research during the COVID-19 pandemic. *European Journal of Education Studies*, 7(11). doi:http://dx.doi.org/10.46827/ejes.v7i11.3336

**Trotsky, L.** (1932). *The History of the Russian Revolution*. Pathfinder Press. ISBN: 9780873488297.

**Un-authored.** (2012). Advancing a human-centered approach to development: Integrating culture into the global development agenda. *United Nations*. Retrieved April 17, 2020, from https://www.un.org/en/development/desa/policy/mdg_workshops/tashkent_mdgs.shtml

**Un-authored.** (2018). Center for Innovation and Impact. *USAID*. Retrieved from https://www.usaid.gov/cii

**Un-authored.** (2018, June 28). Kenya 8th on extreme poverty list. *Business Daily Africa*. Retrieved at https://www.businessdailyafrica.com/economy/Kenya-8th-on-extreme-poverty-list/3946234-4635310-79pa9rz/index.html

**Un-authored.** (n.d.). Timeline of ancient Egypt. *Timeline of Ancient Egypt*. Institute of Egyptian Art & Archaeology, The University of Memphis. Retrieved April 3, 2022, from https://www.memphis.edu/egypt/resources/timeline.php

**UN Sustainable Development Goals Knowledge Platform**. *United Nations*. Retrieved from https://sustainabledevelopment.un.org/index.php?page=view&type=20000&nr=414&menu=2993

**USAID. (n.d.)**. *Development Innovation Ventures. USAID*. U.S Global Development Lab.

**USAID.** (n.d.). *The Journey to Self-reliance - Country Roadmap/Kenya. USAID*. Retrieved from https://selfreliance.usaid.gov/country/kenya

**Wilson, T., & Blood, D.** (2019, August 13). Rwanda: Where even poverty data must toe Kagame's line. *Financial Times*. Retrieved May 8, 2020, from https://www.ft.com/content/683047ac-b857-11e9-96bd-8e884d3ea203

**Wallerstein, I. M.** (2006). *World-Systems Analysis: An Introduction*. Duke University Press.

**Wasike, A.** (n.d.) Kenya: Exodus from cities creates anxiety in rural areas. Retrieved December 14, 2020, from https://www.aa.com.tr/en/africa/kenya-exodus-form-cities-creates-anxiety-in-rural-areas/1907564

**Weber, M.** (2002). *Protestant Ethic and the Spirit of Capitalism*. Penguin Press.

**Weston, M.** (n.d.). How to tackle coronavirus in slums. *Global Dashboard Blog covering international affairs and global risks*. Retrieved February 14, 2021, from https://www.globaldashboard.org/2020/03/27/how-to-tackle-coronav irus-in-slums/

**WHO**. (2021, February 23). Ebola Virus Disease. *World Health Organization.* https://www.who.int/news-room/fact-sheets/detail/ebola-virus-disease

**World Bank Group, Christiaensen, L., & Beegle, K**. (2019, October 9). Accelerating poverty reduction in Africa. *Open Knowledge Repository.* Retrieved March 12, 2020, from https://openknowledge.worldbank.org/han dle/10986/32354

**World Population Review**. http://worldpopulationreview.com/countries/ken ya-population/

**www.president.go.ke**

# Index

industry professionals, xvii
informal settlements, xv, xviii, xxi,
 xxv, xxvii, xxviii, 1, 6, 7, 10, 11,
 12, 14, 15, 16, 17, 19, 20, 21, 22,
 23, 24, 25, 26, 27, 28, 29, 30, 31,
 33, 34, 35, 36, 38, 40, 41, 43, 45,
 48, 51, 52, 53, 54, 56, 61, 62, 64,
 65, 73, 77, 78, 82, 83, 84, 87, 91,
 93, 96, 99, 104, 107,108, 109, 111,
 113, 114, 116, 119, 123, 124, 125,
 127, 128, 130, 132, 133, 135, 136,
 137, 139, 140, 141, 142, 143, 146,
 147, 148, 149, 150, 151, 152, 166,
 178, 187, 188, 189, 190, 191, 192,
 193, 194, 195, 197, 199, 200
innovation, xxv, 101, 142, 149
interdisciplinary approach, xxv
International Bank for
 Reconstruction and
 Development, xix
international development, xv, xvii,
 xxii, xxv, 3, 46, 158
International Development
 Research Center, xix
International Monetary Fund, xix
International Relations, xviii, xxii,
 xxiii, 62
inter-sectoral, xxix

## J

Johnathan, Kevin, and Maxwell B.,
 xviii

## K

KENSUP, xix, 28, 29, 56, 66, 72, 95,
 114, 119, 136, 178, 191, 192
Kenya, xv, xix, 1, 6, 9, 10, 11, 16, 17,
 18, 19, 20, 21, 24, 25, 27, 31, 32,
 33, 35, 36, 37, 38, 39, 40, 41, 42,
 53, 62, 66, 67, 72, 74, 81, 82, 87,
 91, 92, 95, 110, 111, 118, 120,
 121, 122, 123, 127, 132, 133, 134,
 136, 137, 138, 140, 146, 148, 151,
 166, 182, 183, 184, 185, 199
Kenyan Census, xxvii, 132
KISIP, xix, 66, 114, 191, 192
knowledge, xxv, xxix, 44, 64, 77
Koltai (2016), xxviii
Kuhn (1962), xxviii

## L

Lancaster (2006), xxviii, 50, 57
land tenure, 25, 103, 112, 113, 116,
 150, 198
literature, xvii, xxvii, xxviii, 16, 36,
 43, 47, 48, 49, 51, 55, 56, 57, 58,
 60, 62, 65, 66, 67, 80, 87, 101,
 111, 115, 133, 143
lived experiences, xviii, xxv, xxvii,
 6, 11, 14, 47
local missions, xxv
low-income, 9, 14, 35, 38, 46, 64,
 98

## M

male, 1, 25, 79, 93, 109, 159
marginalized, xviii, 9, 30, 35, 46,
 63, 65, 127, 152
Marimba (1994), xxviii
maternal and child health, xxv
MCC, xvii, xviii
men, 79, 80, 93, 133, 144, 149, 154
MENA, xix, 57
methodology, xvii, 50, 68, 73, 79,
 87, 119
Middle East and North African, xix
Millennial Development Goals,
 xxviii
Millennium Challenge
 Corporation, xvii, 17

76, 81, 82, 83, 94, 97, 100, 109,
110, 113, 115, 125, 126, 127, 128,
135, 137, 140, 146, 147, 151, 152,
178, 190, 194, 195
PPP, xix, 26
practitioner, xxix, 15
praxis, xxix, 44, 45, 47, 64, 78
Pre-colonial, 17, 36
primary research, xxv, 62
program planning, xxv, 12, 47
proletariat, 1, 6
psychologism, 45, 46, 47, 75, 76,
78, 89, 90, 97, 99, 140, 172, 173,
177, 178, 200
Public-private Partnership, xix

## Q

quizzes, xxv

## R

radicalization, 45, 46, 47, 75, 76, 78,
83, 90, 97, 99, 100, 103, 142, 200
Recommendations, xxix, 135, 148
Request for Proposal, xx
research questions, xxvii, xxix, 65,
79
RFP, xx, 59
Rodney, xxviii, 11, 18, 50, 53
Rostow, 36, 38
Ruben Center, 67, 74, 75, 79, 80,
95, 114, 136, 137, 178, 192
Rural, 36, 52, 127

## S

Scott (1985), xxviii, 50
SDG, xx, 4
SDI, xx
sectarianism, 45, 47, 75, 76, 78, 90,
96, 99, 102, 200

self-reliance, 36, 43, 47, 64, 145,
146, 152
Sen (1970), xxviii
similarities, xv
slum communities., xv
slum dwellers, xv, xxiii, xxix, 6, 24,
102, 134, 141
Slum Dwellers International, xx
slum fires, xxiii
slums, xv, xviii, xxi, xxii, xxiii, xxvii,
1, 6, 14, 33, 38, 39, 47, 84, 104,
105, 113, 114, 117, 118, 128, 129,
130, 134, 165
slums of Nairobi, xviii, xxii, 14
social capital, xviii, xxviii, 40, 56
social discord, xxviii
social norms, xxix
socioeconomic background, xxvi
students, xxii, xxv, xxvi, 15, 47, 67,
104, 158, 199, 200
subjectivism, 45, 47, 75, 76, 78, 90,
96, 97, 99, 102, 173, 177, 200
successful, xv, 6, 28, 30, 49, 51, 52,
54, 66, 80, 99, 113, 126, 133, 140,
142, 151, 177
Survey variables, 89, 131
sustainable development, 60
Sustainable Development Goal,
xx, xxvii, 146

## T

Tanzania, xxi, 10, 129
Taylor (1985), xxviii
technological, 24, 71
theoretical, xv, xxvii, 13, 43, 81, 82,
143, 148
theory, xviii, xxvii, xxviii, xxix, 6, 7,
11, 12, 15, 16, 17, 30, 43, 45, 47,
51, 56, 62, 63, 64, 65, 68, 71, 78,
83, 87, 135, 137, 141, 143, 145,
148, 152, 153, 200

ingЧЧ

www.ingramcontent.com/pod-product-compliance
Lightning Source LLC
Chambersburg PA
CBHW071854270326
41929CB00013B/2227